THE UNION SOLDIER IN BATTLE

THE UNION SOLDIER IN BATTLE
Enduring the Ordeal of Combat

Earl J. Hess

 University Press of Kansas

973.741
HES

Published by the University Press of Kansas (Lawrence, Kansas 66049), which
was organized by the Kansas Board of Regents and is operated and funded by
Emporia State University, Fort Hays State University, Kansas State University,
Pittsburg State University, the University of Kansas, and Wichita State
University

Library of Congress Cataloging-in-Publication Data

Hess, Earl J.
    The Union soldier in battle: enduring the ordeal of combat / Earl
J. Hess.
    244 p.   cm.   (Modern war studies)
    Includes bibliographical references and index.
    ISBN 0-7006-0837-0 (alk. paper)
    1. United States—History—Civil War, 1861–1865—Psychological
aspects.   2. Combat—Psychological aspects—History—19th century.
3. Soldiers—United States—Psychology—History—19th century.
4. United States.   Army—History—Civil War, 1861–1865.   5. United
States.   Army—Military life—History—19th century.   I. Title.
II. Series.
E468.9.H58   1997
973.7'41—dc21   96-45652

British Library Cataloguing in Publication Data is available.

Printed in the United States of America

10 9 8 7 6 5 4 3 2 1

For Pratibha,
a great soul,
with love

Contents

(photo insert follows p. 72)

Preface

This book is an attempt to understand how the Northern soldier dealt with combat in the Civil War. It is not a fully developed study of soldier morale but an interpretive essay about the experience of battle in the Civil War and the mechanisms whereby the Northern soldier was able to emotionally face the shock of battle, master his reactions to it, and continue to effectively serve the cause. I do not ignore the significant minority of men who failed to some degree to master their fears, but I focus on the great majority of soldiers who obeyed orders, stayed in line, and somehow found the resolve to endure battle after battle in this long, costly war.

The factors that enabled those men to endure combat naturally varied from one individual to the next, but they ranged from ideology to religion, from the comradeship of the army community to support from home, from the pragmatic habits of those who were nurtured in a working-class culture to successful efforts to overcome fear by comparing battle with typical peacetime experiences. The interpretive framework is based on an acknowledgment that although battle is a frightening and disorienting experience, the majority of Northern soldiers were able to psychologically and emotionally endure it. They learned to manage their responses to an apparently unmanageable situation. The soldiers came to recognize the horrors of the battlefield but succeeded in retaining faith in the ideals or motives that had impelled them to go to war. They continued to retain that faith even after the conflict ended and they sat down to evaluate what had happened to them from the perspective of time. The soldiers of the Union were not victims, as twentieth-century authors tend to portray soldiers in all wars, but victors over the horrors of combat.

Only a few other books deal satisfactorily with combat morale in the Civil War. Gerald F. Linderman's *Embattled Courage: The Experience of Combat in the American Civil War* (1987) addresses only one theme—the

ideal of courage—with respect to a select group of Northern and Southern soldiers. Linderman takes a decidedly negative view of ideology and
ideals and portrays Civil War combat as an unmasterable experience
that warped the view of its participants. I offer a completely different
interpretation of the impact of battle on Northern soldiers, an interpretation that makes use of a great deal of the primary literature that Linderman does not mention.

Other recent books about the Northern soldier, such as Reid Mitchell's
Civil War Soldiers: Their Expectations and Their Experiences (1988), James
I. Robertson's *Soldiers Blue and Gray* (1988), and Randall C. Jimerson's
The Private Civil War: Popular Thought During the Sectional Conflict (1988),
are mainly concerned with politics, social history, or philosophy. They
offer valuable and suggestive insights into the minds of men on both
sides but only marginally touch on the experience of battle. Joseph Allan
Frank and George A. Reaves, in *"Seeing the Elephant": Raw Recruits at the
Battle of Shiloh* (1989), come closer than any other authors to a comprehensive approach to combat morale in the Civil War. Their research is
thorough, and their grounding in the work of historians who have studied other wars is solid. Yet they study only Shiloh and do not address
the postwar attitudes of veterans.

Nor do older Civil War studies address the larger issues involved in
combat morale. Pete Maslowski, "A Study of Morale in Civil War Soldiers" (1970); Michael Barton, *Goodmen: The Character of Civil War Soldiers* (1981); and Bell Irvin Wiley, *The Life of Billy Yank* (1952), address
such issues in some ways, but all three works have their limitations.
Maslowski and Barton employ statistical analysis of a small range of primary sources. Neither author focuses on battle but looks at the full range
of issues involved in soldier morale. Wiley's social history of the Northern soldier is still impressive in many ways, but he also fails to study
the experience of combat in depth. Published in 1952, Wiley's book is
also outdated.

Combat morale in more recent American and European wars has been
far more widely studied than in the Civil War. Much of this work began
with the appearance of John Keegan's *The Face of Battle* (1976), a book
that offered new insights into how military historians ought to think and
write about their subject. Keegan's primary concern was to reconceptu-
alize our understanding of the relationship between the soldier and the
physical environment of the battlefield. Most of the historians who were

inspired by Keegan's work failed to follow up on this point but went on to write about the psychological and emotional impact of battle on the soldier. Although given a great boost by the publication of *The Face of Battle,* this sort of inquiry did not begin with Keegan's work. John Baynes's *Morale: A Study of Men and Courage* (1967) and Lord Moran's *The Anatomy of Courage* (1966) are excellent studies of the British soldier in World War I by veterans of that conflict. Whereas Baynes covers all aspects of morale, Moran focuses mostly on combat. A different kind of study, produced by academic authors, deals with the total experience of war as it affected the consciousness of soldiers in both world wars. Eric J. Leed's *No Man's Land: Combat and Identity in World War I* (1979) is the best book in this category. Paul Fussell, author of *The Great War and Modern Memory* (1975) and *Wartime: Understanding and Behavior in the Second World War* (1989), offers interesting insights into the psychology of the soldier and often deals with the impact of combat.

This book, therefore, is intended to fill a gap in Civil War studies. The first three chapters describe the experience of battle, the following five chapters explore the factors that enabled soldiers to endure battle, and the final chapter discusses postwar attitudes toward the experience of war. The book is based on a careful reading of the primary literature, the letters, diaries, and memoirs of the soldiers. As all students of the Civil War know, Billy Yank wrote voluminously of his experiences. Blessed with a high rate of literacy, unencumbered by military censorship, and fully aware that they were engaged in a larger-than-life endeavor that could change their country forever, the mass of Northern soldiers produced the most valuable collection of personal accounts ever used to document a phase of American history. A considered evaluation of what they had to say, shorn of modern prejudices, ideological faddishness, and a desire for political correctness, is the only proper way to understand the soldiers of the 1860s and to honor their suffering and their success.

A study of this kind begs comparison with the Confederate soldier's experience. In many ways, Johnny Reb responded to the war in exactly the same manner as his Northern counterpart. The nature of combat and the factors that enabled him to emotionally endure battle were the same. A major difference lay in the reflections of Confederate veterans on the meaning of their war experience. They interpreted the conflict differently, arguing that different issues were involved and that important aspects of American culture were lost in it. I chose to concentrate on the men who fought the war to save the Union because I wanted to study the experiences of a successful army. This is not an insult to the Confederate soldier, who fought as hard as the Northern soldier did and suffered the additional agony of seeing his society wrecked by the war. In most ways, the war experience of Northern and Southern soldiers was similar, but it is also important to acknowledge the ways in which their experiences differed. They fought for profoundly different causes and had to deal with divergent outcomes. Moreover, unlike opponents from foreign nations, they had to live with their former enemies after the war ended. They were belligerents as well as brothers, and an appropriate way to remember their war is to keep that tension in mind.

Many of the points made in this book were presented in a paper I read at the Southern Historical Association conference in Lexington, Kentucky, in November 1989. I wish to thank Professors Herman Hattaway and Drew Faust for their comments on it. In September 1990, the same paper was read at the Tennessee Historians' Conference, and Professor Patrick D. Reagan of Tennessee Technological University kindly offered comments on it as well. Most of the material in chapter three was presented at a conference entitled "On the Road to Total War: The American Civil War and the German Wars of Unification, 1862–1871," sponsored by the German Historical Institute in April 1992. That paper was published as chapter twenty-two in a collection edited by Stig Förster and Jörg Nagler, *On the Road to Total War: The American Civil War and the German Wars of Unification, 1861–1871* (Cambridge University Press, 1996), reprinted here with the permission of the German Historical Institute, Washington, D.C. Most of the research for this book was conducted many years ago while I was a graduate student at Purdue University. While there I was generously supported by grants and fellowships and encouraged by the mentorship of Professor Harold D. Woodman. Professor William L. Shea, a co-conspirator of mine in the production of a book on Pea Ridge a few years ago, encouraged me in this study. He also contributed material from his own research and aided in the writing of chapters one and two. Also, the reviewers who read the manuscript for various presses suggested helpful ways to improve it. I am grateful to them.

1

Innocents at War

You wanted to know how we felt in the battle. I don't know as I can tell you how I do feel. I have a dread of it at first when I know I have to go in, but when you come to see the wounded carried by you and . . . hear the shouts of them that are at it, it isn't long before you won't think or care whether you are in it or not and as was the case at White Oak Swamp, I wanted to go in and give the Rebs a try, but it is awful work.

John Burrill
2d New Hampshire Infantry

Who but a living witness can adequately portray those scenes on Shiloh's field, when our wounded men, mingled with rebels, charred and blackened by the burning tents and underbrush, were crawling about, begging for someone to end their misery? Who can describe the plunging shot shattering the strong oak as with a thunderbolt, and beating down horse and rider to the ground? Who but one who has heard them can describe the peculiar sizzing of the minie ball, or the crash and roar of a volley fire? Who can describe the last look of the stricken soldier as he appeals for help that no man can give or describe the dread scene of the surgeon's work, or the burial trench?

William T. Sherman

It was the first time I had ever been on a field of battle. After the heat and excitement of the day were over I lay down and tried to sleep. But the din of the engagement was still in my ears, and kept up a perpetual buzzing that I could not drive away. I had a bad headache, my throat was parched, my eyes were aching. I could not sleep.

Thomas H. Evans
12th U.S. Infantry

In the spring of 1861 a nation of innocents went to war. Few of the young men who so boldly offered their lives to the cause of the Union had an accurate conception of what combat was like. Only thirteen years had passed since the nation's last major military conflict in the Mexican

1

War, but that had been a foreign affair, conducted many hundreds of miles from Northern territory. The War of 1812 had witnessed the invasion of American soil by columns of British regulars, but that conflict was a half century in the past and had largely been fought on the margins of a vast and sparsely populated country. Northerners had to reach back to the War of Independence to find a conflict that had racked the heartland of the nation and involved so great a proportion of its young men. That bitter struggle had much to offer an innocent people yearning to know war's lessons. It had killed a large percentage of the American population, laid waste to farms and businesses, and embittered a generation of Americans. But few Northerners realized or remembered these things in 1861. Already more than eighty years in the past, the War of Independence had become more legendary than real in the minds of most citizens of the Republic.

Because few Northerners had any personal experience with war, they relied on a number of secondhand sources of information. The most pervasive and probably the most influential was the array of history textbooks read by schoolchildren. These tomes paid lip service to pacifism, declaring war to be a terrible waste of life that should be avoided if possible. Nevertheless, they made it clear that Americans had not hesitated to fight for the right cause. The authors of these texts seriously undermined their peaceful veneer by devoting much space to colorful and dramatic descriptions of battle. One widely used textbook, published in 1839, devoted no fewer than 144 of its 432 pages to military operations in the War of Independence and the War of 1812.[1]

Conflict was the overwhelming image of America's past presented to students in the antebellum period, but this image of conflict was unrealistic. The excitement, drama, color, and heroism of war were stressed; its darker aspects were downplayed or overlooked. Impressionable boys and young men were easily seduced by this romanticized view of history. Soldiering was an adventure; death in battle was a glorious sacrifice for country and a good cause. Antebellum schoolbooks thus inadvertently prepared young men to accept and even to embrace the idea of going to war. The foremost historian of public education in the nineteenth century noted that textbook descriptions of armed conflict gave the impression that "war is a natural and normal relationship between nations; it is dreadful but inevitable. And its horror is full of interest."[2]

Illustrated media such as newspapers, prints, and broadsides were another source of information about war. These publications also failed to provide an accurate description of combat. "In all the pictures of battles I had seen before I ever saw a battle," recalled one Union soldier, "the officers were at the front on prancing steeds, or with uplifted swords were leading their followers to the charge." Later, he was surprised to learn that most officers remained in the rear of their commands.[3]

The illustrated media could even mislead young men about such matters as the age and physical appearance of soldiers. Oliver Wendell Holmes, Jr., went to war in 1861 assuming that most soldiers were older men. "I remembered a picture of the revolutionary soldier . . . representing a white-haired man with his flint-lock slung across his back. I remembered one or two living examples of revolutionary soldiers whom I had met, and I took no account of the lapse of time." Only after he had seen much service did Holmes realize that war was largely the business of the young.[4]

Many young Northerners relied on their childhood games as a reference point when contemplating the nature of battle. Like boys in any society, they were fascinated by the glitter of military life and the excitement of massed conflict. Seventeen-year-old Benjamin Smith of Illinois believed that combat would be something like the game he and his friends had played, "armed with clods and turfs." They had divided into opposing armies and engaged "in a battle royal charging each other until our ammunition was exhausted . . . some of us would get a black eye or bloody nose now and then, which we did not mind much."[5]

Samuel P. Jennison, who would rise through the ranks to become the lieutenant colonel of the 10th Minnesota, recalled a similar experience. When imagining what combat would be like, he mixed impressions of mock battles fought during his youth with his more adult but no less unrealistic image of the fighting in Kansas territory in 1856. He assumed that the Civil War would be "a desperate hand-to-hand struggle, much like the Kansas border ruffian war, except on a broader scale." And, like almost everyone, he expected the war to be decided in one engagement. "I suppose it was a sort of likening of a battle to the fights of which I had some knowledge among boys, an expectation that the promised hand-to-hand, bowie-knife, clubbed-musket, knock-down-and-drag-out method of warfare would decide the event." Not everyone was so naive. William W. Belknap of the 15th Iowa remembered that at least some volunteers at the beginning of the war had a vaguely accurate notion of the nature of combat. "They had a dim, uncertain thought of a real action in the field," he recalled. "They knew that bullets were to fly, shells to burst, and men to be wounded and killed." But even for these relatively perceptive individuals, reality proved to be a grisly shock.[6]

The vast majority of Union soldiers were to learn that combat bore little resemblance to their rather childish conceptions of it. A gigantic gulf existed between those men who had been in combat and those who had not. Battle was such a unique experience that only those who had personal exposure to it could know what it was like. Crossing this gulf, becoming an initiated warrior, was essentially a matter of learning that battle was an experience of the senses. It involved placing the body in an environment made deadly by modern weapons. Until they were physically thrust into that environment, few soldiers were able to conceive of the sounds, sights, smells, or tactile sensations produced by battle. They had to cross over the gulf that separated naive imagination from brutal reality in order to understand combat. Only by effectively dealing with the fear, excitement, horror, and exaltation known by the warrior could they become real soldiers.

CROSSING OVER

The process of learning war was complex and dangerous, but it proceeded at a pace common to most soldiers. From the time of their enlistment and mustering in to their transfer toward the theater of operations, their lengthy waiting in camps, and their initial exposure, Northern volunteers had some opportunity to acclimate their senses and emotions to the novel experience of war. No matter how much they mused, however, battle could shock them with incredible force. And it was not necessarily the first battle experience that jolted the most. Subsequent engagements could take even veteran soldiers to a new level of physical knowledge of combat. Although fairly uniform for all men, the experience of crossing over could be more intense or prolonged for some than for others.

Enlistment did not immediately thrust the new warrior into the brotherhood of men at arms. Most regiments were raised locally, where the men were issued uniforms, arms, and equipment and received some rudimentary training. Discipline was lax, and officers and men often went home to eat and visit or entertained civilian visitors at their camps. This initial phase of military life, almost pleasant when viewed in retrospect, ended as the regiment marched through town past blaring bands and cheering civilians, then embarked on a train or ship or riverboat for Washington or St. Louis or Cincinnati. This was the step that severed the soldier from his previous existence and brought him to the front-line Northern cities, a transition zone on the threshold of combat.

These cities displayed a marked and exciting military presence. Railroad stations, wharves, commercial districts, and arteries of transportation were transformed by the unending logistical demands of thousands of men and animals. Streets were crammed with busy soldiers. Earthworks, sprawling camps, and enormous accumulations of wagons and artillery ringed the cities. The change in landscape for the new soldier was abrupt and startling. "Suddenly, now that I had set foot in the capital the war that I had heard so much about became real," observed a future photographer of the Far West named William H. Jackson, who had traveled to Washington, D.C., with his regiment from faraway Vermont. "So far it has been a war of distant armies identified by the names of their generals. Now it was a war of soldiers—who ate and drank and smoked and swore and slept afloors, like me." Another Union soldier was similarly impressed with the sense of having moved from one world to another. "Things began to look warlike to me," observed George P. Metcalf, a young New Yorker. "The immense forts covered and bristling with cannon, the white tents covering thousands of acres, the tramping of thousands of men, the bugle-call, the playing of innumerable bands—all was like a new life to me."[7]

For most Union soldiers, the front-line cities were a brief stopover before plunging into active campaigning. Here they saw for the first time the scale and scope of the war. Here too they encountered veterans of Manassas and Wilson's Creek and other early clashes, many identifiable by their weathered uniforms and tanned faces. Others were equally obvious by their mutilated forms as they recuperated from wounds or awaited transportation home. Eventually the soldiers piled once again onto trains or boats or set out on narrow and dusty roads, advancing into the Confederacy. From that point onward, every hour brought them closer to the enemy.

Sooner or later, soldiers learned that battle was imminent. This knowledge provoked a frenzy of activity and a clamor of contrasting sounds. "Oh! it is an awful sight a host arming for battle," remembered a soldier on the eve of a major engagement. "The packing of knapsacks, the examination of cartridges, the ringing of the rammers in the muskets to see that all is ready for the dread conflict, the orders of the officers, the hasty couriers and aides riding their horses to the utmost speed, the forming in ranks to *right face,* and *forward march!!!* All tell of the *dead work to come.*"[8]

Nearly every battle of the Civil War was fought on ground that was partly open and partly covered with dense woods. Typical European battlefields—level expanses of cropland or pasturage where small armies could be drawn up in full view of each other—were rare in America. The huge field armies of poorly trained men that fought the Civil War were forced to deal with difficult, cluttered terrain. Because of the dense foliage, their movement toward the enemy could be nerve-wracking. Troops might approach the battlefield on a narrow lane that meandered inside a tunnel of vegetation. Visibility was often limited to only a few hundred yards. Soldiers could hear the rumble of artillery and crackle of rifle fire and sometimes smell the acrid scent of black powder before they could see anything but the backs of their comrades. Deployment from marching columns into lines of battle often meant plunging into a mass of vegetation that swallowed up entire units and severely impeded movement, communication, and combat effectiveness. Nowhere was the foliage more tangled or more impenetrable than in a second-growth forest in northern Virginia, the location of the battles of Chancellorsville and the Wilderness. "We at once entered the forest," wrote a New York soldier of his first encounter with Southern vegetation, "but found the scrub pine so closely grown together with their branches extended out from the ground up and so interlocked we could not advance in company front. It was even difficult for a single man to move ahead in the thicket."[9]

The first visual evidence of a battle was often the casualties, usually individuals struck down in the early stages of the engagement. Such sights generated powerful, conflicting emotions, especially in the minds of untried soldiers. "We met some of the New York Fire Zouaves coming out" of the fighting near Gaines's Mill, recalled Pennsylvanian James C. Miller. "One big fellow was wounded in the shoulder and had his breast bared and the blood streaming down it. I believed I was surely going to be wounded, and wondered where I would be hit and whether I would be killed. As we passed the big Zouave I almost imagined I felt a bullet strike me in the same place too, but at the same time I would have resented the inference that I felt like running away." The sight of enemy corpses brought the same thoughts to other soldiers. Harvey Reid of Wisconsin marched past a dead Confederate whose face was covered with blood, a sight he remembered more vividly than any other at the battle of Thompson's Station, Tennessee. "It served to give a proper idea of the *effect* of a battle." In a fight near Goldsboro, North Carolina, Samuel C. Day of the 3d New York Light Artillery saw a Confederate soldier lying "close to the road, just alive, with a sabre cut in the side of his head four inches long, and his brains were running out on to his coat. O! How sick I felt, though I did not show it, but I could have been on the out side of my dinner very easily. I thought to myself, if I got sick at the sight of one dead man what would I do on a battle field."[10]

When Union troops moved from the periphery toward the center of the battlefield, they often had to advance directly over the fallen bodies of other Northerners. Major Francis E. Pierce of the 108th New York had to take care to avoid stepping on mangled blue-clad forms as his regiment marched toward the blazing Confederate position at Fredericksburg. It struck him that "their ghastly gaping death wounds" were a prediction "of what might be in store for us." Small battles were no less unsettling. Illinois artilleryman Patrick H. White first saw action at Belmont. He stated that "our own dead who had dyed in the full flush of health, had turned black and we had to move them so as not to crush them with our cannon wheels." Dragging the corpses of his comrades out of the road made an indelible impression on this untried soldier whose mother had recently died. "I will frankly say to you the thoughts that came to my mind then were: this may be my last day and I may see my mother before night."[11]

Rice C. Bull of the 123d New York used straightforward prose to capture the unexpected sensations that greeted him while moving into combat.

As we neared the front there were all the evidences of battle, wounded men being brought back, ammunition wagons and ambulances hurrying to the front, cowardly skulkers who would not stay on the firing line except a bayonet was at their back getting to the rear, men, horses, and even mules wild with excitement. There is nothing that tests men's nerves more than marching up to a line of battle that is already engaged; they know they are soon to take their place on the firing line. While making the advance they can see, hear, and think, but can do nothing to take their minds off the dreadful work they know is before them. Until their own battle line is formed and they are facing the front and firing their nerves are almost at the breaking point; then the strain relaxes and the fear and nervousness passes away.[12]

Daniel McCook relied on a more self-consciously literary style to describe an escalating series of horrors as his command marched into the second day's fight at Shiloh.

The first dead soldier we saw had fallen in the road; our artillery had crushed and mangled his limbs, and ground him into the mire. He lay a bloody, loathsome mass, the scraps of his blue uniform furnishing the only distinguishable evidence that a hero there had died. At this sight I saw many a manly fellow gulp down his heart, which swelled too closely into his throat. Near him lay a slender rebel boy—his face in the mud, his brown hair floating in a muddy pool. Soon a dead Major, then a Colonel, then the lamented Wallace, yet alive, were passed in quick and sickening succession. The gray gloaming of the misty morning gave a ghostly pallor to the faces of the dead. The disordered hair, dripping from the night's rain, the distorted and passion-marked faces, the stony, glaring eyes, the blue lips, the glistening teeth, the shriveled and contracted hands, the wild agony of pain and passion in the attitudes of the dead—all the horrid circumstances with which death surrounds the brave when torn from life in the whirlwind of battle, were seen as we marched over the field, the beseeching cries of the wounded from their bloody and mirey beds meanwhile saluting our ears and cutting to our hearts. Never, perhaps, did raw men go into battle under such discouraging auspices as did this division. There was every thing to depress, nothing to inspirit, and yet determination was written upon their pale faces.[13]

Despite their different styles of expression, Bull and McCook successfully conveyed the unfamiliar, disorienting, and harrowing impressions soldiers received as they marched toward the sound of the guns. They had begun crossing over the gulf that separated green recruits from veterans who realized that combat could be understood only as an experience of the senses. Seeing, hearing, and physically feeling battle made it real.

SEEING BATTLE

In the most literal sense of the term, a Civil War soldier often had difficulty "seeing" the battle swirling around him. In many cases, nature and technology combined to obscure the combatants from one another. Theodore Lyman, a staff officer in the Army of the Potomac, aptly characterized the battle of the Wilderness.

> I had taken part in two great battles, and heard the bullets whistle both days, and yet I had *scarcely seen a Rebel* save killed, wounded, or prisoners! I remember how even line officers, who were at the battle of Chancellorsville, said: "Why, we never saw any Rebels where we were; only smoke and bushes and lots of our men tumbling about": and now I appreciate this most fully. The great art is to *conceal* men; for the moment they show, *bang, bang,* go a dozen cannon, the artillerists only too pleased to get a fair mark. Your typical "great white plain," with long lines advancing and maneuvering, led on by generals in cocked hats and by bands of music, exist not for us. Here it is said: "Left face—prime—forward!" and then *wrang, wr-r-rang,* for three or four hours, or for all day, and the poor bleeding wounded streaming to the rear. That is a great battle in America.[14]

Paintings and prints familiar to antebellum Americans usually portrayed military engagements as relatively smokeless encounters with cloudlike billows hovering high in the background. Consequently, few soldiers were prepared for the reality of a Civil War battlefield where visibility was often severely limited. When opposing lines met each other, the smoke produced by thousands of rapidly firing muskets and cannons often obscured soldiers who were only a few yards apart. At Peach Tree Creek, visibility was effectively nil on a fine summer day. "During the afternoon the enemy made five charges on our line, coming at times within one hundred feet," reported Rice C. Bull, "yet I did not see a single Johnnie. The clouds of smoke from the muskets of both sides . . . poured down on us to hide everything but the flash of the enemy's guns that gave us their position." James Wright of the 1st Minnesota recalled that on another bright summer day at Gettysburg, troops along his section of the Union line fired at the feet and lower legs of the approaching Confederates, "which was about all we could see of them at the time, as all above their knees was covered with the smoke from their own guns." A soldier in the 5th Iowa, Samuel H. M. Byers, fought at Champion's Hill, where his regiment advanced to within a hundred yards of the enemy. "The rebels in front we could not see at all. We simply blazed at their lines by guess, and occasionally the blaze of their guns showed exactly where they stood."[15]

Problems of visibility were more than just annoyances. Combatants became disoriented and confused. This was an especially acute problem for artillerymen, whose relatively distant targets often were only vaguely seen through the haze. Lieutenant William Wheeler, 13th New York Battery, told his mother of such an episode on the first day at Gettysburg. The captain of an adjacent battery could not see whether the smoke-shrouded figures in his front were friends or foes. He shouted, "Wheeler, which are the rebels and which are our men?" Caught up in the grim excitement of combat, Wheeler responded "with the same answer as that with which the showman so triumphantly crushed the little boy. 'You pays your money and you takes your choice.'"[16]

Smoke and vegetation so obscured some battlefields that combatants fought as much by ear as by eye. At Second Bull Run, the 12th U.S. Infantry fired at an approaching Confederate line shrouded in smoke. The Union soldiers could see little, but they knew their shots "went home, as we could tell by the outcries." Officers standing or sitting on horseback a short distance behind the firing line generally saw even less than the men in the ranks. During the battle for possession of Fort Harrison, a part of the Richmond defenses, the Confederates launched an ill-fated counterattack. Brigadier General Edward H. Ripley commanded the Union brigade that bore the brunt of the assault. "It was close range for the rifles of Stannard's Division, and instantly there burst forth from those double lines of breechloaders the most awful fire troops ever had to face. We could see nothing until a cheer went up, which told us that the charge was broken and the Rebs were going back."[17]

Soldiers often had to be satisfied with only indirect evidence of the enemy's presence. At Chancellorsville, the 132d Pennsylvania advanced through the tangled woods. The Confederates heard the Federals crashing through the underbrush and fired a volley in their general direction. "The morning was lowering and misty and the air very light," recalled Frederick L. Hitchcock, "so that the smoke made by the rebel volley, not more than fifty yards away, hung like a chalk line and indicated their exact position." The Pennsylvanians were ordered to aim below the layer of smoke and responded with a volley of their own that drove the Confederates away.[18]

The blindness that many soldiers endured on the battlefield heightened their fears. "There is a feeling of uneasiness in the stoutest heart in facing danger that one cannot see and know," remarked Sergeant E. B. Tyler of the 14th Connecticut. "The mystery is doubly intensified by the sudden, silent dropping dead . . . of men on either hand that somehow does not seem to connect itself with the constant roar of musketry that is going on." Sergeant Thomas H. Evans of the 12th U.S. Infantry agreed. "Up to this time I had not seen a single soldier of the enemy," he wrote of Second Bull Run. "The woods and the smoke hid them entirely. To me this brings always a most disagreeable feeling, akin to awe, at this fighting the unseen. We know that there are 100,000 men in front of us, probably half as many more. We know they are close on us, by the force with which the minie bullets strike. We know that they intend to have a hard fight by the dispositions they have made, their point of attack, and the large force of artillery they have in play. But by feeling and hearing alone are we judges of this."[19]

Imagine how startled Union soldiers could be when they did see Confederate troops in plain view. This occurred nearly as often as seeing only trees and bushes, for even the more thickly vegetated battlefields had cleared fields and homesteads. Federal soldiers peering into wafting billows of smoke or groping through tangled vegetation would come face-to-face with the enemy. The first sight of Confederate troops under such nerve-wracking circumstances could be a memorable experience. Vinson Holman of the 9th Iowa was startled at how suddenly the enemy appeared at Pea Ridge. One moment, the smoky slope in front of his position was empty, the next it was "covered with rebels." At Corinth, the 52d Illinois had a different but no less unsettling experience. The Federals emerged from a thicket onto the open right-of-way of the Mobile and Columbus Railroad. There they stumbled upon a thin screen of Confederates. "I saw one of the rebel skirmishers step upon the track some sixty rods distant," wrote Colonel John S. Wilcox. "I had stopped, he stepped one step back, squatted and took aim at me. I stooped down by the horses neck and the bullet whistled over me. This was the first ball near me [and] the first fired at our Regiment." Wilcox had the comparatively rare experience of actually seeing an enemy soldier fire at him, an event that made battle seem intensely personal.[20]

On a few battlefields, massed enemy formations could be seen at a considerable distance, at least before the firing began in earnest. Robert G. Carter of the 22d Massachusetts wrote of the sight of oncoming Confederates on the second day at Gettysburg: "The indistinct form of masses of men, presenting the usual, dirty, greyish, irregular line, were dimly visible and moving up with defiant yells, while here and there the cross-barred Confederate battle flags were plainly to be seen." Rebel lines also were fully visible at Antietam, Franklin, Bentonville, and a number of other engagements.[21]

Union soldiers did not often see their own immediate formations. On a few memorable occasions, however, soldiers were heartened by the sight of long lines of blue-clad troops stretching as far as the eye could see. Two such episodes took place in northwestern Arkansas. During the climax of the fighting at Pea Ridge, the Union army was visible from flank to flank. A dazzled Union officer called the bristling array of men at arms "the grandest sight that I had ever beheld." The entire Union army also could be seen deployed across the grassy expanse of Prairie Grove. "I have not the power of description sufficient to tell you of the grand magnificent sight presented when all our batteries opened, and our whole line for more than a mile in length commenced," wrote Major William G. Thompson of the 20th Iowa. Such rare vistas gave Union soldiers enormously enhanced confidence in the strength of their side and were a welcome relief from the nerve-wracking experience of fighting blind.[22]

Ironically, the best view of an engagement often was from a considerable distance, when the terrain allowed soldiers on one part of a battlefield to view developments on another part. At Fisher's Hill, in the rolling Shenandoah Valley, men of the 12th Connecticut watched a distant Union brigade advance up an open grassy slope toward a wooded hilltop. "Suddenly a grey field of smoke lined the edge of the woodland and clung there silently for several minutes," wrote Captain John W. DeForest. "Then the line of blue went to bits, staggered in groups and dots down the slope, and halted behind a low crest of earth. There it took shape again, laid down in ranks and opened a file fire, as we could make out by the frail spouts of smoke."[23]

The most spectacular sights of battle occurred at night, when muzzle flashes and exploding shells mesmerized men. They compared such scenes to a fireworks display, perhaps forgetting for the moment that they were not at a county fair. "After dark the rebels opened fire on some of our men," recalled New Jerseyan Alfred Bellard of a night battle, "and going into the road to see what was the matter, we saw a splendid show of fireworks. On the edge of the woods where our men were posted a continuous stream of fire seemed to shoot into the woods accompanied by the roar of musketry, while a stray flash was seen in the woods, wherever the trees or bushes were rather thin." Charles Cowell of the 9th Illinois described the situation at Corinth before dawn on October 4, 1862, in a different fashion. "The shells were flying through the air like mosquitos of a summer night and I thought they were the prettiest thing a busting in the air I ever saw, most especially when they did not come close."[24]

The siege of Vicksburg offered Northern soldiers a stunning view of the beauty and power of the huge mortars fired from vessels in the Mississippi River. Jacob Switzer of the 22d Iowa left a graphic description.

The firing of the gun or mortar caused a flash of light in the west, similar to a faint flash of lightning; immediately a beautiful star would arise from the horizon and mount into the sky, ascending to a great height; just as it reached its highest point and turned to descend, the roar of the gun would be heard, and the swish or roar of the shell as it mounted was terrific and continued long after explosion of the shell. The star would continue to descend until it reached a height of probably one hundred yards and then a puff of smoke would be seen, but still the roar of the oncoming shell would continue for some time until the sound had time to traverse the

intervening distance when the noise of the explosion would be
heard, and then the buzzing, whizzing sound of the pieces as they
flew in every direction over the Confederate works. I have lain for
hours of a beautiful starlit evening when all other firing had ceased
except for the occasional shots of the mortars—about one per
minute—watched these stars mount to the zenith, descend and
explode, and counted the time from the puff of smoke at the explosion of the shell until I would hear the noise of the explosion, and
thought that no more beautiful sight could be witnessed, not giving a thought to the death and destruction contained in each one of
the terrible missiles.[25]

Soldiers of every rank and background were impressed by the terrible
aesthetic appeal of combat, especially when distanced from it. Awesome
displays of power were enormously seductive.

Soldiers sometimes were thrilled by the color, excitement, and drama
of battle. Such a grandiose human endeavor, no matter how lethal, had
the potential to awaken an appreciation that was based on stimulation
of the senses. A Missouri cavalry officer genuinely felt sorry for his wife,
for she had "none of the excitement of the camp the march and the battle field" to take her mind off the anxieties felt by those who remained
at home. He described a fight at Osage, Missouri, in October 1864 as
"one of the most beautiful battles that was almost ever fought being on
an open smooth prairie. . . . You may think it strange but it is worth a
lifetime to see and live through such a fight as that was. I often think
that if there had been an artist there that he could have got some beautiful sketches for pictures."[26]

These grand, sweeping vistas were striking but uncommon. More typical of the soldier's experience were remembered images, sometimes
only details, that somehow stood out amid the chaos of battle. As his
unit advanced toward a Confederate position during the Bayou Teche
campaign in Louisiana, Captain John W. DeForest looked up, fascinated
by the effects of artillery fire: "the shells hummed and cracked and
fought each other in flights over our heads, dotting the sky with the little globes of smoke which marked their explosions, and sending
buzzing fragments in all directions." Certain memories of battle were
remarkably mundane, almost irrelevant to the grim matter at hand.
Deployed in a wheat field at Gettysburg, Robert G. Carter of the 22d

Massachusetts distinctly remembered "standing waist deep in the beautiful yellow grain, the blue [of his uniform] strongly contrasting." These little memories fixed the swirling imagery of combat in the soldier's mind, capturing its irony in microscopic detail that was as poignant as it was pristine.[27]

HEARING AND FEELING BATTLE

From a considerable distance, a clash of Civil War armies did not sound particularly ominous. The muffled boom of artillery fire was almost indistinguishable from thunder, and the irregular crackle of musketry hardly seemed threatening. Many soldiers compared musketry to a ripping or tearing sound, but Wilbur Fisk of the 2d Vermont offered a homely analogy. "It sounds, when it is a good ways off so that you can just hear it, like popping corn."[28]

Participants in a battle, however, found the noise of battle to be much more impressive. "Oh! the rush and roar of the battle!" wrote David E. Beem of the 14th Indiana after Antietam. "I wonder if the dreadful sounds will ever get out of my ears!" Leander Stillwell of the 61st Illinois eloquently described the dissonance that greeted a soldier's ears at Shiloh. "His sense of hearing is well-nigh overcome by the deafening uproar going on around him. The incessant and terrible crash of musketry, the roar of the cannon, the continual zip, zip of the bullets as they hiss by him, interspersed with the agonizing screams of the wounded or the death-shrieks of comrades falling in dying convulsions right in the face of the living." Soldiers did not recover physically from such an ordeal for some time. "Many of our Company were affected by the continuous roar of the artillery only twenty feet from where we were," recalled a New York soldier after one of the battles outside Atlanta. "For two days our hearing was almost gone; it was several days before it was normal again."[29]

When attempting to describe the noise of a battle, writers often made comparisons with sounds familiar to a population that lived in a relatively quiet age. The rattling of sheet iron, an apt metaphor for an industrializing society, or the noise made by "ten millions of firecrackers" was used by different soldiers to describe the sound. Music, oddly enough, was another popular metaphor. Captain Joseph J. Scroggs of the 5th U.S. Colored Infantry described skirmishing as "the musical overture of battle," and other participants often referred to the sounds of combat in symphonic terms.[30]

The sounds of bullets and artillery projectiles fascinated soldiers. Probably no other aspect of the aural experience of battle inspired such inventive descriptions. Men variously reported "a most villainous greasy slide through the air" or a "hoarse leisurely humming." During the siege of Jackson, Mississippi, Charles C. Paige of the 11th New Hampshire made an extended study of enemy small-arms fire. "Some bullets would pass, cutting the air like a knife . . . others with a zip which we did not relish; while others went by singing, awhew, awhew, awhew, which would provoke a laugh from the veteran soldier." Another man, Vermonter Wilbur Fisk, used a marvelous array of folksy examples as he cataloged the sounds of bullets passing over his head at Cold Harbor. "Some of them come with a sharp 'clit,' like striking a cabbage leaf with a whip lash, others come with a sort of screech, very much as you would get by treading on a cat's tail. Then there are others, the sharpshooters' bullets we suppose, that whistle on a much higher key, and snap against a tree with as much force as if the tree had been struck by a heavy sledge hammer. Some strike in the dirt with a peculiar 'thud,' others fly high in the air and make a noise similar to a huge bumble bee. They do not tarry long by the way." Bullets sounded so different to so many soldiers because of the differences in caliber, velocity, and shape. Ricocheting bullets often became deformed and tumbled through the air at relatively slow speeds, adding to the variety of sounds. An observant man who could temporarily set aside his fear could find much interest in listening to the sounds of rifle fire.[31]

Inexperienced soldiers, of course, first had to realize what those sounds were. Recruits almost never had an opportunity to recognize the screech of a bullet until they entered their first battle. Nearly all of Ulysses Grant's men at Fort Donelson were green. As Henry Dwight of the 20th Ohio remembered it, many of them were under fire some time before they realized what was happening. "Next we discovered that as we moved on, the air was full of objects that flew like birds, and seemed to whisper softly as they went. When once or twice we heard these flying objects hit trees with a sharp crack, it occurred to us that they were bullets from rebel guns."[32]

The sound of artillery fire was very different from that of small arms. The muzzle blast of a cannon and the shriek of a large projectile were distinctive, dominating noises that stood out sharply against a more or less continuous backdrop of crackling musketry. Green New York troops at Chancellorsville were startled by a sound "like a great bird fluttering over the Regiment." They wondered what it was, until something crashed and exploded in the woods behind them. There was no doubt now, and the New Yorkers ducked and jumped as more shells came over, some making hideous noises that inspired even more nervous reactions.[33]

Soldiers soon came to realize, sometimes with a fascinated awe, that munitions did not account for all the noises heard on the battlefield. Projectiles hit and tore inanimate objects on the field much more often than they hit men, making distinctive sounds. During the fighting on the Rose farm at Gettysburg, Robert G. Carter of the 22d Massachusetts never forgot the "melancholy ring" caused by stray enemy bullets striking a bell mounted atop the farmhouse. The shingles of a residence on the field of Fair Oaks, during the Peninsula campaign, absolutely "rattled with the hail of Rebel bullets," according to one astute observer. Trees covered so much of the land where firing took place that trunks and limbs were torn, splintered, and rocked by all kinds of fire. As Confederate artillery sprayed the woods at Chancellorsville with canister, it produced a singular sound. Wilbur Fisk compared it to a noise familiar to his childhood experience. "At every discharge the grape could be heard rattling against the trees like throwing a handful of pebbles against the side of a building."[34]

The combined effects of explosions made up the most impressive sound of battle. "It seemed as if earth and heaven were coming together, such was the roar of cannon," wrote Gavin A. Lambie of the 146th New York. Participants wrote of the "unearthly shrieking of the shells as they flew over our heads on their mission of death elsewhere, and the constant explosion of them in our very midst; the uninterrupted roar of hundreds of cannon, and the report of thousands of muskets made indeed, till darkness closed the horrid scene, a pandemonium, a Hell Upon Earth!" Although sometimes described as coherent, the noise of small arms and artillery struck most soldiers as "the grandest discord of sound" imaginable. It was so loud and insistent that the roar of battle made it nearly impossible to communicate. Soldiers standing only a few feet apart could not hear orders or shouts of encouragement. At Gaines's Mill, frustrated members of the 12th U.S. Infantry gave up shouting and used exaggerated facial and hand movements to communicate. "We judged what the message was from lip motions and gestures."[35]

Interspersed in this swelling wave of sound, filling up the lulls and softly punctuating its contours, were the noises made by the participants themselves. Soldiers shouted during battle to relieve stress, encourage themselves and their comrades, or intimidate their opponents. The Confederates often attacked "with a yell and a fury that had a tendency to make each hair on one's head to stand on its particular end," a practice that never failed to impress Union soldiers. "Yelling like savages and swearing like demons" was how Lieutenant Colonel Charles E. Lippincott of the 33d Illinois described attacking Southerners at Cache River, Arkansas. During a Confederate assault at Pea Ridge, Captain Robert P. Mathews of the 25th Missouri was surprised to hear the "cheers and yells" of the oncoming Rebels "rising above the roar of the artillery," something he had not thought was possible. The psychological impact of Confederate screeching was never greater than in the darkening woods at Chancellorsville. "The Rebels yelled tremendously and all was confusion, we could not see how many there were for the extensive forrests." Union soldiers also cheered and shouted in battle but generally did so in a lower register.[36]

The sounds of the battlefield could not be ignored or forgotten. They were summed up poignantly in a short description penned by William C. Kent, one of Berdan's Sharpshooters, after he survived the Seven Days battles. Rebel infantry were "delivering their fire in crashes, lengthening into long rolls, above which one could hear the yells of the rebels, and the cheers of our men, and every little while, would come a silence, far more awful than any noise, when nothing could be heard, but the shrieks and groans of the wounded."[37]

Seeing and hearing battle were impressive parts of the battle experience, but soldiers soon learned that it was possible to feel battle as well. Projectiles could miss flesh so closely as to brush a man's skin with air pressure, toss him about, or sear him with heat. Small-arms and artillery rounds flew promiscuously about the battlefield, randomly hitting or missing any object within range. Thus, near misses by projectiles and the suffocating atmosphere created by clouds of powder smoke could affect soldiers without killing or maiming them.

During the New Madrid campaign, a Scots immigrant in the 10th Illinois had a close call when a shell from a Confederate gunboat landed in his trench and exploded beside him. "I thought for a short time that I was killed," reported John H. Ferguson. "I was perfectly serviceable but could not move or scarcle breath attal; it was caused by the pressure of the air striking me with such force that I was left without power to move for a minnot." Thomas H. Evans, an immigrant from Wales, resigned himself to fate when contemplating the play of projectiles around him at Gaines's Mill. "There is no use trying to dodge shot. No one hears the whistle of the ball that hits him, any more than a man sees the flash of lightening that kills him. He is aware, however, of those that pass him so closely that he is certain he will be hit, and to which the strongest nerves seldom acquire sufficient steadiness to prevent an involuntary shrinking movement." The smoke generated by combat not only clouded vision but cloaked the soldiers' other senses as well. The battle of Antietam occurred on a late summer day. Musketry blanketed the rolling landscape with smoke so thick it made "breathing difficult and most uncomfortable" for Frederick L. Hitchcock and his comrades. "The day was excessively hot, and no air stirring, we were forced to breathe this powder smoke, impregnated with saltpeter, which burned the coating of nose, throat, and eyes almost like fire." The sulfurous air combined with heat and the ebbing effects of adrenaline to dull the senses and cause intense fatigue. Soldiers came to realize that battle was a comprehensive experience of all the senses, not just of sight and sound.[38]

THE GULF OF EXPERIENCE

"I must write to you of actual combat with armed rebels (for I am writing the day after the battle), and how like a dream it seems," wrote Harvey Reid after the engagement at Thompson's Station. "I cannot realize that I actually have stood where rebel balls were flying around me, that shrill hum which still seems ringing in my ears was actually rebel shells, that those noble hearted men with whom I have been associated so many months are really all still in death on the hills of Tennessee, languishing in hospitals from bloody wounds inflicted by rebel missiles or suffering the hard fate of prisoners of war." Henry M. Cross of Massachusetts groped for the proper way to express his feelings of surprise and disgust after experiencing his own introduction to war. "A battle is a horrid thing. You can have no conception of its horrors. I never did before." These veterans now had something in common. They had crossed over the gulf of experience, leaving behind relatives and friends who could not know what had happened to them.[39]

Once they got through the searing experience of combat, survivors found themselves set apart from other people, even those closest to them. Daniel Holt, surgeon of the 121st New York, wrote to his wife about Chancellorsville and grew impassioned as he struggled to make her understand.

> You have asked me to give a description of a field after the Angel of Death has passed over it; but I can no more do so than I can give you an idea of anything indescribable. You must stand as I have stood, and hear the report of battery upon battery, witness the effect of shell, grape and canister—you must hear the incessant discharge of musketry, see men leaping high in the air and falling dead upon the ground—others without a groan or a sign yielding up their life from loss of blood—see the wounded covered with dirt and blackened by powder—hear their groans—witness their agonies, see the eye grow dim in death, before you can realize or be impressed with its horrors.

Studying what he had written, Holt realized the impossibility of bridging the gulf of experience by writing a letter. "Notwithstanding all this, you do not see it in its true light."[40]

Letters written to homes in every Northern state contained similar declarations of futility. Written words seemed such inadequate vessels to convey the confusion of battle. Edwin W. Payne of the 34th Illinois wrote to his parents that a description of Shiloh was beyond his literary skills. "If I should live to get home I will try to tell you about how it looks on the battlefield but [I] can hardly expect you to credit the truth as it really is." Even when soldiers wrote only for themselves in their diaries, they reiterated the same futility. The nightmare of Chickamauga caused Captain James P. Suiter of the 84th Illinois to write, "I shall not attempt to describe what I saw, of dead wounded and suffering. It would be an absolute impossibility and if it were possible my heart would shrink from such a task." After Malvern Hill another soldier wrote: "I wonder if any living man of ordinary perceptions and feelings ever dared tell of the horrors of a battlefield. Those who have lived through a battle and passed the night afterwards upon the ground where it happened, would understand, if they were men and not demons, why never, for any slight cause, should war be inaugurated."[41]

In other modes of expression as well, men considered it impossible to adequately describe war to audiences that had never seen it. The furious fighting at Gaines's Mill produced "a scene that is impossible to describe either for a writer or artist," declared Sergeant Reuben T. Prentice of the 8th Illinois Cavalry. Even if it were possible for a gifted soldier-artist to draw combat, believed another Illinois soldier, "the task would be too unpleasant to be performed by me."[42]

Even if they could not describe combat, soldiers tried to assess the meaning of their shared trials. For many, the Civil War seemed to be a particularly ferocious rite of passage. "We had started out as boys with all the enthusiasm and ardor of youth," declared Rice C. Bull. "We had returned feeling that we were men, that the dividing line between boyhood and manhood had been passed by us on the field of Chancellorsville." Oliver Wendell Holmes, Jr., was more perceptive. The future Supreme Court justice realized that military service not only separated men from boys but also separated veterans from the rest of the population and bound them together. Of this powerful, almost mystical, form of comradeship he wrote, "We have shared the incommunicable experience of war."[43]

2

Paying for Victory

As we neared the firing line the noise was deafening, the air was filled with the fumes of burning powder; the lazy whining of bullets almost spent, the shot and shell from the enemy batteries tearing through the trees caused every head to duck as they passed over us. With all this tumult could be heard the shouts of our men and the yells of the enemy.

Rice C. Bull
123d New York Infantry

I heard the grating sound a ball makes when it hits a bone instead of the heavy thud when it strikes flesh.

Thomas H. Evans
12th U.S. Infantry

Our loss is heavy and the sight is sickening, to look over the field and see the dead wounded and dieing laying all over wallowing in their blood, and many hallowing for godsake to help them where no help could reach them close to the enemys work. Their only chance was to lay there and die.

John H. Ferguson
10th Illinois Infantry

The air was filled with groans, moans, shrieks and yells. Prayers were offered and curses pronounced. Piteous appeals were made for water, for help, for death. The sounds came from everywhere, distinctly heard from those near by, and growing fainter and more indistinct until lost in one constant low, far-away moaning sound. Occasionally, by the flashing of the lightning, you could see a dark form rise from the ground as some poor wretch by a super-human effort would attempt to rise, and then it would disappear. These spectacles covered acres and acres of ground. I see them now when my eyes are shut, and hear the sounds I cannot describe whenever I let my mind dwell upon that night of all nights, as I lay among the dead and dying on the night of July 3rd on the battlefield of Gettysburg.

George P. Metcalf
136th New York Infantry

Seeing, hearing, and feeling battle were only the first steps a soldier took
on his journey across the gulf of experience that separated the grizzled
veteran from the jingoistic civilian. The Northern soldier began to reach
a new level of awareness when he first became a target of enemy fire,
watched as his comrades were hit, or was wounded himself. His experience in the hospital or his observation of death on the battlefield carried him farther and faster across the gulf of experience than anything
he had undergone before. These were the ultimate experiences of war,
bringing the Northern soldier to the full status of veteran. Up to this
point, all soldiers shared the same experience, whatever had led them
to join the army in the beginning. And even if they later came to believe
that the war had been fought for nothing, that their suffering on the battlefield had been wasted, they could still look back on an experience that
had made them all equals amid the dangers of war.

UNDER FIRE

At Chancellorsville, the men of the green 123d New York waited
uneasily as the fighting slowly approached their position in the woods.
"We continued standing unengaged in line, a trying time for even veteran soldiers, almost unendurable for us new recruits," recalled Rice C.
Bull. "Looking down the line of our Company as the yelling of the
enemy came nearer and nearer to us, I judged that everyone felt about
as I did; there was no levity now, the usual joking had ceased and a great
quiet prevailed. I could see pallor on every face as we brought hammer
to full cock. I believe every arm trembled as we raised our guns to our
shoulders to fire but all eyes were to the front, not one looked back." The
crackle of gunfire came closer and closer as the Confederates steadily
drove the Union skirmishers. Suddenly the skirmishers burst into view,
scrambling through the tangle of trees and briers as they dashed for the
dubious safety of the main Union line of battle. An anxious moment
passed, then the enemy emerged from the dappled shadows of the forest and fired a volley. "We were warned not to fire before ordered to do
so but as soon as the Johnnies opened on us some of the men commenced. Most of us, however, held our fire until we saw the line of
smoke that showed that they were on the ridge; then every gun was
fired. It was then load and fire at will as fast as we could. Soon the ner-

vousness and fear we had when we began to fight passed away and a feeling of fearlessness and rage took its place."[1]

Coming under fire was, of course, an unusual experience for the Northern soldier, and it became the subject of extended commentary in his writings about battle. Men described with fascination what they saw, heard, and felt while being fired at by other men who meant to kill them. Almost invariably, they relied on the common but effective metaphor of precipitation. Confederate musketry often seemed to produce a "rain" or "perfect shower" of minié balls. A lethal hail of fire would knock down twigs and leaves, chip the bark off tree trunks, and kick up dust along the ground. If the leaden shower of bullets crept over a stationary regiment, such as happened to the 52d Illinois at Corinth, the sensation was much like getting caught in a hailstorm. "Thicker faster they came until it was one continuous humming about our ears," described Colonel John S. Wilcox. "It was wonderful, thick and close they flew. The men lay like snakes on the ground."[2]

If a regiment had to advance into such a shower, the comparison with precipitation seemed even more appropriate. During the terrible fighting in the Wilderness, the 20th Maine was posted at the edge of a clearing in the scrubby forest. The men watched as "spurts of dust" were "started up all over the field by the bullets of the enemy, as they spattered on it like the big drops of a coming shower along a dusty road." When ordered to advance, the Maine veterans pulled their caps down over their eyes as if to shield their faces from the leaden storm.[3]

The random fall of bullets meant that getting hit was largely a matter of chance. Near misses were much more common than deadly hits; soldiers often spoke of projectiles cutting their clothing, denting or puncturing their equipment, and knocking weapons out of their hands. "The bullets from ten thousand rifles went whizzing through the air over our heads, [along] side of our heads, and striking the ground all around," wrote George P. Metcalf of the 136th New York about Gettysburg. Another New Yorker found that bullets not only struck the ground around his feet but also passed close enough to move the hair on his head. The play of minié balls around Wilbur Fisk of the 2d Vermont at the Wilderness was not uncommon. "I had a bullet pass through my clothes on each side, one of them giving me a pretty smart rap, and one ball split the crown of my cap in two, knocking it off my head as neatly as it could have been done by the most scientific boxer."[4]

Soldiers often were amazed that they could endure this kind of exposure and remain unscathed. Robert F. Braden of the 26th Indiana took part in an unsuccessful attack at Prairie Grove. "As we came off the field," he reported, "the bullets were flying suming by as thick as hail and nearly every one was struck either in his person or clothing. I was one of three in my company who did not receive a mark of a bullet." Lucius W. Barber of the 15th Illinois seemed to collect nonlethal hits at Shiloh. One bullet shattered his rifle stock, another bullet perforated his canteen, and a third cut the straps on his haversack. "Thick as hailstones the bullets whistled through my hair and around my cheek, still I remained unhurt." Henry Houghton of the 3d Vermont duplicated Barber's unnerving experience at the Wilderness. "One man at my left fell dead, and a bullet went so near the face of the man in my rear that it took an eye out, two bullets went through my haversack and one through my canteen, another passed so near my neck that it burned the skin then entered my blanket and when I unrolled it I found nineteen holes in it."[5]

Oliver Wilcox Norton of the 83d Pennsylvania was the victim of many close shaves, grazes, and minor wounds at Gaines's Mill. While at close range with the attacking enemy, Norton's musket was ruined when a minié ball smashed into the barrel. "The ball flew in pieces and part went by my head to the right and three pieces struck just below my left collar bone. The deepest one was not over half an inch, and stopping to open my coat I pulled them out and snatched a gun from Ames in Company H as he fell dead." But this replacement gun was not immune to enemy fire either, as another ball splintered off a piece of the wooden stock. Yet a third ball struck Norton's canteen and glanced off into his groin. "I pulled it out, and, more maddened than ever, I rushed in again." Only a few minutes later, the muzzle of his musket was smashed by a bullet, and the rammer of his third gun (taken from a wounded soldier) was bent by a ball. Because guns were easier to find on the battlefield than rammers, Norton secured his fourth weapon of the day and tried to blaze away. Another projectile of some kind hit his head, making only a "slight scratch" in the area of his left eyebrow. Norton survived all this, but he could hardly believe it. "It seems to me almost a miracle that I am yet alive and able to write."[6]

When near misses were replaced by hits, soldiers took another step toward realizing the lethality of combat. Their descriptions of battle assumed a more pathetic tone. For the first time in their lives, young men saw relatives, friends, and other comrades killed or grievously wounded at close hand. "Every five or six seconds some poor fellow would throw up his arms with an 'Ugh!' and drop; then pick himself up, perhaps, and start for the rear," wrote Theodore A. Dodge of the 119th New York regarding the first day's fighting at Gettysburg. "Another would drop flat on his face, or his back, without a sound; another break down, and fall together in a heap. Still another would let drop his gun, and holding his shattered arm, would leave the ranks; or perhaps, stay by to encourage his comrades." According to other observers, a man would "flop" to the ground or sink into the mud "like a log." Some men did not die so easily. A particularly gruesome death was viewed by a number of unwilling witnesses at the Wilderness. A soldier was struck in the head, fell to the ground, struggled to his feet, and, to the horror of his comrades, "with blood streaming from his head he staggered aimlessly round and round in a circle, as sheep afflicted with grubs in the brain do." Within a few seconds, the mortally wounded man was put out of his misery by a second bullet.[7]

At times the sight of a comrade getting hit could be very close and personal. Frank Wilkinson of the 68th Indiana Infantry saw 150 of his regimental comrades fall in only fifteen minutes of fighting on the first day at Chickamauga. His friend Robert Price was hit three times. One ball passed between his right arm and his body, tearing his clothes considerably, and another struck a glancing blow to his left shoulder. Price was so surprised by the second hit that "he turned his head partly round and pointing to the wound said to one of his sergeants *'look at that will you'* just as he said this and while his head was still turned a ball struck on the right side of his face." Price was mortally wounded by this third ball.[8]

The impact of artillery fire on a closely packed line of battle was much more spectacular than that of minié balls. "Death from the bullet is ghastly," wrote Augustus Van Dyke of the 14th Indiana, "but to see a man's brains dashed out at your side by a grape shot and another body severed by a screeching cannon ball is truly appalling." Infantrymen dreaded solid shot, even though the solid iron balls caused relatively few casualties compared with canister. "It is a pitiful sight to see man or beast struck with one of those terrible things," explained George C. Parker of the 21st Massachusetts. "That terrified look of surprise on the face of a man—the upraised quivering arms and slow dropping of them to the side—makes a man sink. 'Oh God' comes to a mans lips unconsciously." Frederick L. Hitchcock saw an officer decapitated at Antietam. "His poor body went down as though some giant had picked it up and furiously slammed it on the ground." The sound of a solid shot striking a respected comrade made a man's heart sick, particularly if it would "hardly leave a trace of his existence behind." A single projectile, a solid shot or shell that failed to explode, often caused multiple casualties. At Malvern Hill, a Confederate shell ripped through the ranks of the 5th New Jersey with ghastly effect. "The shell went through the breast of one man, cut the lower part of the body off another, and took the hand off from the third after which it ploughed its way in the ground without bursting, thus saving more of us."[9]

Canister, an antipersonnel round that spewed several iron balls in a shotgun pattern at short range, was even more devastating. The 7th New York Infantry was hit by a round of canister at Antietam at the short range of seventy-five feet. It killed and injured nine men. Indeed, the concussion of the discharge at that range blew Henry Gerrish, a German native, some thirty-five feet to the rear before he fell unconscious. After he recovered and had an opportunity to recall this terrifying incident, Gerrish believed that he had been close enough to "see half way into the bore of the gun."[10]

Whether fired from artillery or small arms, millions of lethal projectiles filled the air on every Civil War battlefield. Sometimes the barrage of missiles was so intense that men went down in heaps. A Union soldier at Gaines's Mill described his experience in the present tense. "Directly in front of me six men fall in quick succession, so rapidly that I have to pause an instant to avoid trampling on them." Massachusetts soldier Henry M. Cross used a remarkable metaphor to describe the loss of many of his comrades in an unsuccessful assault on the defenses of Port Hudson. "You have seen, in a bowling alley or the beach, a ball rolled into the pins and all but two or three fall. So have I seen human beings fall around me and I left standing." The rain of missiles randomly knocked men down and traumatized any part of their bodies that chance allowed, "from the Crown to the Sole of the foot." One limb might be struck by several bullets, canister balls, or shell fragments while the rest of the body remained untouched. Given the widespread practice of recruiting regiments from the same locality, the cost of a single fierce engagement to a community might be appalling. When Francis E. Pierce of the 108th New

York described the battle of Fredericksburg to his brother, his account read like a town registry. "Bob Collins had his left leg taken off close to his body and it was cut into four times besides and the foot was cut into. It made a ghastly looking wound. Charles Clark had his left arm knocked to pieces, also his left thigh and knee. Frank Downing struck in the hip; John Sanders . . . struck in about four or five places. It was awful."[11]

Observant soldiers not only saw their comrades become casualties but could often hear it as well. The sound of bullets and other projectiles striking human flesh was a particularly macabre aspect of the experience of battle. During a skirmish along the Mississippi River, Captain John W. DeForest heard "a sharp crack of broken bone, followed by a loud 'Oh' of pain and horror" to his immediate right. "I glanced that way," he recalled, "and saw Color Sergeant Edwards fall slowly backward, with blood spurting from his mouth and a stare of woeful amazement in his eyes. A bullet had shattered his front teeth and come out behind his left jaw." John W. Appleton, an officer of the 54th Massachusetts, first noticed this dreadful sound at Fort Wagner. "One of Napoleon's marshals once said that he could hear the bones crack in his division 'like window-glass in a hail-storm.' In our case also the shock and rattle of the canister upon the persons and arms of the men could be distinctly heard." The noise could be poignant—"a thud, a sickening, dull cracking sound." As bodies tore apart under the impact of artillery fire, they added further to the sounds of battle. Captain William Wheeler of the 13th New York Battery watched an infantryman's leg ripped off by a solid shot at Gettysburg. The limb "whirled like a stone through the air, until it came against a caisson with a loud whack."[12]

Few recruits of 1861 could have guessed that parts of their comrades would become projectiles or smother them on the battlefield, but that was exactly what happened. Artillery fire in particular could dehumanize a soldier by literally breaking him apart and turning him into just another physical obstacle for his brothers-in-arms to sidestep or clean up. Brigadier General Edward H. Ripley discovered this while standing directly behind an artilleryman during the battle for Fort Harrison, a part of the Richmond defenses. Suddenly he was "dashed in the face with a hot steaming mass of something horrible" that covered his eyes and filled his nose and mouth. "I thought my head had gone certainly this time," the badly shaken general wrote afterward. "A staff officer happened to have a towel with which he cleaned away the disgusting mass from my face and opened my eyes; unbuttoning my sabre belt and throwing open my blouse, I threw out a mass of brains, skull, hair and blood. As I opened my eyes the headless trunk of the artillery man lay between my feet with the blood gurgling out."[13]

Being under fire, observing the effects of bullets and shells, wondering if the next round would find him, the Northern soldier was deeply impressed by the sights and sounds associated with death and injury on the battlefield. Four decades after the conflict, Robert G. Carter vividly recalled the death of a comrade in the 22d Massachusetts who had been struck in the head by a bullet. "He was gasping in that peculiar, almost indescribable way that a mortally wounded man has. I shall never forget the pleading expression, speechless yet imploring."[14]

GETTING HIT

One of a soldier's greatest fears, beyond watching others fall, was that he might become a casualty himself. No matter how optimistic the youthful volunteer, he could hardly see hundreds of men fall in successive battles and still assume that he was invulnerable. "So we have an indefinable dread," reported a Maine artilleryman, "our nerves subjected to a continual strain which we know cannot end till the war ends, or we are all wiped out." As the years of combat dragged on, more men experienced "unnatural dreams" in which they suffered horrible wounds leading to blindness, amputation, or death. "I would be in battle and charge to the mouth of a cannon, when it would fire and I would be blown to pieces," recalled James O. Churchill of a recurring nightmare. Even worse was the surrealistic horror that haunted the 11th Illinois soldier for weeks after he suffered a serious injury at Fort Donelson. "I dreamed that two officers came and sat by me," he informed his parents from a hospital in St. Louis. "I swallowed them both and they passed down and into my fractured leg, took out their swords and commenced hewing their way out. At this grand 'finale' I would awake with such a start that I would throw my whole body out of position."[15]

For thousands of Union soldiers, the possibility of a serious or fatal wound became a horrible reality. How did it feel to be hit? "The first sensation of a gunshot wound is not one of pain," explained a veteran of the 7th Michigan Cavalry named A. B. Isham. "The feeling is simply one of shock, without discomfort, accompanied by a peculiar tingling, as though a slight electric current was playing about the site of injury. Quickly ensues a marked sense of numbness involving a considerable area around the wounded part." Other soldiers reported differing sensations. Ebenezer Hannaford was struck in the upper shoulder, near the base of the neck, at Stones River. "I remember no acute sensation of pain, not even any distinct shock, only an instantaneous consciousness of having been struck; then my breath came hard and labored, with a croup-like sound, and with a dull, aching feeling in my right shoulder, my arm fell powerless at my side, and the Enfield dropped from my grasp."[16]

Colonel Adoniram Warner of the 39th Pennsylvania was hit in the right hip at Antietam by a rifle bullet. His nervous system was so jolted by the blow that his brain registered conflicting impressions of what had occurred. "The sensation I felt when the bullet hit me was that of a tremendous thump on the hip bone and I thought a grape shot had smashed in the bone, but the sensation was soon gone and I thought I was not much hurt." Vincent B. Osborne of the 2d Kansas had a similar experience at Wilson's Creek. "The feeling when it struck my leg was like striking it with something blunt without any sharp pain in the vicinity of the wound," he remembered. "It caused a slight dizziness at first and I thought I was shot both in the foot and leg." Casting about for some familiar metaphor, he concluded, "The feeling in my foot was about the same [as if] one had hit it with a hammer."[17]

The experience of getting hit was particularly vivid for James Tanner of the 87th New York, who lay on the ground at Second Bull Run with the rest of his regiment, taking Confederate artillery rounds. Tanner saw a shell explode in front of him and ducked his head so hard that it "struck the sod sharply," but he had much more to worry about than a bump on the head. He had always, according to his mother, had the habit of crossing his legs while lying down and now had both feet tangled. He knew that a fragment of the shell had hit him but he had no idea how badly he was injured until someone nearby screamed, "'My God! Look at that poor boy with both feet gone!'" Tanner's comrades seemed to be paralyzed by the shock of this spectacle and did nothing to help him. "Don't let a fellow lie here until another one comes and takes his head off," pleaded Tanner. This broke the spell, and he was carried off to a field hospital, where surgeons discovered that the fragment had severed his right leg except for a bit of skin and flesh and had so cut up his left leg as to force its amputation.[18]

Alonzo Abernethy of the 9th Iowa was hit by a bullet or canister ball just above the ankle at Pea Ridge. He felt as if he had been struck by a club. "The instant I felt the stroke, there came to me, probably for the first time since early childhood, the recollection of stories to which I had listened, related by returned soldiers of the Mexican War, that a cannon ball might take off a leg or a foot with no more pain at the instant, than of a limb benumbed by a blow or bruise. I looked down and found the foot still there." Injured soldiers groped for appropriate metaphors to describe the initial sensations. One man felt "as though an immense timber had struck me end first, with great force." Another wrote that it was as if he "had gotten into a wreck of some kind and that a cowcatcher had battered my leg in no gentle manner." Still others likened the moment of impact to being struck by a hammer or "shocked as if by a galvanic battery."[19]

The thoughts and emotions that coursed through a soldier's consciousness after receiving a wound were vividly documented by many Northerners. Oliver Wendell Holmes, Jr., an officer in the 20th Massachusetts, was severely wounded in the chest at Ball's Bluff. To those around him he seemed "light-headed," but Holmes never thought more clearly or more quickly than during the period immediately following his wounding. At first he felt afraid, but then he said, "By Jove, I die like a soldier anyhow—I was shot in the breast doing my duty up to the hub—afraid? No, I am proud." Then he dwelled on his religious faith, coming to the conclusion that his near death had not changed his mind. He still did not know if he had a soul and had no intention of making a last-minute confession of faith. Holmes put his trust in a blind belief that whatever happened was meant to happen, and therefore it was right. With such weighty matters out of the way, he turned his mind to women—"one of the thoughts that made it seem particularly hard to die was the recollection of several fair damsels whom I wasn't quite ready to leave." He also wondered whether he should make some gesture toward other wounded men, offering to let them be evacuated to the hospital first, but never brought himself to do so. Finally, Holmes tried to imagine exactly how he might die from his chest wound, recalling a fictional story he had read about a man shot through the lungs by a robber. All these impressions and thoughts came to him in a short space of time, and of course, Holmes survived not only his wound at Ball's Bluff but the war itself to become one of America's most famous jurists. He was "struck with the intensity of the mind's action and its increased suggestiveness, after one has received a wound."[20]

IN HOSPITAL

When the guns fell silent and the haze of smoke drifted away, the landscape of battle appeared littered with human wreckage. Wounded soldiers quickly passed the first few minutes of their newfound status as casualties. The numbness around their wounds dissipated and was replaced by searing, throbbing pain. Thirst set in quickly as the body strove to replace fluids lost as a result of the trauma. Days might pass before overworked stretcher-bearers made their way to all corners of a far-flung battlefield. The waiting seemed longer as injured men began to wonder whether anyone would ever come to their aid. For the less seriously hurt, there was time to gaze upon letters or photographs from home and think about those who would be most affected by their death. For the badly injured, there was only precious time counting away as blood flowed and life slipped away.

After the Seven Days battles had ended, Captain Edward A. Acton of the 5th New Jersey labored to describe the sounds he had heard during the night following the engagement at White Oak Swamp. Some of the hundreds of wounded strewn across the field called repeatedly for drink. "For Gods sake bring me some water!" Others screamed for help. "Doctor! Doctor! Oh! my God where is the Doctor? Others again groaning aloud in their anguish and calling piteously upon the name of some friend who could not go to him! And I would hear a boyish voice calling in a sobbing and pleading tone for something or somebody, the sobs choking his utterance, so that at the distance I lay I could not distinguish his wants! Again I would hear weeping voices bewailing their fate and begging for some relief from their sufferings and alas! What was more terrible than all, many were blaspheming and cursing most horribly." Clearly shaken by the experience, Acton added an emotional postscript. "No voice can convey the faintest idea, no pen can describe in any but the most imperfect manner, no tongue however eloquent could portray but in the feeblest style, nor could any language, no matter how chaste and powerful, illustrate the terrible fearfulness of those cries of anguish."[21]

Rescue from the field of battle did not mean an end to suffering, despair, and death. Nowhere was the horrible cost of battle more apparent than in the primitive field hospitals hastily established behind the lines. They usually were located in farmhouses, barns, and other outbuildings, where sanitary conditions were poor. In the aftermath of a large engagement, the farmsteads of an entire locality were commandeered for this pathetic work. The amateurish Union army was ill prepared to handle large numbers of wounded until late in the conflict. Surgeons were mostly civilian doctors who joined volunteer units or who contracted directly with the army to work at assigned posts, usually large hospital complexes in Northern or occupied Southern cities. The administration of field medical care was woefully inadequate, as was the general state of medical, especially surgical, knowledge in the 1860s. A regiment could suffer hundreds of casualties in a single morning with only a surgeon, an assistant surgeon, and a handful of untrained medical orderlies available to deal with the emergency. The system of field medical care was swamped after every serious engagement, overwhelmed by the enormity of battle.

Rufus Meade of the 5th Connecticut saw a field hospital at its worst following the battle of Peach Tree Creek. He beheld "the suffering and dying conditions of the poor fellows that lay there wounded in every part of the body, some crazy and raving and others suffering all that mortals can. Doctors were busy cutting off limbs which were piled up in heaps to be carried off and buried, while the stench even then was horrible. Flies were flying around in swarms and maggots were crawling in wounds before the doctors could get time to dress them. . . . Suffice it to say that the 20th of July 1864 was the saddest day I ever saw, I think I never saw half the suffering before in one day."[22]

The conditions in the field hospitals were unavoidably primitive. Barns, tents, and living rooms were improvised dressing stations, hardly fit for the surgical procedures needed during the hours immediately following a battle. If a wounded soldier survived the first few days, he could look forward to transportation to base hospitals and general hospitals in Northern-controlled cities. These facilities often were constructed from the ground up and thus were well-planned and adequately equipped with beds, wooden floors, and medical supplies.

They also were manned by better nurses—women volunteers from the North, even members of religious orders who were specially trained in medical care. The squalor and confusion of the field hospital were replaced by order and cleanliness.

Yet even in these comparative havens, a soldier's wound could cause him much pain and anxiety. Colonel Adoniram Judson Warner of the 39th Pennsylvania Infantry survived his severe wound at Antietam only to endure many months of painful recovery in Northern hospitals. In January 1863, he received the first of two operations for his wound. The ether dulled his senses and he felt no pain, but the anesthetic produced a whirlwind of horrible imagery while the surgeon cut into his mangled body. "I fancied that I was wafting at an inconceivable velocity over space through regions of every degree of darkness and of light now in one and now in another and whirled round and round at a rate so horrible that I shudder to think of it and still I thought there was no end to this and that these wild pangs that I felt would last forever." Warner experienced in his mind a bewildering contrast between calm and terror. "At one moment all would be light and glorious—the universe radiant all over with rainbow light and then in a moment, as it seemed to me, all was black and dark and the universe seemed filled with all loathsome things—serpents, lizards . . . crockodiles—monstrous beasts of all shapes mixing their slime in their gnashing for me and sounds that no letters will spell greeted my ears."

Perhaps the worst aspect of this experience was that this initial operation had to be followed by a second one. Warner was so terrified by his drug-induced visions that he initially refused to take ether for his second operation, which was more risky than the first. The surgeon had to give him chloroform, a much milder anesthetic, to ease him into the harsher drug. Fortunately for Warner, it worked. He later admitted that he could not have withstood the second operation without ether, which he credited with saving his life.[23]

Soldiers who received major injuries had to struggle for life no matter what hospital they were treated in. Warner won his battle, and so did another seriously injured man, Ebenezer Hannaford of the 6th Ohio Infantry. Hannaford was hit near the throat during the battle of Stone's River. At first he only wanted to crawl to a safe place on the battlefield to die, but the dull ache in his right shoulder and his breath, which came "with a croup-like sound," did not feel so bad after a time. He managed to make his way to a field hospital, where he received emergency care.

But this was only the beginning of Hannaford's ordeal. Carried to a base hospital at Nashville, where he would spend the next three months, Hannaford discovered the true nature of his sacrifice for the cause. "It was there that Death drew near and bent over my pillow, so close that I could feel his icy breath upon my cheek, while in mute, ghastly silence we looked steadfastly each in the other's face for weeks together." More than a month after the battle, Hannaford nearly died when his wound suddenly began to bleed. "I could feel myself sinking rapidly away; a quiet, painless lethargy was stealing over my brain; fixed upon the wall opposite, my eyes saw objects dim, trembling, spectral; in my ears were strange, unearthly ringings, such as I know not how to liken. Earth was receding—eternity at hand." As the surgeon and a nurse entered his ward, Hannaford invited death and closed his eyes with a tired but calm feeling. The doctor managed to stop the flow of blood, however, and Hannaford slowly regained consciousness. It was a "strange, weird sensation, that vague, dreamy return to consciousness." His first thought was to berate the surgeon for saving him. "Those moments of syncope, when over my soul had rolled the waters of oblivion, I seemed to feel had been a very heaven of delight, and it was pitiful service to recall me thence to life and suffering again." Yet he was destined to live and recount his story in vivid detail for a popular news magazine later that year.[24]

The doctors who tended soldiers like Warner and Hannaford were warriors too. Their job was to try to save the thousands of wounded men streaming rearward during and after an engagement. They came face-to-face with the direct results of combat and tried desperately to deal with physical trauma much more diverse, more terrible, and more voluminous than anything they had encountered in small-town medical practice. "I have been hard at work today dressing wounds," wrote surgeon Seneca B. Thrall, 13th Iowa, to his wife. "The unutterable horrors of war most manifest in a hospital, *two weeks* after a battle, is terrible. It required all my will to enable me to properly dress some of the foul, suppurating, erysipelatous fractured limbs." Most surgeons were incapable of working under these conditions without being moved. Kentucky surgeon Claiborne J. Walton was immersed in blood and suffering following the unsuccessful Union assault at Kennesaw Mountain. The wounded of his regiment were forced to lie in the hot sun between the lines for most of the day, and some were nearly covered with maggots by the time they were retrieved. Many who reached the field hospital alive were hardly recognizable as the healthy young men who had volunteered for military service not so long before. "You may well suppose that their suffering is immense," Walton told his wife. "Such as arms shot off—legs shot off. Eyes shot out—brains shot out. Lungs shot through and in a word *everything* shot to pieces and totally ruined for all after life. The horrors of this war can never be half told. Citizens at home can never know one fourth part of the misery brought about by this terrible rebellion."[25]

Like the soldier, the surgeon came to realize that a gulf of experience separated him from a home-front population that could not possibly imagine the stream of torn bodies flowing toward a primitive field hospital. Some doctors admitted they were powerless to convey the sense of poignancy that surrounded the care of the wounded. Surgeon Frederick Winsor of the 49th Massachusetts tried hard to inform civilians of the grim reality of combat medicine. In a magazine article, Winsor stressed that the military surgeon had to rely on all his senses. He encouraged his readers to imagine themselves in his hospital after an unsuccessful assault at Port Hudson. In order "to realize the surgeon's experience you must not only see with his eyes and hear with his ears, you must *feel* with him; for he and his patients are all *feeling;* they feel the suffering; he feels with the sense of touch, the skilled touch. Perhaps none but a blind man can know how all sensation seems to centre in the surgeon's finger at such times, as it takes up the momentous investigation where the eye fails." Winsor grew more earnest as he tried to reach his unseen and uncomprehending audience. "Try—for it is worth an effort—to realize how he longs for strong and steady daylight, all the while compelling himself to be firm and patient, that he may do for each sufferer his very best."[26]

Soldiers visiting wounded comrades in field hospitals were exposed to the same sights, sounds, and smells as the surgeon, but they usually had more difficulty accepting them. William Wheeler found a man whose wound had so affected his nervous system that pain "came in great wrenches and spasms that made him gnash his teeth and beat on the bed in agony." Wheeler acknowledged that this gruesome scene made him so ill that he had difficulty walking to the door. Even a hardened campaigner could falter in the face of what a regimental surgeon encountered in numerous cases.[27]

Perhaps the most terrible tragedy of the Civil War was that it took place less than two decades before medicine was revolutionized by a series of major biological and technical advances. The use of antiseptics and sterilization, and the implementation of higher professional standards for doctors and nurses, would have saved thousands of lives. Unfortunately, during the Civil War, wounded men far too often had to rely on chance, their own determination, or the uncertain skills of overworked and undertrained medical personnel to decide their fate. The most remarkable feature of the medical history of the Union army was the large number of soldiers who survived their wounds. The horrors of the battlefield were great, and the horrors of the hospital may have been even greater, but many soldiers somehow endured and returned to the ranks or to civilian life.

DEAD ON THE FIELD

Soldiers came to realize that after the excitement and danger of combat had passed a battlefield was a melancholy but compelling sight. The chance for glory had passed, and the necessary task of cleaning up had begun. Human remains had to be interred, abandoned weapons and equipment gathered up, and dead horses and mules dragged into piles and burned. By far the most disturbing part of a wasted field of battle were the bodies of the dead, scattered carelessly over the landscape and displaying every possible type of injury. Some men seemed asleep; others were dismembered or disemboweled. Blood, body parts, and personal belongings were everywhere. Battlefields became charnel landscapes, and the hapless soldiers assigned to clean them up became undertakers of the hopes and dreams of many young men far less fortunate than they.

Curious soldiers recorded in vivid detail what the landscape of war looked like immediately following an engagement. Robert Carter of the 22d Massachusetts scoured the countryside west of Bit and Little Round Top and Cemetery Ridge after the fighting ended at Gettysburg. "In every direction among the bodies was the debris of battle—haversacks, canteens, hats, caps, sombreros, blankets of every shade and hue, bayonets, cartridge boxes—every conceivable part of the equipment of a soldier. . . . Corpses strewed the ground at every step. Arms, legs, heads, and parts of dismembered bodies were scattered all about, and sticking among the rocks, and against the trunks of trees, hair, brains, entrails and shreds of human flesh still hung, a disgusting, sickening, heart-rending spectacle to our young minds."[28]

Blood was everywhere after a battle. Dead and wounded men, and those who came in contact with them, were saturated with it. On many occasions, seemingly exaggerated phrases such as "blood-soaked fields" and "blood flowing in streams" were literal descriptions of battlefields. Hamlin A. Coe of the 19th Michigan traversed the path of several Confederate assaults at Peach Tree Creek and carefully noted in his diary what he saw. "In front of our regiment the boys have buried nearly two hundred [rebels], and thousands have been wounded. I noticed several places where the blood has run in st[r]eams down the hillside, and go where you will, there are pools of blood." The phenomenon was even more pronounced at Cedar Creek. "Here and there were splashes of blood, and zigzag trails of blood, and bodies of men and horses," reported a Connecticut officer. "I never on any other battlefield saw so much blood as on this of Cedar Creek. The firm limestone soil would not receive it, and there was no pitying summer grass to hide it."[29]

In this kind of setting, it was impossible to view death as a neat, structured part of life. On the battlefield, death had the appearance of chaos. Its connotations were those associated with sordidness, randomness, and lack of respect for the mortal remains of good men. An Iowa veteran mused on the nature of what he called "ordinary death," that which he had grown familiar with during his civilian life before the war. Then, death had been neat and orderly, part of the normal course of affairs. The deceased neighbor or relative was laid out in a formal manner in his or her home. The body was cleaned and presented in the best possible fashion, loving hands gently laid it in the grave, and the plot of ground became sanctified. But he realized that such ceremony was irrelevant to deaths on a battlefield. "In the 'grim visage of war' we saw more. We saw the gaping mouth and glaring eye. . . . But here a still worse picture met the eye in face contortions; in brainless skulls; in limbless and headless bodies; here an arm, there a leg, and close by, two booted and stockinged feet, still standing in their place but from which had crawled away the mangled body, leaving the red stains as the life blood gushed out."[30]

Some men in blue gained an unwanted familiarity with the dead on the field. Robert and Walter Carter took shelter behind two corpses, piled one atop the other, at Fredericksburg. The brothers lay behind their impromptu breastwork for hours while enemy fire swept the field. "The fixed and glassy eyes stared us in the face, and the stench from our comrades of clay became repulsive to the last degree," remembered Robert with a shudder. He also recalled the "peculiar dull thud in the dead flesh" caused by Confederate bullets. George P. Metcalf achieved an even more intimate contact with the dead when he advanced toward the abandoned Confederate position along Seminary Ridge after the battle at Gettysburg. He tripped and fell forward onto the body of a soldier, killed and stripped one or two days earlier, that had lain in the rain all night. "I was going so fast that when I fell on my face I slid the whole length of this dead body, and a sort of slimy matter peeled off and stuck to my face." Metcalf not only saw and smelled death but touched it as well.[31]

If a soldier happened upon a particularly concentrated scene of death on the battlefield, the vividness of mortality could be intense. Ira Merchant of the 28th Illinois had the opportunity to examine the interior of Fort Henry immediately after its capture. The fort had been heavily bombarded by Union gunboats before the enemy evacuated it, and Merchant marveled at the way the shells had riddled sandbags and huts. The sight of torn, dismembered bodies was even more amazing to him. In one gun emplacement, "a shot had struck the muzzle[,] glancing off, breaking the carriage and killing four men. Their bodies still lay where they had fallen. One had his head blown off leaving the neck bones protruding[;] another had the upper part of his head torn off leaving the lower jaw and teeth perfect. The third was struck . . . in the breast and the fourth had his head partly torn off and seemed to have been hurled back with such violence as to half bury the body in the mud. His beard was extraordinarily heavy and his face looked like nothing but a buffalo robe tramped in the mud."[32]

Over the course of four years of deadly warfare, many soldiers saw death repeatedly. The images could begin to lose their context of time and place, becoming only vivid mental snapshots taken on some dimly recalled battlefield during any campaign. Some soldiers remembered the dead "with countenances distorted, hands grasping leaves and sticks, others placid and one with a pleasant smile on his face." They recalled that some dead soldiers were drained immediately of their blood and their faces shined "white like alabaster." Others found corpses lying with their heads lower than their feet, causing the blood to drain into their necks and faces, turning them into "an awful looking object." On other occasions, Northern soldiers found their dead comrades only after the enemy had had an opportunity to roam the battlefield, stripping them of shoes, clothing, and equipment. It was not unusual for Federals to find bodies that were completely naked. If they had to stand picket the night following a hotly contested battle with unburied dead littering the ground, many soldiers found that the darkened, moonlit terrain added a poignant tone to the vision of death. Such a situation "made the scene appear more heart-sickening" to Harrison Chandler of Illinois. Chauncey Cooke of Wisconsin found it so "ghastly" that one of his comrades covered the face of a corpse to hide it from sight.[33]

Death was bad enough when it was fresh, but as the hours passed, the victims of battle became awful in appearance. Bodies decomposed quickly in the hot, humid southern climate. As the pathology of death set in, corpses turned black and emitted a disgusting smell. Pictures of dead soldiers taken by Civil War photographers, about a hundred in number, clearly show this process. Corroboration of the unnatural appearance and odor of the dead can be found in numerous accounts by survivors, who referred to the "blackened swollen decaying bodies of the dead, festering in the hot sun poluting the air with a foul sickening stench." Amazed observers noted that the eyes of the fallen often swelled "out of their heads," and their bodies became bloated until "they were twice their natural size." Even friends of the fallen often could not identify their comrades because the swelling and the blackening had so distorted their features. Indeed, many soldiers could hardly tell their white comrades from African Americans. Clothes often burst as bodies continued to expand. The smell from hundreds of rotting corpses—animal as well as human—created a pall that haunted every battlefield for days after an engagement.[34]

Besides the transformation of the dead into something that hardly resembled humanity, death on the battlefield was sometimes seen in another seemingly unnatural way. Soldiers often commented on the fact that corpses could be found that did not appear to be corpses at all. These individuals had died in such a way that their bodies experienced instant rigor mortis. They remained in whatever position they had maintained in the last moment of life. It was a peculiar and startling way for a survivor to see death, and many soldiers initially were unable to recognize death for what it was. They spoke to individuals who seemed perfectly alive—sitting upright, casually leaning against a tree, or even loading a cartridge into a musket—before realizing that life had long since deserted them. Surgeon John H. Brinton carefully recorded a number of such cases on the Antietam battlefield. Brinton looked on the phenomenon from a medical or professional viewpoint. Surprisingly, so did George Carrington of the 11th Illinois. After observing many cases of instant rigor mortis during the Vicksburg campaign, in which the percentage of head wounds was unusually high due to the nature of siege operations, Carrington concluded that it was caused by projectiles entering the part of the brain that controlled motor activities. Most observers of instant rigor mortis ignored the pathology of the phenomenon and merely commented on the uniqueness of it. Death could be exhibited on the battlefield in an amazing variety of ways.[35]

Burying the dead was a gruesome task, unpleasant under the best conditions. It was less so if the bodies were interred before too much decay had taken place. Then they could be quickly buried in single, shallow graves where they lay or gathered at a central location on the battlefield, laid out, and placed in mass graves. There seldom was the time or inclination to put the body in a winding sheet, blanket, or box. Normally they were laid in orderly fashion atop one another in a large trench. As a Pennsylvania soldier remembered it, "Two would be laid side by side, then two on top reversed so their heads would rest on the feet of those making the lower tier." Confederate dead normally were given the same treatment, but always in separate plots.[36]

If the burial parties were delayed in covering the battlefield, their work became much worse. The process of decay was relentless. Bodies often rotted so badly that they could hardly be moved without disintegrating, and the living had to exercise great care. Several thousand men perished in the battle of Gettysburg, and hundreds of them lay exposed to the warm summer temperatures for four or five days before being interred. Burial parties found many corpses so badly decomposed that they had to be lifted and moved with fence rails. When these bodies dropped into a burial trench, they often ruptured and emitted a horrible stench that nauseated the living. Men in the burial parties soon learned how to deal with this problem. They ran away the instant a body slid over the edge of the trench, then repeated the process at other trenches some distance away until the smell at the first location had dissipated.[37]

In short, battlefields were not merely scenes of desperate conflict but also huge graveyards. The hastily interred remains of once vibrant men all too often resurfaced after a few hard rains had fallen, turning the landscape of battle into a macabre place where the reminders of death were everywhere. Captain Samuel H. M. Byers found Champion's Hill, site of the principal engagement of the Vicksburg campaign, to be a weird place to camp. But that was exactly what he and his Iowa comrades did only six weeks after the battle. They camped on the same part of the battlefield where they had lost ninety-four men. Byers had a strange feeling as he set up his tent, for he knew that in the darkness all around him were the graves of his comrades. After dinner, a group of men sang a particularly melancholy version of "We're Tenting Tonight on the Old Camp Ground." Byers noticed an unpleasant odor that lingered all night. He discovered the source of the smell the next morning in a nearby ravine, where he found the partially exposed remains of hundreds of men. Many of the corpses had been savaged by wolves and dogs and were missing limbs. Byers remembered the image of this eroded graveyard for the rest of his life.[38]

A year earlier, the battle of Shiloh had cost twice as many Union casualties as the conflict at Champion's Hill. A few months after the earlier engagement, Henry Dwight of the 20th Ohio examined the Shiloh landscape in detail. The experience nearly overwhelmed him.

The trees are scarred, and splintered rusty shells or exploded fragments, rusty guns bent or broken, rebel bowie knives, twisted bayonets, splintered swords, bits of leather belts, ammunition boxes, battered camp kettles, broken shovels, tin cups, knives, forks, and spoons, playing cards, leaves of Bibles and hymn books, lie scattered in every direction, and every few steps are graves with rough boards for tombstones to testify that such a one was killed in action April 6th or April 7th or died of disease in a hospital. Nor is this scene limited to any small space. A tramp of four or five miles would not take one out of the silent and polluted woods, the rotting debris of an army, or the all-pervading stench of decay. On turning to flee to a hill-top for a chance to breathe with full lungs, there also is the pile of dead horses among broken trees which tells the story of a stubborn artillery fight. In a gulch at the foot of such a hill I found a rough board nailed to a tree which bore this inscription:

137 DeD rEBeLs BuriED here

And as I stood to look at it, I cast my eye to the ground and saw a
piece of skull covered with hair, and a little way down the gulch a
bony hand protruded from the ground with the tattered grey uniform still hanging from its withered wrist.[39]

Every Northern regiment engaged in a daily ritual known as roll call.
Its purpose was to maintain adequate records and to provide information on how many men were present for duty on a regular basis. Yet it
could become a painful reminder of the war's terrible cost. The sergeants of the 26th New Jersey, Ira Seymour Dodd's regiment, could call
out their men's names without referring to the roll book, but they could
not always remember to avoid calling the names of men who had
recently died. Even when they did remember, the omission was just as
obvious. The men who were left behind struggled with a "feeling of
solemn thankfulness" or a "rush of sad remembrance" when this happened. "Oh, those silent names!" wrote Dodd long after the war. "For
days, yes, for weeks and months every now and then you seem to hear
them at evening roll-call, and somewhere, close beside you it may be,
an unseen presence seems to whisper: 'Here!'"[40]

Death on the battlefield was the final and most intense manifestation of
the effect of combat on the men who had volunteered to save the Union.
Of the more than 364,000 Northern men who died in the conflict, 110,100
lost their lives in combat. Another 275,175 Northern soldiers were
wounded but survived, many of them crippled and disfigured. A generation of young men was marked by the war. When the soldier had
seen, smelled, and touched death, he had completed his rite of passage
across the experiential gulf that separated the civilian from the veteran
volunteer. He could not return to innocence any more than his nation
could undo the tangled web it had begun to weave when it chose war
as the response to secession.[41]

Citizen soldiers had to deal emotionally with the cost of combat, and
many of them could not avoid dwelling on it. Darwin Cody, a gunner
in Hubert Dilger's Battery I, 1st Ohio Light Artillery, was haunted by
what he had seen at Chancellorsville. "It was an offal sight to see so

many fine young & old men piled up in heaps, to keep them out of the way of the horses. Then to go to the hospital & see the legs & arms amputated." More than a month after the battle he mused in a letter to his cousin Sarah, "Only think how many fine young men are killed every day." For Cody and many other soldiers like him, this line of thought had to be explored before the worth of the Northern war effort could be placed in its proper context.[42]

3

The Nature of Battle

The idea almost everyone forms of a battle is something like a vast chessboard (at least that was always my inexperienced idea) on which the masses of infantry are pawns, the cavalry, light artillery, and commanding officers the pieces, and the commanding generals the players. Such may be the case in the Old World, but a new system was inaugurated in the New World. Cavalry, always playing such a conspicuous part in European battles, was here a dead letter. . . . The ground was impracticable for evolutions, and the foe is wherever he is least expected, till he comes on with a mad rush . . . that nothing can resist.

Thomas H. Evans
12th U.S. Infantry

It does not require a well drilled soldier to fight well. Some men who have been with the regiment 13 months have never been in a fight yet. All that is needed is plenty of courage, a good gun and ammunition for it and I will insure the fight.

Frederick Pettit
100th Pennsylvania

I am sick. Yes sick and tried of bloodshed. Weary and worn out with it. We have been on this campaign fifty-six days and it has been almost one continued scene of *carnage* from day to day. I am not out of much of the groans of the wounded from morning till night. My hands are constantly steaped in blood. I have had them in blood and water so much that the nails are soft and tender. I have amputated limbs until it almost makes my heart ache to see a poor fellow coming in the Ambulance to the Hospital.

Surgeon Claiborne J. Walton
21st Kentucky

SHERMAN WAS RIGHT

Having crossed the gulf of experience from the status of a green volunteer to that of a veteran, the Northern soldier was in a position to know

45

and understand battle. That knowledge brought with it a deep appreciation of chaos, for that was one of the most pervasive aspects of combat.
The sights, sounds, and emotions assaulted their senses, nearly wrecked
their ability to perceive coherent patterns in the world around them, and
forced them to confront an alien experience for which most of them had
no prior reference points. Battle created an environment that most soldiers described with images of dissonance, confusion, and frightening,
nearly demonic fear. Combat tested their sensory, their emotional, and
even their moral abilities to the fullest. They came to know that Sherman was right when he said, "War is hell."

Soldiers experienced what Captain James Franklin Fitts of New York
termed "the awful demonism of battle" every time they entered combat. "Oh that horrible tempest of fire in those few moments!" vividly
recalled Ebenezer Hannaford of his experience in the battle of Stones
River. "Then the incessant din of musketry, the ringings in one's ears,
the smell and the smoke of gunpowder, the defiant cheers, the intensity
of intellection, the desperation even at last!" After enduring his first battle, Pennsylvanian Jacob Heffelfinger concluded that "the horrors of war
more than counterbalance the glory."[1]

The nature of battle became all too palpable to soldiers, but only the
more articulate could describe it with the necessary complexity and sensitivity. Lewis M. Hosea, an officer in the 16th U.S. Infantry, entered the
weird, dangerous world of combat on the second day at Shiloh.

The first shock of battle is appalling. The rattle deepens into a roar
as men get down to the work of loading and firing rapidly; but it is
not alone the *noise* of firing that appeals. The vicious 'whizz,' and
'zip' past the ears; the heavy blows—all these make up a horrible
din that has no parallel on earth. But with it all is the realization that
this is but the accompaniment of a leaden blast of hell sweeping
into one's face as though it were a sort of fierce and deadly wind
impossible to stand against; and the rain of leaves and twigs cut
from the trees, and the occasional fall of larger branches, heightens
this impression of a raging storm. After a little the smoke obscures
everything and the battle goes on in an ever-increasing arrid fog that
would make breathing impossible were it not for the frenzy of battle that seizes upon every other faculty, physical and mental, and
makes one oblivious to all other surroundings.[2]

Battle was a comprehensive physical experience of the senses that surrounded the soldier with a lethal, chaotic environment. He had no control over that environment and often had great difficulty controlling his
emotional response to it. Historian Eric J. Leed, in writing of World War
I, described the soldier's perception of himself as an autonomous player
in a world that could be manipulated. He was used to living this role in
civilian life but found that in the trenches of the Western Front, those
safe assumptions were no longer valid. The result could be a breakdown
of something essential to morale.[3]

The Civil War soldier never quite became entrapped in the kind of
physical environment of combat that the unlucky veterans of World War
I found themselves in, yet he and all soldiers in combat faced the same
problem: how to deal with an environment over which he had little control. Chaos was the theme most consistently used by Northern soldiers
in their descriptions of combat. On all levels—from the smoke-
enshrouded vision of the individual to the confused movements of companies struggling through brush-entangled terrain—the soldier
struggled against chaos and strove to create a coherent vision of battle.

Soldiers often found that combat wrecked the most reassuring element of order in military life: the linear tactical formations that were the
foundation of movement on the battlefield. "It is astonishing how soon,
and by what slight causes, regularity of formation and movement are
lost in actual battle," mused David L. Thompson of the 9th New York.
"Disintegration begins with the first shot. To the book-soldier all order
seems destroyed, months of drill apparently going for nothing in a few
minutes." Thompson admitted that the presence of the enemy was the
most important factor in the breakdown of order in the ranks, but it was
also caused by vegetation and the terrain. A clump of trees, for example, could cause one portion of a line to lag behind the rest, skewing the
whole or even resulting in the line losing its direction and advancing to
a point its commanders had not intended.[4]

As Thompson indicated, the chaos of battle was not caused solely by
the dangers of flying lead threatening frail bodies; it was also the result
of the natural arena on which Civil War battles took place. The South
occupied a vast geographic area with a variety of terrain and natural
growth. Generally, about half the land on any given battlefield was covered with vegetation, ranging from open woods to thickets of scrub trees
choked with dense brush and briers. Maps of several battlefields large

and small—from Wilson's Creek, Pea Ridge, and Prairie Grove in the Trans-Mississippi; to Shiloh, Corinth, and Chickamauga in the west; to Second Bull Run, the Wilderness, and Five Forks in the east—show a mixture of open fields, choked thickets, and grand forests. Long battle lines typically spanned this mixture, part of them moving freely in the open and the rest struggling through jungle matting. Infantry units clawed their way through woods until they burst out into fields and then wormed their way once again through thick growth. Civil War field armies were so large that they could not fit onto the small farms and pastures of the South but sprawled across the landscape. Theodore Lyman, an aide on Major General George Meade's staff, commented on the difficulties of keeping the 5th Corps line straight during the early phases of the Petersburg campaign. It "was not straight or facing properly. That's a chronic trouble in lines in the woods. Indeed there are several chronic troubles. The divisions have lost connection; they cannot cover the ground designated, their wing is in the air, their skirmish line has lost its direction, etc., etc."[5]

Vegetation had an enormous impact on Civil War tactics. It broke up formations, nullified the power of shock on the battlefield, and allowed firepower to dominate the action. This greatly intensified the problem of controlling the movements of individual regiments, brigades, and divisions. Lateral coordination broke down, leaving units unsupported on their flanks and commanders frustrated over the lack of control they could exercise over their own men. Vegetation severely limited visibility, thus reducing the range of rifle fire. Soldiers often had to wait until the enemy was seventy-five, forty, or even twenty yards away before catching glimpses of gray-clad figures. Heavy growth often nullified the effectiveness of artillery fire, for projectiles that hit trees lost considerable velocity and were deflected from their course. Most important, thick vegetation hid targets, and Civil War artillerymen could fire only at what they saw. It also made the cavalry even more irrelevant on the battlefield than it had already become due to the rifle musket. On open ground, cavalry was decimated by rifle fire when it attempted to launch mounted assaults against infantry; in brush-entangled terrain, cavalrymen had no chance to employ shock tactics against infantry.

Trees, bushes, and grasses of all kinds were such ever-present elements on the battlefield that they became unintended targets. Civil War battle had an enormous, awe-inspiring effect on vegetation, ripping the natural growth like a great reaping machine. Soldiers were nearly as astonished by this as by the destruction of human bodies. Lieutenant Colonel Alexander W. Raffen of the 19th Illinois looked with amazement at the field of Chickamauga several months after the battle. "The trees in some places are cut down so much by the artilerly that it looks as if a tornado had swept over the field, all the trees and stumps are pluged all over with bullits it is astonishing to think that any one could have come of safe without being hit." Such destruction led an Indiana soldier to remark of Shiloh, "Thare is some places that it Looks as if a mouse could not get threw alive."[6]

Captain John William DeForest of the 12th Connecticut, an educated and highly literate observer of the military experience, was very sensitive to the sublimity of this part of battle. Industrialized warfare shattered the natural environment of the battlefield, representing in DeForest's mind the growing power of man over the wilderness. It was a power that he felt must be viewed with ambivalence. Observing the effect of Confederate artillery fire during a Federal assault on the defenses of Port Hudson, DeForest noted that "every minute or two some lordly tree, eighteen inches or two feet in diameter, flew asunder with a roar and toppled crashing to earth. For some minutes I admired without enjoying this sublime massacre of the monarchs of the forest."[7]

Few soldiers could actually enjoy seeing nature destroyed, partly because it meant that the stable placement of natural objects around them was also destroyed. Their sense of disorder and the inability to control their immediate environment was heightened when they saw great trees shorn and splintered. It was physical proof that nothing, not even the "monarchs of the forest," could withstand combat unscathed. And it was not only the trees that suffered; astonishingly, even bushes, underbrush, and blades of grass were clipped as if by shears and scissors in the storm of rifle fire that swept the battlefield.

The most famous instance of nature suffering at the hands of soldiers engaged in combat occurred at Spotsylvania on May 12, 1864. In one of the most horrific battles of the war, massed Union and Confederate formations poured fire at each other all day long while locked into static positions on opposite sides of an earthen parapet. Late that night, an oak tree some twenty inches in diameter fell; its trunk had been so pared by the rain of rifle balls that it could no longer stand. In falling, the oak knocked a South Carolina soldier unconscious and grazed several other men. For the soldiers, this tree came to symbolize the awesome destructive power of combat. The trunk was quickly cut up by Federals eager for a relic of the great battle, and the stump was removed to find its way many years later into the Smithsonian Institution's National Museum of American History.[8]

It seemed rather odd to Northern soldiers that trees, bushes, and grass could become casualties of war. That is why so many of them commented on this aspect of combat. Indeed, considering the small size of field armies and the usually short duration of engagements in America's previous wars, the Civil War was the only conflict fought on American soil in which the natural environment was decimated by artillery and small-arms fire. The destruction of natural growth was yet another example of the bizarre chaos generated by battle. Nothing was safe from the lethal fire unleashed by massed formations of determined men.[9]

Virtually no man was safe from that lethal fire either. One of the great untold stories of the Civil War was the tragic deaths of Union soldiers from what twentieth-century writers would call "friendly fire." The Union army made no attempt to determine how many of its members became victims at its own hand. Much of it was the result of poor artillery fire and faulty equipment. The ever-observant Theodore Lyman of Meade's staff noted the frequency of this occurrence: "Not a battle is fought that some of our men are not killed by shells exploding short and hitting our troops instead of the enemy's, beyond. Sometimes it is the fuse that is imperfect, sometimes the artillerists lose their heads and make wrong estimates of distance."[10]

The majority of friendly casualties, however, resulted from small-arms fire. "A lot of Maine Conscripts fired into us the other day wounding several of the boys," complained William Ketcham of the 13th Indiana. Nervousness and lack of training led to the unintended deaths of thousands. Musing on the death of a "wicked profane boy" who nevertheless was a "good soldier" (he was struck in the back of the head by a Federal ball while standing picket duty), Thomas White Stephens of the 20th Indiana complained, "It is a shame that men can not keep cool in time of battle, but fire into one another." The religious Stephens took this philosophically, but many others were greatly embittered by such an unexpected loss of their comrades.[11]

None of the green volunteers who flocked to the recruiting stations in 1861 could have guessed that battle would consume men in this fashion. As they came to know it, some of the glory went out of the sacrifice, and the soldier's awareness of the chaotic nature of battle increased. He had to be concerned not only with fire to the front but also with the potential of fire to the rear.

Beyond the disorder caused by tangled terrain and friendly fire, the ultimate chaos of combat occurred when soldiers engaged in hand-to-hand fighting. When soldiers were exchanging blows with clubbed muskets or lunging at each other with bayonets and swords, all order broke down. Officers found it impossible to direct or control their men, and soldiers found themselves surrounded on all sides by an enemy who was close enough to knock them down with their fists. Hand-to-hand combat created an environment of brute survival unequaled by any other form of battle.

Lieutenant Holman Melcher, commanding Company F, 20th Maine, took part in a classic example of personal combat during the battle of the Wilderness. His company had advanced too far into the thick scrub timber and had become separated from its regiment. He and seventeen men were forced to retreat through Confederate lines. They crept through the brush to within fifteen paces of the Rebels, then fired and rushed into the scattered Confederate line. Although most of the Confederates fled rather than engage his men, some accepted the challenge. After seeing one man pin a Rebel to the ground with a bayonet, Melcher swung his sword at the back of another Confederate who was about to fire his musket, but he was barely close enough to do any damage. "The point cut the scalp on the back of his head and split his coat all the way down the back. The blow hurt and startled him so much that he dropped his musket without firing, and surrendered." Melcher's little band made it safely back to Union lines.[12]

Melcher discovered what most soldiers knew: hand-to-hand combat was so confusing, so threatening, and so unpredictable that men seldom allowed themselves to be caught in it. An unusually reflective civilian, Sidney George Fisher, came to the same conclusion, and his thoughts were confirmed by a long conversation he had with a veteran of McClellan's Peninsula campaign. "I said it seemed to me that the most terrible thing in a battle must be a charge of bayonets, that a confused melee of furious men armed with such weapons, stabbing each other & fighting hand to hand in a mass of hundreds, was something shocking even to think of. He said it was so shocking that it very rarely happened that bayonets are crossed, one side or the other almost always giving way before meeting."[13]

Fisher was unique, for few civilians realized that battle seldom involved close-range fighting. It was the most personalized form of warfare, and soldiers avoided it. To kill the enemy at a distance was safer and easier. Depersonalized combat represented the true nature of modern warfare, making the killing easier to do and to endure. "We hear a great deal about hand-to-hand fighting," complained Henry Otis Dwight of the 20th Ohio during the Atlanta campaign. "Gallant though it would be, and extremely pleasant to the sensation newspapers to have it to record, yet, unfortunately for gatherers of items, it is of very rare occurrence. . . . When men can kill one another at six hundred yards they generally would prefer to do it at that distance than to come down to two paces."[14]

The chaotic elements of battle were also evident in night fighting. It was nearly as rare as hand-to-hand combat because of the difficulties it posed. Although field commanders could operate effectively without seeing the enemy, they had to see their own units and the terrain. Darkness cut the typically poor visibility of the common soldier down to nearly nothing, increasing his sense of confusion and fear. Thus when night fighting did occur, it was usually incidental to daylight operations, the fighting continuing beyond dusk until exhaustion or the impenetrable darkness forced an end to it.

A few commanders planned and executed night operations to achieve surprise. One of the more famous such battles occurred on the night of October 28–29, 1863, at Wauhatchie, in the valley of Lookout Creek near Chattanooga. Union forces had just opened a new supply route into this beleaguered city and had barely assumed positions to safeguard the flow of supplies when Confederates under Lieutenant General James Longstreet attacked them in the dark. Some of the toughest fighting was done by Brigadier General John W. Geary's division of the 12th Corps. His command was struck from the north, the opposite direction from which it expected an attack, at 12:30 A.M. "The moon was fitful and did not afford light sufficient to see a body of men only 100 yards distant," wrote Geary. The darkness covered the Rebels' approach. When they opened fire, it startled Geary and his staff members, who were overseeing the formation of an improvised battle line. The general and about twenty horsemen rode furiously out of the way, cutting through the ranks of the 149th New York, which was marching to take its place in the line. Several wagon teams and ambulances also shattered the formation of the New York unit. For three hours Geary's division fought in a twilight world lit only by musket flashes. Artillerymen and infantrymen directed their fire at these fleeting lights, their only indication of the location of the enemy. To add to the confusion, Geary's teamsters fled their posts and allowed mules and horses to scatter all over the field; some of them were hit by stray balls, and their crumpled bodies dotted the area. Despite the complications, Geary's command held the little knoll that had become the focal point of its position. Night fighting may not have been an effective way to conduct an offensive, but it certainly intensified the swirling chaos of battle.[15]

Eighteen-year-old Chauncey H. Cooke of the 25th Wisconsin survived a night battle during the Atlanta campaign and was forever impressed by the devilish nature of it. While his unit held the line at Dallas on May 29, 1864, Confederate forces suddenly jumped out of their trenches only a few hundred yards away and stumbled forward through the darkness. They began at 9 P.M. and attacked several times without doing significant damage to the Federal position. "It was a night of dazzling, glaring, shrieking sounds," Cooke informed his parents. "The earth seemed crashing into ten thousand atoms. The sky but an hour ago so pitchy black, seemed boiling with smoke and flame. And the horrid shrieking shot, and bursting shells, then the shouting of commanders and cheering of men, mingled with the sputter of muskets and the roar of batteries, made the world about us seem like a very hell. . . . They may tell of hell and its awful fires, but the boys who went thru the fight of Dallas with all its scenes, are pretty well prepared for any event this side of eternity." After the firing died down, the cries of the wounded filled the dark air. This "murdered all sleep" for Cooke, who lay awake the rest of the night pondering the significance of each death in this war as a "sacrifice to the crime of slavery."[16]

For Chauncey Cooke, night fighting became a real hell, not just a figurative one. The darkness that cut his visual contact with other members of his regiment, the brilliant and uncontrollable flashes of light, the cacophony of threatening noises, and then the awful silence of the night, ruined only by the cries of the lost as they lay dying between the lines, combined to turn this field of battle into a worse nightmare than daytime combat.

Northern soldiers knew that chaos was a key and unavoidable characteristic of battle. But as they came to know combat, they also came to know the utter frustration of striving mightily to achieve few results, for another key and unavoidable characteristic of Civil War battle was indecision. Commanders and members of the rank and file learned through hard experience that the war was not to be won by a single great engagement but by a long, seemingly endless series of campaigns to grind down the Confederate armies. The naive assumptions of 1861 were replaced by the hardened acceptance of costly, determined offensives that would take the lives of tens of thousands of Northern men but inevitably would take the life of the slave empire as well.

IN SEARCH OF VICTORY

Northerners had the precedents of earlier conflicts to bolster their belief that the war against the rebellion would be short. The war with Mexico had lasted only a year and a half and had resulted in minimal loss of life, and American armies had driven deep into the heartland of Mexico. An even more encouraging historical example was the series of wars between France and a host of European allies from 1792 to 1815. Napoleon's wars, in particular, demonstrated that massed armies could still win quick battlefield victories that convinced their opponents to negotiate peace.

But Northern volunteers did not appreciate the unique situation they faced. The army had an unprecedented task: to eradicate a government and subdue a large, hostile population scattered over a vast geographic area—in short, to reclaim half the United States. No previous American war had been like this one. It was a twentieth-century conflict being fought by an eighteenth-century military force. American politicians had crafted an army designed for wars of short duration and limited goals, consisting largely of green troops who had to be mobilized, armed, and trained after the war began and before any significant fighting took place. Long delays and bitter setbacks were inevitable.

These strategic and policy factors greatly lengthened the Civil War, but tactical factors were just as important in frustrating Northern hopes for a quick victory. As indicated earlier, the defining characteristic of Civil War combat was the indecisive nature of battle. During the Revolutionary War, it had been possible for one army to nearly annihilate another in only an hour of fighting, as at the battle of Cowpens. During the Napoleonic conflicts, much larger armies had fought much longer, yet one of them could break up, scatter, and render its opponent militarily ineffective. The latter scenario was uncommon during the Civil War; the former was impossible.[17]

Historians have long attributed this dramatic change in tactics to the adoption of the rifle musket by the American army in the 1850s. It was more accurate and had a greater range than the smoothbore musket of previous wars. With the smoothbore, the army that took the tactical offensive had as good a chance of victory as the army that took the defensive. Because the volume of fire was limited, shock was as important as firepower in deciding victory. A spirited assault by infantry in a column or line could overwhelm the defender before his musketry could stop it. Historians have argued that the rifle musket made firepower dominant on the battlefield, tipping the tactical balance in favor of the defense.[18]

Even if the defender was outnumbered or attacked from three directions simultaneously (as happened at the battle of Atlanta), the defender had an excellent chance of doing more damage to the attacker than he received. While retreating, an army could maintain its fighting integrity by deploying, halting a pursuit, and continuing to withdraw. The introduction of breech-loading and magazine weapons, such as the Spencer and Henry, further increased the rate of fire a soldier could deliver on his target, but these advanced weapons were not distributed widely enough among Northern regiments to replace the Springfield and Enfield rifle muskets as the primary arms of the Union soldier.[19]

The range of fire, ironically, remained consistent. Pre–Civil War armies fired their smoothbore muskets at ranges of less than a hundred yards. Northern soldiers continued that practice, although they had weapons capable of hitting targets at five times that distance. This was partly due to the rugged terrain and dense vegetation that reduced visibility. More important, habit dictated their decisions to wait until the enemy was close by. Thomas L. Livermore, a veteran of two New Hampshire regiments, recalled that any officer who ordered his men to fire as far as the true range of the rifle musket "would have been looked upon as light-headed."[20]

The short range did not lessen the defender's ability to repel an attack as long as the rate of fire was high. The maximum firing rate of the rifle musket, three rounds per minute, was possible only under ideal conditions, but even when circumstances were less than perfect, Civil War soldiers could pour in fire. Charles C. Paige of the 11th New Hampshire Infantry was able to shoot 200 rounds over a four-hour period during the battle of Fredericksburg—nearly one round per minute. He had to stop halfway through the battle and swab the barrel with his handkerchief. Later, he accidentally fired off his ramrod and had to find an abandoned one to replace it. Yet Paige and his comrades were able to maintain this rate of fire despite these problems. "They fired with great deliberation and coolness, and stood at their posts in an unbroken line till ordered to retire," their colonel proudly reported.[21]

When the terrain and vegetation allowed the troops to fire at longer ranges, they could maximize the damage done to attacking forces. At the battle of Franklin, Confederate divisions advanced over open, rolling ground for a mile before they attacked heavy fortifications. The Federals were ready for them and opened fire as soon as they could. Andrew Moon of the 104th Ohio scampered over the battlefield that night before his regiment pulled out of the works. "Well, for 400 yards in front, I could hardly step without stepping on dead and wounded men. The ground was in a perfect slop and mud with blood and, oh, such cries that would come up from the wounded was awful."[22]

The linear tactical formations used in the Civil War have been blamed for some of the indecision on the battlefield. They presented massed targets for men firing modern weapons at short ranges. Only the skirmishers—few in number and deployed with several yards between them—could take cover and fight as individuals. The battle line was effective against short-range, smoothbore muskets. The only way to deliver a significant volume of fire onto an attacker was to mass men in broad, shallow formations and fire in unison. It has long been portrayed, however, as a tactical formation whose day had passed.[23]

More recent studies have shed new light on the roles of the rifle musket and linear tactics in the Civil War. Given the normally short ranges at which battles occurred and the similar rate of fire compared with the prewar smoothbore, the rifle musket did not significantly alter the tactical picture. Also, linear formations were exactly the right tactics for the rifle musket. The weapon that would foster a change in tactical formations was the breechloader or a magazine-fed weapon, such as the Sharps carbine or the Spencer repeater. These weapons dramatically increased the rate of fire of the individual soldier and made massing personnel on a broad front unnecessary. Single soldiers or groups of men could take cover and deliver heavy volumes of fire from prone positions. These weapons, which were not widely used in the Civil War, demanded loose-order formations, which would become common following Appomattox.[24]

The most important reason that Civil War battle was indecisive was the lack of training among field commanders, who found it difficult to effectively manage huge armies that sprawled across the rugged landscape of the battlefield. This was the fault of the military system of the country and was felt on both strategic and tactical levels. It was not surprising that the tiny professional army was incapable of adequately training the gargantuan volunteer force, for it was dwarfed by the sheer size of it. Because the volunteer regiments were organized by the state governments, politics and favoritism dictated the creation of this unique force. With only 16,000 officers and men, the regular army could not mold a force that would number nearly 300,000 by the summer of 1862. At best, it could only try to ensure that soldiers were properly uniformed, armed, and drilled in the intricate maneuvers of linear formations. Far too often, volunteer officers had no regular officers to serve as mentors. Most of them had to study on their own, reading drill manuals the night before trying out the next maneuver on their unsuspecting men. No matter how inspired by ideology or adventure, no army of this type could be expected to win a large, complicated war quickly.[25]

Far worse than the regular army's inability to thoroughly train the volunteers was its failure to properly train its own personnel. West Point was not a true military school. Rather than rounding out the cadets' knowledge with intensive study of strategy, tactics, logistics, administration, and planning, the curriculum focused on subjects its graduates could use in civilian society, such as engineering. Given the country's traditional distrust of a large professional army, a holdover from the days of the Revolution, West Point could not get the support to turn out well-trained generals. Many West Point graduates in the Union army rose above their training, but none could claim to have been adequately prepared for commanding large forces in the field.[26]

The most serious deficiency in academy training lay in administration. The army had no general staff to plan strategy or properly coordinate logistics. Although the administrators generally worked wonders in the areas of supply and communications, it was done without the aid of a modern administrative apparatus similar to the kind being perfected in Prussia.[27]

In addition to the institutional deficiencies of the service, Civil War commanders faced a nearly insurmountable difficulty on the tactical level that heavily contributed to battlefield indecision. The huge size of their field armies led to a chronic problem: lack of control. Linear tactics had been perfected by the small armies of the eighteenth century, which usually numbered ten thousand to thirty thousand in strength. Napoleonic armies were greatly expanded in size, but massed linear tactics were still effective because field commanders interspersed columns into the battle line. This broke up the linear formations into shorter segments that were still connected to each other. The mix of column and line diversified the formations, giving generals the option of delivering both shock and firepower. The result was added flexibility.[28]

Civil War commanders relied almost solely on the line. There was little experimentation with column formations, probably due to the shortcomings of their West Point training. The size of their field armies was equal to that of Napoleon's, but they failed to use his innovations. The result was that on dozens of battlefields, lines stretched for miles over rough, broken terrain and through dense thickets. Generally, a battle line of ten thousand men covered one mile. The thick vegetation that smothered many battlefields was hardly a fit environment for even a small unit, yet armies of nearly one hundred thousand men formed battle lines nearly ten miles long across this imposing terrain.

It was impossible to maintain control over armies deployed under such conditions. The result was a persistent breakdown of coordination between regiments, brigades, divisions, and corps. On the offensive, units found it difficult to coordinate their movements and far too often engaged in piecemeal attacks that the enemy easily stopped. The breakdown of lateral coordination reduced the shock effect of the assault and enabled the defender to better use his firepower to overwhelm the attacker. On the defensive as well, a breakdown of lateral coordination could endanger a field army if the attacker managed to maintain his control. The problem of lateral coordination was so pervasive that it even infiltrated the inner ranks of the regiment. On many battlefields, a regimental commander's control over his ten companies broke down, and the basic unit of Civil War field armies fragmented into tiny pieces while advancing on or defending a position.[29]

Consequently, field officers on all levels of command often relied on small-unit action. They sent one or two regiments or brigades to do work better left to divisions or corps. This was particularly true in the first half of the war, when both officers and men were relatively untried in maneuvering under fire. In battle after battle, men were forced to wait and watch as a single regiment went forward alone and unsupported against a force several times its number, with the predictable result.[30]

On the defensive, the field commander's habit of relying on individual regiments and brigades was often effective in blunting an attacker's momentum. At the battle of Perryville, the 21st Wisconsin was placed at least seventy-five yards in front of the rest of Starkweather's brigade, which held a key hill in the face of a driving assault by Maney's brigade. The Wisconsin men were exposed between the opposing lines, battling four Tennessee regiments with only marginal fire support on their flanks. They quickly lost over one hundred men and were forced to retire. Michael Fitch, a member of the regiment, wrote: "The enemy had lapped both flanks and were in addition firing in front. The regiment was compelled to retreat over a high fence and up the face of a bare hill which the enemy could sweep with terrific effect." Its ranks were broken during the retreat but rallied behind the cover of Starkweather's fresh regiments atop the hill. Despite their exposed, outnumbered condition, the Wisconsin men had delivered enough fire to temporarily halt Maney's brigade. Given the inherent power of the defensive, piecemeal deployment could be effective but unusually costly.[31]

Not surprisingly, flanking movements designed to bypass a strongly defended position were risky. If coordinating the movements of units that were within sight and sound of each other was difficult, one can only imagine how hard it was to coordinate the movements of units that were marching thousands of yards, even miles, from each other. Frontal attacks often became the simplest, but deadliest, maneuver a field commander could use. The extensive reliance on frontal assault also contributed to the dominance of firepower, not shock, on the battlefield. Defenders could more easily detect frontal attacks and get ready for them. Given the effectiveness of the rifle musket, one of the few ways an attacker could employ shock was to strike unexpectedly and on the flank or rear of a surprised and unprepared enemy.[32]

Even when Civil War armies achieved some success in reducing the fighting capacity of their enemy, they usually failed to capitalize on it.

Generals were notorious for not adequately following up tactical victories. There were a number of reasons for this, including the impact of vegetation. Recalling the Atlanta campaign, William T. Sherman wrote that "habitually the woods served as a screen, and we often did not realize the fact that our enemy had retreated till he was already miles away." The exhaustion of the troops was a common factor as well. Field commanders typically had to employ all available men during the course of a battle, leaving no sizable rested reserve to fully exploit a tactical success.[33]

One of the most decisive defeats of a field army during the Civil War occurred at the battle of Nashville on December 15–16, 1864. The Federals launched a vigorous pursuit with cavalry, but the Confederate army not only escaped but also regrouped, moved hundreds of miles over a broken-down transportation system, and fought again at Bentonville, North Carolina. It was much easier for a Civil War army to escape a battlefield than to pursue and catch its enemy. The only time it happened in the open field was Grant's capture of Lee's Army of Northern Virginia. With this unique tactical success, the war effectively came to an end.[34]

But that final military triumph of Union arms was preceded by years of inefficient and costly handling of troops on the battlefield, which produced defeats of stunning proportions and victories of dubious value. Within each major battle of the Civil War were dozens of case studies which proved that the conflict was so long and so bloody in large part because of commanders' inability to handle their men, compensate for the difficulties of the terrain, and find a solution to the devastating power of massed rifle musketry. One such case study involved a single assault conducted by Colonel James Nagle's brigade of Reno's Division, 9th Corps, of Major General John Pope's Army of Virginia. Late on the afternoon of Friday, August 29, 1862, at the battle of Second Bull Run, Nagle's men were sent forward into action. Their experience was a microcosm of combat, involving all the elements that made Civil War battle distinctively deadly and frustrating.

Nagle's three regiments, totaling about fifteen hundred men, arrived on the battlefield at noon. During the next four hours, they waited on Dogan Ridge, the staging area for the repeated Union assaults that had been taking place nearly all day, munching hardtack and watching the stream of wounded return from the failed attacks. Finally, orders came from Pope to clear Groveton Woods of Rebel skirmishers who were annoying the Federal artillerists. These woods lay east of an unfinished railroad cut in which the Confederates had posted their main line. Nagle deployed his brigade into two lines—the 6th New Hampshire on the left of the first line, and the 2d Maryland on its right. Fifty yards behind, the 48th Pennsylvania constituted the second line. At 4 P.M., the three regiments stepped off Dogan Ridge, which was little more than a small rise in the ground, and began to march the several hundred yards of mostly open terrain that lay before them. When they reached the edge of the woods, they not only were harassed by the scattering fire of the Rebel skirmishers but also had to cross a fence. Nagle pushed his men over the obstacle and sent out skirmishers. Once inside the woods, he took time to re-form his ranks before resuming the advance. His skirmishers spread out before his battle line, driving the Rebels back.[35]

Among the skirmishers was Captain Henry Pearson's Company C, 6th New Hampshire. They found the woods to be a thick cover of small white oak with a fairly dense layer of underbrush. Nagle's battle line faced west, and the late afternoon sun shone directly into his men's eyes. Visibility was limited; Pearson could not see the Rebel skirmishers until he was at least seventy-five yards from them, but Nagle's regiments had no trouble steadily pushing them toward their main line. Both sides fired repeatedly as they moved. At the railroad cut, Isaac Trimble's and Alexander R. Lawton's Confederate brigades could see relatively little of the action. Not only the woods but also their position in the cut, which placed their eyes at ground level, prevented them from realizing that Nagle's main line had arrived. By now the Federal skirmishers had rejoined their regiments, and the 48th Pennsylvania had moved up between the 6th New Hampshire and 2d Maryland. The 6th had obliqued to its left during the advance to create a space for the 48th. Nagle now had a front of three regiments, about seven hundred yards wide. They advanced to the brink of the cut, angled their muskets downward, and fired two volleys at point-blank range into the faces of Trimble's and Lawton's men. Many Confederates were hit, and their bodies littered the floor of the cut; the rest fled. Nagle ordered his units to cross the cut and continue westward through woods that were as thick as those they had just left. After struggling for a hundred yards, they could see through the woods into an area of open fields beyond.[36]

This was as far as they would get, for Nagle's brigade was unsupported on its flanks. The Confederates quickly realized this and reacted quickly to take advantage of it. Bradley Johnson's brigade now advanced from its position to the right of Trimble's brigade and some three hundred yards west of the railroad cut. Marching at the left oblique, Johnson's men hit the left flank of the 6th New Hampshire and began to get into Nagle's rear. Believing all the movement to his left to be that of friendly troops, Colonel Simon Griffin of the 6th sent Henry Pearson to investigate. Pearson hurried back to the cut and was stunned to find that the masses of men to the regiment's rear were enemies. In fact, Pearson barely survived the fire that Johnson's Rebels had begun to send toward the New Hampshiremen's rear. Pearson rushed back to Colonel Griffin, who still could not bring himself to believe it. The doubting colonel lifted the regimental flag high into the air, where it was riddled with Rebel balls. Finally convinced, he ordered the regiment to retire. The men ran back to the railroad cut and then followed it northward for a distance. When safely out of sight of Johnson's men, they left the cut and moved quickly eastward through the woods to Dogan Ridge. The 48th Pennsylvania and 2d Maryland were forced to do the same.[37]

The aftermath of Nagle's sortie nearly proved disastrous for the main Union position on Dogan Ridge. Marching only a few minutes behind Nagle and following his line of march was a supporting unit, Nelson Taylor's brigade. Many of Nagle's retreating men ran through the ranks of one of Taylor's regiments, but a much more dangerous threat was posed by Johnson's Confederates, who struck Taylor's left flank and rear. As Taylor retired, Johnson received support from other Rebel units, and the Confederates continued to advance in an impromptu assault toward the main Federal position. With only Nagle's and Taylor's shattered brigades in the way, Union officers scrambled to find any stray batteries or infantry units to slow down the Rebels. Johnson and his supports had no trouble dealing with the small, isolated opposition thrown in their path, but they could not overcome the same problem that Nagle had been unable to surmount. Their advance was not meant to be a full-scale penetration of the opposing line but a limited strike that was uncoordinated with the rest of the army's movements. Federal forces north and south of the area toward which Johnson advanced began to deliver fire on his unsupported flanks as he neared Dogan Ridge. The Confederates were forced to withdraw to the railroad cut. The crisis on both sides of this field of battle was over, and nothing had been accomplished by either side except to litter the ground with hundreds of casualties.[38]

Nagle's regiments had suffered shocking losses for their work, which had lasted little more than an hour. The 6th New Hampshire was the hardest hit. "As it came out and gathered around the flag, it was a sorry-looking handful of men," moaned Lyman Jackman. Of the 450 members, 210 had fallen, a casualty rate of nearly 50 percent. The other two regiments suffered a combined loss of about 250 men. The unusually heavy loss suffered by the 6th New Hampshire scarred that unit forever, according to Jackman. He was wounded when the regiment drove Trimble's and Lawton's Confederates out of the railroad cut. Jackman noted with pride that his comrades felt good about having done their best under difficult circumstances, but he sadly noted that "our regiment never fully recovered from the terrible loss suffered here."[39]

The attack and retreat of Nagle's men illustrated much that was typical of Civil War combat. Captain Henry Pearson was absolutely right when he complained that "at all points we were out-generaled." Pope sent Nagle's brigade to do a limited task in a deadly environment, to drive skirmishers from a wooded area that was well within rifle range of the Confederate main line. It easily did this but then found itself forced to continue its advance for self-protection, making an impromptu but major assault against a heavily defended position with no support to its right or left flanks. The men bravely punctured that line but were in turn outflanked and sent scattering. Pearson once again accurately summed it up. "We lost the battle Friday because one brigade or division at a time was sent into the woods to be slaughtered." They did not even have artillery support. Pearson blamed this on linear tactics, believing that the use of columns could have opened fields of fire for the guns. As it was, the heavy loss of valuable manpower produced no significant results and severely reduced morale. "The whole army is disgusted," complained Pearson, and his comrades began to despair of winning the war.[40]

But soldiers like Henry Pearson and his comrades did not give up. Dedicated and tough-minded, they went on to the next campaign willing to accept the fact that one or two battles could not decide the victor in this war. They were sustained by a resilient, sometimes sullen belief in eventual Union victory. Oliver Wendell Holmes, Jr., rightly called this "The Soldier's Faith," a belief that was "true and adorable" and that led "a soldier to throw away his life in obedience to a blindly accepted duty, in a cause which he little understands, in a plan of campaign of which he has no notion, under tactics of which he does not see the use." The Union soldier would endure and try again.[41]

Northern soldiers found themselves fighting a war with little possibility of quick victory on the battlefield. They would have to pay a deadly price for their nation's insistence on maintaining a small, poorly trained professional army in peacetime. The only thing they could do was to obey orders and move forward into yet another costly and probably futile assault that should not have taken place. The volunteer army had no institutional means of self-examination. There were no military commissions charged with finding out why battle was indecisive and offering recommendations for dealing with the problem. The regular army was too small, poorly trained, and overwhelmed with other duties to fulfill that important role.[42]

By 1864, in response to the persistent deadlock on the battlefield, Northern commanders developed a policy of continuous campaigning, a major innovation in the course of American military history. This led to another innovation, the use of sophisticated field fortifications. The first innovation failed to make battle decisive, but it did wear down the Confederate army in a strategy of exhaustion that shortened the war. The second innovation was a major reason that the tactic of continuous campaigning did not lead to dramatic breakthroughs on the battlefield. The North would win the war with continuous campaigning, but its casualty rate would mount exponentially. Although the horrors of constant fighting and trench warfare would be lessened in the western theater compared with the eastern, the last year of the Civil War would dramatically foreshadow the nature of warfare in the twentieth century.

Continuous campaigning was a new experience for Northern soldiers. During the first three years of the war, operations had centered on the pitched battle, a distinct engagement lasting from a few hours to a few days, each engagement separated by weeks if not months of preparation, maneuvering, and idleness. The Army of the Cumberland, for example, spent six months recuperating from the horrible battle of Stones River before resuming the series of campaigns along the railroad line that penetrated the southeastern portion of the Confederacy. Nearly all field armies entered winter camps rather than exhaust themselves by struggling over mud-engulfed roads. In Europe, where geographic distances were shorter and improved road systems offered armies a greater opportunity to achieve strategic gains in a shorter time, seasonal campaigning did not unnecessarily prolong conflicts. But in America, with its dirt roads and great geographic expanses, seasonal campaigning prolonged the fighting and loss of life. Ulysses Grant's promotion to commander of all Federal armies in March 1864 changed this pattern. Grant intended to apply continuous pressure on the two major Confederate armies in Virginia and Georgia in order to wear down their strength and prevent them from taking the strategic offensive into territory already cleared of Rebel troops. The war would be more vigorously pursued, and losses would be great for the immediate future, but the war would be shortened and fewer lives sacrificed in the long term.[43]

As a result, the campaigns of 1864–1865 would be a new and terrible experience for the Northern soldier. The pitched battles of 1861–1863 had been extremely costly. That would not change. Essentially, Grant's strategy would pack several battles with the intensity of Gettysburg and Chickamauga into a compressed time span, each one linked by only a few hours or days of maneuvering into new positions while under the guns of an alert and desperate enemy. The war would shift into overdrive, and the pressures placed on the common soldier would dramatically intensify.

The practice of continuous campaigning fostered another key feature of modern warfare: the extensive use of earthen field fortifications. Earthworks had been widely used from 1861 through 1863, but primarily to protect fixed assets such as towns, artillery emplacements, and river passages. The nature of pitched battles, which lasted only a few hours or a few days, discouraged the construction of even temporary earthworks in the field—soldiers usually had no time to dig them and lacked the incentive to rely on them if they knew that the battle would end soon.

When armies remained in longer contact with each other, both the time and the incentive appeared. Living, fighting, even marching within sight of the enemy placed a premium on protection. Soldiers learned to construct earthworks quickly, often doing so while under fire. Henry Dwight of the 20th Ohio explained this tactical development in an article published in 1864. "Wherever the army moves, either in gaining the enemy's work, or in taking up a new line of attack, the first duty after the halt is to create defensive fortifications. . . . It is now a principle with us to fight with movable breast-works, to save every man by giving him cover, from which he may resist the tremendous attacks in mass of the enemy."[44]

Taking personal charge of the Army of the Potomac, Grant began the new campaign in the first week of May 1864. Robert E. Lee's Army of

Northern Virginia struck the Federals in a densely wooded area known as the Wilderness, fifty miles north of the Confederate capital of Richmond, Virginia. The Wilderness was as bloody and indecisive as previous pitched battles had been, but Grant surprised his men by continuing the advance southward instead of retreating northward to recuperate. The Federals cheered as they realized that they were marching toward, not from, the enemy. They knew the futility of engaging the Rebels in costly battles only to allow them a chance to recover by withdrawing to fight another day.[45]

Those men who cheered their commander on that pleasant day in spring had no idea what Grant's new strategy would mean to them by the hot and humid days of summer. In mid-May, Grant's and Lee's armies met in an even more intense battle at Spotsylvania Courthouse. For fourteen days, soldiers tore at each other in some of the most vicious combat Americans had ever endured, climaxed by a massed assault on a bulge in the Confederate lines known as the Mule Shoe Salient on May 12. As at the Wilderness, the fighting at Spotsylvania was indecisive and costly. The salient was reduced, but the Confederate line held.[46]

Several weeks of maneuvering preceded the next major clash, which came to symbolize the waste of modern war more than any other battle. Confronted by well-entrenched enemy positions near Cold Harbor, Grant threw men into frontal assaults; seven thousand fell in only thirty minutes. Cold Harbor was an ominous preview of World War I, with massed frontal attacks against determined men armed with modern weapons and protected by a sophisticated system of trenches. The casualty rate was roughly similar as well.[47]

The early stages of the Petersburg campaign, which began by mid-June, continued the bloody confrontation that had so far failed to break Lee's army. Offered a chance to capture this small town south of Richmond and force the Confederates to evacuate their capital, the Federals suffered a heartbreaking defeat. The troops were physically exhausted and emotionally drained. Subordinate commanders grew timid in the face of desperate Confederate resistance. By the time both armies settled down into a stalemate in the trenches outside Petersburg, Grant had lost sixty-five thousand men in six weeks of fighting, a number equal to Lee's effective strength at the beginning of May. The Confederates had lost about thirty-five thousand. All that could be shown for the sacrifice, so far, was a tactical and strategic draw.[48]

While the armies grappled in Virginia, William T. Sherman launched his own continuous campaign against Joseph E. Johnston's Army of Tennessee in Georgia. Commanding an army group that outnumbered his opponent nearly two to one, Sherman aimed to wear down the Confederates and capture the important industrial and transportation center of Atlanta. Sherman proceeded with more caution than Grant, relying on maneuvering to pry the entrenched Confederates from one strong defensive position to another, but he did not hesitate to engage the enemy in several pitched battles. Beginning with the engagement at Resaca in mid-May, Sherman's Federals were in almost daily contact with Johnston's Confederates. Large and bloody battles followed at New Hope Church, Pickett's Mill, Dallas, and Kennesaw Mountain before the Confederates gave up northwestern Georgia. Additional conflicts at Peach Tree Creek east of Atlanta, Ezra Church, and Jonesboro took place before Atlanta fell on September 2, 1864. After four months of continuous campaigning and the loss of some twenty-three thousand Union and twenty-nine thousand Confederate soldiers, the western armies knew the hardships of modern warfare as well as the eastern armies.[49]

The effect of this continuous campaigning on the men was dramatic. Previous pitched battles had been traumatic experiences, but the rank and file had always had an opportunity to recuperate between confrontations. Now they had no time to physically rest or to recover their spirits. Campaigning in the field was never easy; now it drove the men to the breaking point. Continuous marching, digging entrenchments, skirmishing, repelling or launching frontal assaults, hastily burying the dead, and beginning the cycle of combat all over again was the rule for months.

The effect of Grant's campaign, in particular, was overwhelming. "Many a man has gone crazy since this campaign began from the terrible pressure on mind & body," reported Captain Oliver Wendell Holmes, Jr. The relentless fighting at Spotsylvania created an exhaustion that severely hampered combat effectiveness. At the Mule Show Salient, two Federal regiments moved up to relieve a third regiment late in the day's fighting. As a modern historian described it:

They took their position along the crest, standing in mud halfway to their knees, with bodies all around them. From there, they fired at the top of the Confederate works until they were numb with fatigue. Some of them sank down into the bloody mud and fell asleep under fire. Their officers, who were just as tired as the men, moved among the prostrate forms, shaking them and shouting at them to resume their places on the firing line. In many cases the officers were exhorting dead men, but they were too numb with exhaustion to know it.[50]

Sherman's campaign was less brutal and wasteful, but it too tested the men past the point of their previous battle experience. Major Stephen Pierson of the 33d New Jersey described how his regiment pushed through the woods at New Hope Church until it could push no more. "But soon through the green of the forest we caught a glimpse of fresh red earth; the strong earthworks were there. Over them we saw leap the skirmish line we had been forcing back, and, the next instant, the storm of shot, shell, shrapnel and minnie burst upon us." As Rebel artillery cut the limbs from the trees, the regiment entrenched with bayonets, hands, and shovels. They remained in this position for a week. The lines were so close to each other that burying the dead was impractical, so bodies "lay there and festered" in the hot May sun. A few men cooked rations behind the lines for their comrades and, under cover of darkness, brought them forward to those on the line. Companies remained on duty until the men had fired off the sixty rounds of ammunition that had been issued to them when they took their places in the trenches. Like nearly all of Sherman's men, the 33d New Jersey performed this kind of routine for four months until Atlanta fell.[51]

The citizen soldiers of the North became instant experts on military engineering. In both Virginia and Georgia, men learned how to strengthen the basic trench with embellishments. Traverses (embankments attached to a trench) were built at an angle to the earthwork to prevent the enemy from outflanking it and pouring a destructive fire into the position. In front of the main trench, men built elaborate obstructions of tree branches, palisades of sharpened stakes, or even wire entanglements—anything to trip up an attacking enemy. Trench lines were constructed to take full advantage of the lay of the land, even incorporating rocky outcroppings into the trench's parapet for added strength. Sometimes trenches were constructed to form a defense in depth, forcing the enemy to deal not just with one trench line but with several lines placed a few yards behind one another. Modern trench warfare, eerily prescient of World War I, became a fact of military life.[52]

Field fortifications hardened the life of the Northern soldier. They fixed the lines in close proximity, intensifying the already fierce nature of Civil War combat. Early in the Petersburg campaign, enterprising Federals devised a plan to dig a mine under no-man's-land, blow up a Confederate fort, and advance through the gap in the Rebel defenses. On July 30, 1864, the mine exploded, creating a crater 30 feet deep, 60 feet wide, and 170 feet long. The attacking divisions went in with inadequate preparation, and the men were awestruck at the sight of the hole and its horrors. The attack was stalled. "Every organization melted away, as soon as it entered this hole in the ground, into a mass of human beings clinging by toes and heels to the almost perpendicular sides. If a man was shot on the crest he fell and rolled to the bottom of the pit." Men struggled for life within a few yards of enemy guns for many hours while the crater became a hellhole. Major Charles Houghton of the 14th New York Heavy Artillery described the scene: "The sun was pouring its fiercest heat down upon us and our suffering wounded. No air was stirring within the crater. It was a sickening sight: men were dead and dying all around us; blood was streaming down the sides of the crater to the bottom, where it gathered in pools for a time before being absorbed by the hard red clay."[53]

The worst example of how fortifications could turn a very small space into a hell of flying metal and desperate survival occurred on May 12 at Spotsylvania. The Mule Shoe Salient, a large bulge in Lee's lines, became the object of a powerful attack by the Federals. Rain fell, keeping the powder smoke low over the battlefield as the Unionists lodged themselves against the outer slope and ditch of the entrenchments while the Rebels clung to the inner slope. The two armies were separated only by an earthen parapet. "Like leeches we stuck to the work," wrote a Federal, "determined by our fire to keep the enemy from rising up." For twenty-three hours the men fought savagely. "So continuous and heavy was our fire that the headlogs of the breastworks were cut and torn until they resembled hickory brooms. . . . The dead and wounded were torn to pieces by the canister as it swept the ground. . . . The mud was half-way to our knees, and by our constant movement the dead were almost buried at our feet." When the inconclusive fighting ended, the men were awestruck by the sight of the horribly mangled corpses. Many were "nothing but a lump of meat or clot of gore," according to Thomas Hyde, a 6th Corps staff member. One man found the body of an acquaintance that had been so riddled there was no untouched spot larger than four square inches. Another man had to rely on the color of a beard and the torn pieces of a letter to identify a friend, for the body "no longer resembled a human being but appeared more like a sponge."[54]

In Georgia, the use of field fortifications also intensified soldiers' suffering. John W. Geary's men of the 20th Corps, who were in action from Resaca to the outskirts of Atlanta, knew this as well as anyone. Geary's division took up positions in the valley of Mud Creek, near Kennesaw Mountain, on June 16, 1864. According to Geary, the stream was aptly named:

> After dark commenced a series of very severe rain-storms, which lasted, with occasional short intermissions, for several days and nights. Our skirmish pits were filled with water, and the occupants suffered much from cramps. All the troops bivouacked in fields of soft, low ground, and without adequate shelter, suffering much from these rains, which were accompanied by chilly winds. Muddy Creek and its small tributaries became swollen to the size and power of torrents, and the low ground adjoining, part of which were unavoidably occupied by my troops in line, were flooded with water.[55]

Although Sherman generally avoided massive frontal attacks against trenches, he duplicated the horror of Mule Shoe Salient on a smaller scale when he launched an assault on a heavily defended Confederate position at Kennesaw Mountain. The focal point of the assault was an angle in the Rebel works called Dead Angle. Some of the best troops in the Confederate army defended this spot against a massed attack on June 27, 1864. In hot and humid weather, the Federals attacked in columns but came up short when they reached the Rebel works, realizing with a shock that the Rebels were much stronger than expected. Many Unionists tried anyway and were killed or taken prisoner as they pushed into the Rebel trench. Others were shot down just outside the parapet, and still others turned and tried to escape. "Men gave up their lives everywhere, it seemed. You could not say or think who would die or be maimed the next instant." During thirty minutes and in a space measuring no more than one thousand square feet, the storm of point-blank rifle fire cut down over nine hundred men in the two brigades that attacked Dead Angle.[56]

Most Federals simply dropped behind a slight crest only a few feet in front of the Rebel line. Here they fortified and stubbornly held on for six days, sniping at the Confederates. They killed or wounded up to fifty Confederates each day. The lines were so close that the Rebels threw rocks and even pieces of cornbread into the Federal trench. Balls ricocheted off the few trees that were left standing and flew into the Union works, killing and wounding men. A truce was called on June 29 to bury the swollen, stinking corpses that had lain since the attack, and then the mini-siege went on. "The men in the trenches were cramped for room, and were unable to sleep except in the most uncomfortable positions. No one dared show a hand or head above the rifle-pits on either side. The hot sun beat down on them by day, and the dews or rain at night. The trenches became muddy and disgusting." The Federals began digging a tunnel in order to blow up the Rebel trenches, but that proved to be unnecessary; the Confederates withdrew from the Kennesaw line on July 3.[57]

For all the horror, discomfort, and disease in the trenches, field fortifications made continuous campaigning possible. Only by digging in could the armies maintain close contact for long periods of time. In addition, living in the trenches itself had a debilitating effect on the Confederates, who were chronically short of men and supplies. During the latter stages of the Petersburg campaign, which lasted eleven months, Lee's army suffered a desertion rate as high as 8 percent per month. Pinned to the cold, bare earth with inadequate food and outnumbered by its opponents, the Army of Northern Virginia suffered an attrition rate between battles that foreshadowed the slow hemorrhage commonly endured by field armies between offensives during World War I.[58]

Ironically, field fortifications also strengthened the power of defense. They provided additional cover for troops and offered a difficult physical obstacle to attacking forces. When defenders enhanced their trenches with obstructions placed in front to trip up enemy troops, they multiplied their ability to hold a position by many times. It would take even more force, determination, and bloodshed to subdue the Rebels than fighting in the open had demanded.

Yet there was no alternative. This new method of pressuring the enemy was the key to the North's military victory. Given the nature of combat in the Civil War, the North could have fought on indefinitely as long as its armies continued the tired routine of fighting, withdrawing, and fighting again. The Rebels had to be ground down in a process of applying continued pressure before peace and the Union could be restored.

This was the environment of combat that the Northern soldier entered. The nature of battle during the Civil War was such that the warrior could expect little opportunity to participate in quick or decisive engagements. Instead, he had to find his way through a vast, often cruel experiment in modernization. The military world in which the Civil War took place was changing, and the average soldier had little opportunity to affect the course of that experiment or even to fully understand it.

This photograph of seven wounded officers, all of whom had a limb amputated near the end of the war, was taken sometime during the summer of 1865. Surgeon C. P. Porter, shown standing on the left, brought their cases to the attention of the Army Medical Museum. All of them were treated at the Armory Square Hospital in Washington, D.C.

Seated on the far left, Captain Charles H. Houghton was wounded at Petersburg in the assault on Fort Stedman, March 25, 1865, by a shell fragment. His right leg was amputated the same day, and he was discharged on July 30.

Next is Captain Edward A. Whaley of the 6th Wisconsin, who suffered a fractured femur by a musket ball at Five Forks, April 1, 1865. He went home on August 15, after having his leg removed.

Third from the left is Lieutenant Moretz Lowenstein, who also was wounded at Five Forks and was on crutches by May 12.

Next to him, Lieutenant W. H. Humphreys was hit by a shell on April 2, 1865, at Petersburg, and lost one of his legs. He went home on August 14.

Fifth from the left is Colonel George R. Maxwell, 1st Michigan Cavalry, whose thigh was amputated because of a wound received at Five Forks. He also was well enough to go home in mid-August.

Next to him, Lieutenant W. C. Weeks of the 5th Michigan Cavalry had an ankle smashed by a ball at Five Forks and "had a firm stump by the latter part of June."

Standing behind his hospital comrades, Lieutenant J. G. Turke's right humerus was smashed during the Confederate attack on Fort Stedman. "He made a rapid recovery after an amputation at the shoulder joint." (Courtesy Otis Historical Archives, National Museum of Health and Medicine, Armed Forces Institute of Pathology, SP 101)

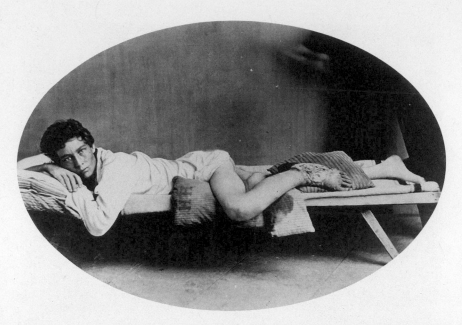

Private John D. Parmenter served in Company G, 67th Pennsylvania. He was wounded on April 6, 1865, in a skirmish at Amelia Springs, Virginia, during the Army of the Potomac's desperate effort to pursue and cut off Lee's army on its retreat to Appomattox. Only three days after Parmenter's wounding, Lee surrendered, and the war in Virginia came to an end. The unlucky private was treated at Harewood Hospital in Washington, D.C., by Dr. R. B. Bontecou. The official diagnosis was "gangrenous ulcer on external side of left foot resulting from gunshot wound." The expression on Parmenter's face, the sweat on the pillow supporting his leg, and the foot itself, which was later amputated, tell the story of his private agony as the nation celebrated the end of the war.

(Courtesy Otis Historical Archives, National Museum of Health and Medicine, Armed Forces Institute of Pathology, CP 1073)

This widely reproduced photograph of a Union field hospital at Savage's Station, during the Peninsula campaign, tells a dramatic and tragic story. Most of the men here were wounded at the battle of Gaines's Mill on June 27, 1862. Photographer James Gibson took the view the next day.

The men with the white straw hats were members of the 16th New York. Their colonel's wife had sent thousands of these hats to cover their heads, a thoughtful gift that distinguished them amid the confusion of the battlefield. The regiment played a tough but heroic part in the fighting at Gaines's Mill. When fierce Confederate attacks on the right wing of the Union line, near the McGehee House, began to succeed, the New Yorkers counterattacked. They retook the guns of the 3d U.S. Artillery, which had been captured by the 20th North Carolina. Later, the artillery was captured again by the 5th Virginia. The Federal position at Gaines's Mill collapsed in the face of concentrated Confederate attacks in what was the worst Union tactical defeat of the campaign. But the 16th New York had tried its best, losing 40 percent of its men in the fighting.

On June 29, two days after the battle and one day after Gibson exposed this view, Savage's Station was evacuated as the Federal army continued its long retreat to the James River. Most of the patients in this view had to be abandoned, and they fell into Confederate hands.

Aside from the poignant historical moment captured by Gibson's photograph, the view gives us a marvelous look into the experience of lying wounded at an improvised field hospital during the Civil War. Injured men fill the yard of a house, with outbuildings and tents supplementing the building as shelter. All the men seem to be quietly enduring their injuries, bandages lie scattered about on the ground, and a number of dressed injuries are visible. A surgeon bends down in the foreground to tend to a man's wound. It is an evocative image of the aftermath of battle and the sights one saw while going through the system of care that tended to wounded soldiers.
(Courtesy Library of Congress, LC-B8171-491)

Taken by James O'Sullivan on July 5, 1863, this view of Federal dead at Gettysburg has become one of the most widely reproduced photographs of corpses on a Civil War battlefield. It was one of at least three images taken of the same cluster of corpses on or near the Rose Farm, on the Union left. The casualties depicted fell in the terrible fighting on the evening of July 2. After three days of lying in the sun and under the pelting rain that fell on July 4, the bodies have swollen and become distorted. The Confederates controlled this area during July 3 and 4, and they robbed the dead of their shoes.

This is an evocative view of a battlefield. The grass has been trampled by thousands of feet, and personal possessions lie scattered over the ground. Many photographs of the dead were taken after they had been gathered by burial details and laid out in ordered rows. Other photographs of the dead show only a small number of bodies in a close view. This photograph shows a battlefield before details began to clean it up and order the corpses. It also depicts a wide view, so that the modern student can obtain a true sense of the landscape of the battlefield. The dead lay about in random order, stretching out into the distance. Even the two spectators who are examining the battlefield in the background hardly intrude on the image. This view is about as close as we are likely to come to seeing what an authentic sight of a battlefield was like.

(Courtesy National Archives, 165-SB-36)

No other photograph of battlefield dead better illustrates the effect of artillery fire on a human body. This Confederate soldier was eviscerated by shell fire. His abdomen is gone, his left arm has been severed, leaving his hand lying beside his body. Decomposition over the course of three days has begun to discolor his face. Although the photographer has carefully posed a bayoneted rifle across the knees, he cannot soften the visual impact of a horribly mutilating battle injury. In contrast to other photographs of battlefield dead, this one demonstrates further the dehumanizing effect of fire.

The view was taken by photographer Alexander Gardner on July 5, 1863. The deceased soldier was probably a member of either the 51st Georgia or the 53d Georgia Infantry of Brigadier General Paul J. Semmes's brigade, and fell on the Rose Farm during the fighting of July 2 on the Confederate right wing. It was taken very near a larger concentration of Confederate dead that the Federal army had to bury after Lee retreated from the battlefield. (Courtesy Library of Congress, LC-B8171-274)

On either May 19 or 20, 1864, a group of photographers working for Mathew B. Brady exposed a total of seven views depicting the burial of Union casualties at Fredericksburg. The dead were members of Brigadier General Horatio G. Wright's division, 6th Army Corps, mortally wounded in the vicious fighting at Spotsylvania only a few days before. The division's hospital was located here, and those unfortunates who did not survive found their resting place here as well. It was not permanent, for their bodies were moved to the National Cemetery sometime after the war.

This type of burial was a bit more civilized than that on the battlefield itself. There was a bit more time to make orderly graves, to dig the holes deeper, even to possibly have a chaplain give a prayer. There even was opportunity to provide a coffin for some bodies and to erect headboards. Rather than being located on an isolated farm, the burial ground is literally next door to residences and outbuildings and, apparently, alongside a road. It was about as dignified a burial for Civil War soldiers as they could expect.
(Courtesy Library of Congress, LC-B811-2508)

Taken sometime after the war, this photograph depicts how long it took for the woods at the Wilderness to recover from the buzz saw effect of battle. The spot is inside the Union lines on the north side of Orange Plank Road. The vegetation was second-growth timber, resulting from the progressive cutting of the original timber for fuel in processing iron during the course of the preceding decades. At the time of the Civil War, the battlefield was covered with short, thin saplings and dense undergrowth. Rifle and artillery fire cut and shattered this growth, leaving it surprisingly open in many cases for several years. Note the human bones in the foreground. Many battlefields yielded such remains for decades after the conflict. Civil War combat was devastating to the natural environment, but the effect was localized to areas of intense action. Eventually, the environment healed itself.
(Courtesy Massachusetts Commandery, Military Order of the Loyal Legion and the U.S. Army Military History Institute)

The widespread use of earthworks in the 1864 campaigns greatly intensified the effect of combat on soldiers. It protected those on the defensive and made attacks even more costly and less likely to succeed. When armies remained within firing range of each other for days at a time, a tactic made possible by fortifications, they had less opportunity to rest, eat properly, clean themselves adequately, or even to relieve themselves. Fortifications were a great tactical boon to Civil War armies as well as a hellish way to fight a war.

This photograph depicts a typical Confederate work on the Wilderness battlefield. It was made by cutting small trees, building a revetment (or short wall, supported by upright posts), and then piling earth in front of it. This parapet provided cover for the defending soldiers and was short enough so that they could fire their muskets over it. The earth came from the shallow trench that the man in civilian clothes is standing in, and from a ditch dug in front of the parapet. There may have been headlogs placed on top of the parapet, raised above it so that musket barrels could be stuck beneath the log. This arrangement offered almost complete protection for the soldier. The logs in the foreground, which slant off at an angle from the parapet, are meant to cover the right flank of the line as it stood behind the parapet. The photographer undoubtedly is standing in the roadbed of the Orange Turnpike, looking north.

(Courtesy Massachusetts Commandery, Military Order of the Loyal Legion and the U.S. Army Military History Institute)

In the west as well as in Virginia, Union soldiers found themselves confronted by sophisticated and extensive fortifications as they tried to capture Atlanta. This photograph, taken after the fall of the city, depicts a segment of the defensive line that surrounded Atlanta. It was so strongly built that Sherman refused to attack it directly, preferring to maneuver the Confederate army out of the city by cutting off its supply lines.

The photograph offers an excellent view of many different types of fortifications. It was taken at a redoubt, or fort, an enclosed earthwork built on high ground. The photographer was standing on top of a forward-facing parapet, looking toward the next high ground. An artillery emplacement is in the foreground, with an embrasure cut into the parapet and revetted with small saplings. The gun emplacement is also protected by traverses built to its side for flank protection, and revetted by boards. Another gun emplacement is just to the right of the first one, with another embrasure opened through the parapet to deliver fire in another direction. The interior slope of the parapet is also revetted with boards and posts.

In the middle and background, one can see the connecting infantry trench. It has headlogs on top of the parapet with poles stretching across the trench to catch the headlogs in case they fall off or are rolled backward by artillery fire. There are many traverses behind the infantry trench as well, to serve as flank protection and as living quarters. Poles stretched across the traverses supported tent halves to shield men from the sun and weather. A small redoubt is a short distance from the photographer, and notice the roads that have been well worn behind the trench for communication along the line. There are several rows of obstructions in front of the infantry line, including at least three rows of slanted stakes and a lot of small timber that has been felled to form an abatis. This and several other photographs of the Atlanta defenses amply demonstrate what Rebel earthworks looked like before they were heavily altered by occupying troops seeking firewood.
(Courtesy National Archives, 111-B-4739)

Halfway to Atlanta, Sherman's men crossed the Etowah River to outflank Johnston's army from its stronghold in the Allatoona Mountains. The Confederates were able to shift troops into their path in the middle of a region of rolling terrain and thick, heavy growth. Joseph Hooker's 20th Corps hit the Confederates at a road junction where New Hope Church stood. The resulting battle, fought on May 25, 1864, stopped Sherman's advance. It led to further battles at Pickett's Mill to the east and Dallas to the west, as the Federals tried unsuccessfully to outflank the position at New Hope. For several days, Sherman was stalled in the thickets while his army sniped and fired artillery at the Confederate works. Then, he outflanked the position and continued south toward Atlanta.

Photographer George Barnard exposed this view a few months after the campaign. It shows the dense woods typical of the region as well as a section of the Confederate field works. These were hastily constructed, under fire at times, and were only temporarily occupied. Thus they were not as sophisticated or extensive as the semipermanent works around Atlanta. The parapet was made of logs with earth piled on top, and was beginning to fall apart by the time Barnard arrived. The line ran along the crest of a shallow slope that curved around the junction of the road from Pumpkin Vine Creek with the road to Dallas. Barnard's view is from the front of the works where one of the two roads, almost certainly the Dallas road, crossed them. The photographer's wagon, tent, and assistant are in the background. Also, the effect of the fighting on trees and vegetation was still evident when Barnard took this view. (Courtesy Library of Congress, LC-B8184-8126)

Sherman sent his men into headlong frontal attacks against the Confederate works only once during the Atlanta campaign, on June 27, at Kennesaw Mountain. They assaulted at two places, here, along the Burnt Hickory Road, and about a mile farther south at the Dead Angle. George Barnard exposed this view so as to include the imposing profile of the mountain as well as Union earthworks dug after the assault.

The small eminence on the right is Pigeon Hill, held by a brigade of Missouri Confederates. Next to it rises Little Kennesaw, and on the far left one can barely see the outline of Big Kennesaw. The Burnt Hickory Road approaches from the west and passes Pigeon Hill. Before the attack of June 27, the area where Barnard stood to take this photograph was occupied by Confederate pickets from the Georgia brigade of Brigadier General Hugh W. Mercer. Many of them stood their ground so stoutly in the initial phase of the assault that they were bayoneted in their place. Then, the brigades of Brigadier General Giles A. Smith and Brigadier General Joseph A. J. Lightburn, from the 15th Army Corps, attacked over this ground, Smith north of the road and Lightburn south of it. Although Lightburn was stopped by artillery fire in the open field south and west of Pigeon Hill, Smith's men managed to climb at least part way up the western slope. These meager successes were far too few to make a difference.

This work in the foreground was made for several artillery pieces. Revetted embrasures are clearly visible, and small traverses to flank the gun emplacements are made of earth and logs. In fact, Barnard stood on a traverse to expose this view. Fence rails have also been used to make the parapet, along with boards, saplings, and rocks. Like beavers, the men of Sherman's army have carefully built this work with whatever material was at hand.
(Courtesy Library of Congress, LC-B8184-10402)

Taken during the winter of 1864, before the beginning of the Atlanta campaign, this photograph shows a regiment of the Army of the Cumberland deployed in battle line with a company acting as skirmishers out in front. The flag is barely visible as a blur in the middle of the regimental battle line. This was a sight all too common to Northern soldiers. The linear tactical formations in which they operated are well defined in this view, as well as the wooden huts, complete with canvas roofs and chimneys, they had built for themselves as winter quarters.
(Courtesy Massachusetts Commandery, Military Order of the Loyal Legion and the U.S. Army Military History Institute)

On November 25, 1863, the Federals attacked the main Confederate position outside Chattanooga in an effort to break the Southern "siege" of that strategic city. Grant placed most of his trust on Sherman's assault against the north end of Missionary Ridge, but his subordinate's troops immediately ran into trouble. They were unfamiliar with the terrain and were opposed by the best division in the western Confederate army, led by Patrick Cleburne. The Texans of Cleburne's division were in an excellent position, slightly entrenched atop Tunnel Hill with a steep slope and a spur before them.

This sketch by Alfred R. Waud depicts the attack of Brigadier General John M. Corse's brigade along the spur. Despite fierce small arms and artillery fire, the Federals managed to make it to within fifty feet of Cleburne's position before they were driven back down the slope. Waud's sketch vividly conveys the hazy, imprecise image of the battlefield, swathed in powder smoke and limited by vegetation. No enemy troops are visible, even a portion of the Federal line is obscured by smoke. The neat battle line seen in the drill of the Army of the Cumberland photograph is here a struggling line of men desperately trying to do a job that was too much for them.
(Courtesy Library of Congress, LC-28380-7042)

This is one of the best group photographs of Civil War soldiers ever taken. It was exposed by photographer A. J. Russell and depicts men of Brigadier General William T. H. Brooks's 1st Division, 6th Army Corps, Army of the Potomac. They are resting in trenches dug on the west bank of the Rappahannock River, about two miles south of Fredericksburg, a little before the Chancellorsville campaign. Only a few days later, other units of the 6th Corps stormed the Confederate positions west of town and took them in heavy fighting, in an effort to come to the aid of the rest of the army battling some twelve miles west at Chancellorsville. Brooks's division took part in the fighting at Salem Church, the farthest point the 6th Corps reached in this failed effort to help Hooker. The end of this tragic campaign saw both Hooker and the 6th Corps retreat.

For over a century after Appomattox, this photograph was believed to have been taken in the trenches at Petersburg, during the final few months of the war. But, recent research has proven that it was taken at the midpoint of the war, on the eve of a bloody battle. The expressions on the faces of these men, the close view of their equipment and clothing, the proximity of artillery pieces and earthen fortifications, all present the student a rich opportunity to imagine what it would be like to be in the middle of a regiment on an ordinary day, surrounded by the trappings of war.

(Courtesy National Archives, 111-B-157)

Henry A. Kircher, the son of German immigrants, rose through the ranks to become a captain in the German 12th Missouri Infantry. He was severely wounded in the battle of Ringgold, Georgia, November 27, 1863, at the end of the Chattanooga campaign. Kircher was hit in the right arm, shattering the bone. While he was sitting, immobilized on the ground, another bullet hit his left leg, splitting the tibia so badly that the attending surgeon could put his finger into the fracture. While he was being carried away, a third bullet caused a flesh wound.

His right arm and left leg were amputated and on Christmas day, he returned to his Belleville, Illinois, home. He was carried on the regimental rolls as being on sick leave for the duration of the unit's term of enlistment, which ended in August 1864. But in the meanwhile, Kircher had to try to pick up the pieces of his young life. His uncle, Henry Goedeking, generously offered to help his nephew break into local politics. In March 1865, Kircher announced his candidacy for the position of Circuit Court Clerk of St. Clair County. Goedeking also announced that he would supervise his nephew's work, without pay, and even take over the office if Kircher found it too much for his stamina. In any case, Kircher would have a regular paycheck.

This photograph was circulated as part of Kircher's election campaign. Described by a local newspaper as "a young man, and popular," he remained independent of partisan affiliations and won 4,316 votes compared to his opponent's 2,643.

The election changed Kircher's life. He had been an obscure, nineteen-year-old machinist before the war. Now he became involved in publishing ventures, the board of education, and served as mayor of Belleville. He married in 1880, fathered three sons, outlived his wife, and died in 1908 at the age of sixty-six. Kircher was a good example of a Union veteran who triumphed over his war experience.

(Courtesy Illinois State Historical Library, Old State Capitol, Springfield)

Thousands of Northern veterans journeyed to Southern battlefields after the war to regain contact with their war experience. This photograph depicts one group of them standing on the Orange Plank Road on the Wilderness battleground. The condition of the roadbed and the vegetation are still very close to their appearance in 1864. The choking thickness of the small, scrub trees, with only a narrow opening through them as far as the eye can see, made the Wilderness one of the most difficult landscapes on which to manuever large numbers of troops.

Perhaps that is one reason so many survivors visited the Wilderness. Of all the fierce battles that were fought between Lee and Grant, this one seemed to capture the imagination of the nation more than any other. These men are dressed in civilian clothes and are visibly older than most Civil War soldiers would have been in the 1860s, but their imaginations probably have been taken back to their war experience, for good or bad. Many veterans noted that physically placing themselves back in the environment of the battlefield emotionally brought the war back to them.
(Courtesy Massachusetts Commandery, Military Order of the Loyal Legion and the U.S. Army Military History Institute)

4

Defining Courage

I care not what others may say about having no fear while in danger. I knew enough to know that there was danger on every hand. I could hear men cry out in pain as they were shot, and appreciated the situation I was in. I placed my knapsack, frying-pan, canteen and the butt of my gun between me and the flying bullets and tried in every way to lie as flat on the ground as I possibly could. I remember as I lay there, with death being dealt out on every side, of saying to myself, "What a fool you were to enlist. You need not have come. You were only eighteen years old and could not have been drafted."

George P. Metcalf
136th New York

To the raw recruit the crash of small arms and the roar of cannon are simply appalling; he felt that he was going forward to certain death. With pale cheeks and clenched teeth he held his place, determined to do his duty as best he might. If very much excited, he loaded his musket, and, forgetting to put on the necessary percussion-cap, went through the motion of firing, only to ram a fresh cartridge on top of the first one, when, for the first time using a cap, he was incontinently knocked down by the tremendous recoil of his gun, and believed he was badly wounded. . . . Finally the green soldier discovers that he is not hurt, and that everybody does not get killed in an engagement, so he regains confidence and passes successfully through his baptism of fire.

George F. Williams
New York Volunteers

The man who does not dread to die or to be mutilated is a lunatic. The man who, dreading these things, still faces them for the sake of duty and honor is a hero.

John William DeForest
12th Connecticut

As I look back upon it, it seems astonishing how soon all the natural feelings of apprehension and fear give way to what has been aptly termed the "battle rage," which lifts a man up to a plane where the things of the body are forgotten. Amid the roar and din of musketry and the horrible swish and shriek of shells, the intellect seemed to be disembodied, and, while conscious of the danger of being hurled headlong into eternity at any moment, the pressure upon the brain seemed to deaden the physical senses—fear among them. Fear came later when the fight was over, just as in the waiting moments before it began; but throughout the day while the battle was on I remember having a singular feeling of curiosity about personal experiences. I seemed to be looking down upon my bodily self with a sense of impersonality and wondering why I was not afraid in the midst of all this horrible uproar and danger. I suppose this was the common experience of soldiers, for if it were not so, battles could not be fought.

Lewis M. Hosea
16th U.S. Infantry

The environment of battle offered plenty of danger for the Northern soldier. As he entered into it, he began the process of defining his role in war, of discovering the makeup of his own character. He was forced to find the limits of bravery and of cowardice within himself, to delineate his own personal field of battle.

Most of the men who flocked to the regimental recruiting stations came through this personal reckoning intact. These neophyte soldiers were pushed to the margins of their endurance in their first and subsequent battles, but they managed to remain on the safe side of those margins. They stayed in line, fired their muskets, and obeyed orders. Even those men who flinched in their first engagement were not necessarily lost; they had the opportunity to redeem themselves in the eyes of their comrades in future engagements. There was a tenuous point in every soldier's career when he began to realize that battle was not what he expected it to be and that he would have to come to grips with that new reality. How he acted in that moment determined whether he would become a victim of war or a victor over its horrors.

It may seem obvious to state that most soldiers managed to meet this challenge successfully (for how could the Union have won the war if they had not?), but it is worth repeating. Most, but not all, endured the test. They defined themselves as soldiers capable of dealing with the worst that combat had to offer. But first, they had to define courage itself.

THE NATURE OF BRAVERY

Observant soldiers concluded that most warriors were a mixture of good and bad qualities. William A. Ketcham of Indiana believed that 10 percent of the Northern army were "arrant cowards" who had to be bullied and prodded into battle. They were adept at finding ways to get out of combat and always came up with plausible excuses for their absence. Other commentators placed the proportion of these men as high as 25 percent. Ketcham believed that another 10 percent of the Northern army were genuinely courageous, and the remaining 80 percent fell somewhere in the range between cowardice and bravery. Some of the latter tended consistently to one extreme or the other in every engagement; others waffled in their tendencies from one battle to the next. These men remained within the safe margins of acceptability, however. Whether they gave consistently good service to the cause or limited their contributions, they did not desert, refuse to perform duty, or stage mutinies. They held on, to a greater or lesser degree, to the role of the soldier and pulled the Northern war effort through to victory.[1]

Soldiers often differentiated between moral and physical courage, believing the former to be inspired by a recognition of the terror and danger of the battlefield. The man of moral courage consciously rose above those fears and performed his duty. The man of physical courage responded only to the nervous stimulus of combat; his bravery was the unthinking action of one who foolishly ignored danger and indulged in the rush of sensation. Perhaps a major reason that so many essentially solid and sincere men waffled in their duties during the war was that they could not consistently balance their moral and their physical courage. At times, one force or the other might be weaker or stronger.

Moral courage was widely recognized as the more reliable form of bravery, because it was based on reflection and higher purpose. Physical courage, by nature, could be fickle. Excitement could lead a man to run away as readily as it could inspire him to fight. William T. Sherman believed that the soldier who had "true courage" was one who possessed "all his faculties and sense perfectly when serious danger is actually present." Thus observers were convinced that moral courage was "a daily necessity," and physical courage was needed "only in emergencies."[2]

The lack of physical courage, and of moral courage as well, was strongly illustrated in the case of a gunner who served with William A. Moore in the 3d New York Light Battery. He had been a professional boxer before the war and was full of enthusiasm for a fight. In fact, he constantly bragged about his willingness to take on any man in the battery. But when he first heard Rebel artillery, "he went into convulsions through fear." Moore called him "the only case of constitutional cow-ardice" he had encountered during the war. The deflated fighter was assigned as company cook. In his own way, he aided the Union cause without having to deal with battle.[3]

Like the unfortunate New York boxer, many soldiers found that the hardest part of the test was their first battle. Those men with no previ-ous insight into the psychology of the soldier simply took what battle had to offer and either caved in under its pressure or managed to cope. A few, such as Frank Holsinger of Pennsylvania, sensed enough about the environment of battle before their first engagement to debate with their comrades about how they would react to it. Holsinger argued that if he broke and ran at the first shot, he could forget about becoming a useful soldier. If he managed to stand his ground through the initial vol-leys, he would know that he had passed the test. Holsinger won this contest with his nerves.[4]

Many other new soldiers did not fare as well as Holsinger. The North-ern war effort was characterized by several battlefield reverses involv-ing green troops, many of whom not only retreated under fire but also lost their sense of unit cohesion and turned into masses of uncontrolled men of no use to their commanders. In some cases, these masses became infected with fear and turned into mobs. The impact of these events cast a pall over Northern soldiers' sense of pride and confidence. They had to overcome these setbacks, which were not only battlefield defeats but severe tests of civilian morale on the home front as well.

The first and most famous of these classic disasters occurred at First Bull Run on July 21, 1861. Major General Irvin McDowell's unprepared army of ninety-day volunteers, with a leavening of regular troops and professional officers, began the first of many advances toward Rich-mond. It met a Confederate army of equally unprepared volunteers. After a successful flank march the Federals could not press home their advantage. Their advance faltered, Confederate reinforcements arrived, and the green Yankees began to retreat. It started with the usual strag-gling—individual soldiers sneaking out of line and making their way to the rear. Then entire regiments retreated from the deadly pressure of Confederate advances. Many of them began to break up. "The road was filled with wagons, artillery, retreating cavalry and infantry in one con-fused mass, each seemingly bent on looking out for number one and let-ting the rest do the same," reported one disgusted Federal. This mass became bottlenecked at the crossing of Cub Run. Confederate artillery fire blocked the bridge by causing a team to upset a wagon on it. Panic set in as the desperate Union soldiers bolted for any path that would take them toward safety. Much of McDowell's army atomized; he could only lament its disintegration and accurately reported that his "retreat soon became a rout, and this soon degenerated still further into a panic."[5]

A better example of a Northern field army disintegrating on the battlefield occurred at the battle of Richmond, Kentucky, on August 30, 1862. This was the first engagement of a remarkable Confederate invasion designed to reverse a series of Rebel defeats over the previous six months. A hastily organized field army, consisting of regiments only recently raised, tried to stop an army of men who had seen a year of service. The Rebels were veterans of hard-fought battles such as Pea Ridge and Shiloh, they were eager to take the offensive into Kentucky, and they were commanded by aggressive, experienced officers. In contrast, the Union regiments were willing to do their duty but were pitifully unprepared. The 71st Indiana had been issued ammunition for the first time less than two weeks before the battle; it performed its first battalion drill, loading and firing by company and practicing maneuvers in a regimental battle line, on the morning of August 29. These men were even more green than those who had fled from Bull Run.[6]

At first, the neophyte soldiers did well. They met the Confederates in three separate engagements south of Richmond, putting up stiff resistance each time while on the defensive. But the Rebel army was slightly more numerous and much more skilled in maneuvering. It outflanked the Federals in the first engagement and pursued. As at First Bull Run, the green Yankees could not retreat effectively. The 71st Indiana fled "in great confusion" and lost its two ranking officers. When the army gathered for a stand two miles away, the regiment could not re-form its company organization, and the men "fell into line whare ever it was most convenient." Forced to retreat from this engagement as well, the Federal army practically broke apart and became a mob. When a third stand was made by less than half the original army, the officer who found himself in command of the 71st Indiana decided that forcing his men to fight would result in "our total annihilation or capture." He took what he could gather of the 71st Indiana and left the field. The Confederates sent the few resisting Federals flying and went on to capture Lexington and

Frankfort. About forty-eight hundred of the sixty-five hundred Federals were captured, most of them following the third engagement, when company and regimental cohesion disappeared, and individual soldiers scampered across the rolling landscape of Kentucky bluegrass trying to find a safe place to recuperate from the shock of their first and most traumatic battle. The 71st Indiana took about 800 men into the conflict, suffered 130 killed and wounded, and managed to collect 224 stragglers near Louisville by September 8. It was the worst way for a new regiment to face combat.[7]

Yet these men and their regiments recovered from this introduction to warfare. Captives were exchanged, and stragglers were gathered. All the Federal regiments at Richmond went on to do good service on other fields of battle. They had an advantage in that everyone ran, allowing individuals to find comfort and anonymity in numbers. They felt less guilt and could recover from the trauma as a group rather than as an individual among others who did not run. One of the regiments, the 69th Indiana Infantry, next saw battle at Chickasaw Bluffs in December 1862. The men were ready and performed well, but the memory of Richmond lingered. Alonzo Marshall hoped that the coming campaign would not turn out as disastrously as his first battle. Even though the Federals were repulsed at the bluffs, they did not break or run. Instead, they went on to further operations against Vicksburg, which resulted in its surrender the following July. No matter how badly mauled in their first battle, soldiers always had the opportunity to bounce back.[8]

It was hardly surprising that untried soldiers were particularly vulnerable in their first battle. Taken beyond their naive conceptions of what combat was like, stripped bare of smug patriotism and ideals of glory, many of them reacted to the first shock purely by instinct. Self-survival, that marvelous natural imperative, often moved them. They had no control over their reactions but acted as if in a trance, conscious of their movements but not thinking of them. As Captain James Franklin Fitts of the 114th New York put it, a soldier was "a creature of habit quite as much as of reflection, and what he does in the moment of danger is often the impulse of instinct."[9]

That instinct usually led the soldier to do what he could to avoid getting hit. The sight of dead and maimed bodies littering the field, or the sound of shrieking shells and whirling minié balls, switched on the soldier's survival mechanism, and he found himself squirming to avoid every projectile that came remotely close to him. "My nerves were all unstrung under this altogether new and novel excitement," related one fidgety soldier named Asa Fletcher about his first battle. He became angry with himself because his hands shook so much that he worried whether he would be able to load and fire his musket.[10]

Instinct led George P. Metcalf of the 136th New York to perform some rather jumpy exercises while skirmishing on the wet morning of July 4 at Gettysburg. His company received orders to advance. Stiff and chilled from spending the night in a rain-filled rifle pit, Metcalf crawled out, stood up, and immediately felt a Rebel bullet whistle by his head. Without "any second thought I was back in my pit of water." Metcalf looked about and was relieved to see that everyone else had done the same. Orders were shouted to try again. The New Yorkers screwed up their courage and gathered their nerves, and they all jumped out at the same time, yelling like demons to steady themselves. Metcalf found comfort in using his "trusty old frying-pan and knapsack" as a shield for his face; he somehow convinced himself that they would "stop any unfriendly bullet." It was illogical but effective; Metcalf and his comrades advanced as ordered.[11]

A fascinating example of a man unnerved by his first combat experience and pressed to the hard, unforgiving edge of courage occurred in the 12th Connecticut Infantry in a small fight on October 27, 1862. Captain John William DeForest noticed that while advancing across an open field under fire, the bearer of the state flag suddenly turned around and began moving to the rear. "I never saw anything done more naturally and promptly. He did not look wild with fright; he simply looked alarmed and resolved to get out of danger." DeForest would later realize that this man was not a coward, but in this battle he was "confounded by the peril of the moment and thought of nothing but getting away from it." DeForest set the man straight by rushing to his side, drawing his sword, and threatening to crack his skull open. Still, the conscientious captain had to grab the color-bearer and physically turn him around before the man obeyed "in silence, with a curious dazed expression." Each time the Rebels loosed a volley of fire at the regiment, the color-bearer "fell back a pace with a nervous start; but each time I howled 'Forward!' in his ear and sent him on again." This man, whom DeForest refused to identify in his memoirs, went on to become a reliable soldier in subsequent engagements.[12]

Indeed, many men who found their nerves racked by the first terrible impressions of battle succeeded in enduring their first engagements. They may not have done so with grace, aplomb, or heroics, but they were able to stay in line (perhaps with a lot of help from an officer armed with a sword and a loud voice) and move on to better things in the next battle. Asa Fletcher, George Metcalf, and even the Connecticut color-bearer pulled themselves through the initiation of fire and refined the qualities of a good soldier—steadiness, attention to duty, discipline—by degrees in other battles.

But there were men who did not fare so well under the pressure. Their instinctual reactions led them to act in ways that neutralized their effectiveness on the battlefield. Nerves and reflexive action led them to "pop off their pieces long before there [was] any thing to aim at," particularly if the regiment was facing combat for the first time. This reaction would have an effect on others, and pretty soon half the regiment was wasting "ammunition, courage and morale." In addition to firing at unseen targets, soldiers sometimes became too nervous or excited to load properly. "They drop their cartridges," observed the surgeon of the 2d Maryland Infantry. "They load and forget to cap their pieces and get half a dozen rounds into their muskets thinking they have fired them off. Most of them just load and fire without any consciousness of shooting at anything in particular." John Schofield, who served on General Nathaniel Lyon's staff at the battle of Wilson's Creek, saw a blatant example of this tendency at the height of that bitter, terrible engagement. He found a man who was "too brave to think of running away, and yet too much frightened to be able to fight." All the soldier could do was fire his musket as rapidly as possible into the air, doing no harm to the Rebels. Schofield grabbed his arm, shook him, and told him what he was doing. The man "seemed as if aroused from a trance, entirely unconscious of what had happened."[13]

Reflexive action could bring the soldier to rather odd and unpredictable actions on the battlefield. At Gettysburg, Theodore Dodge of the 119th New York Infantry saw a young man who, although shot in the leg, "sat there loading and firing with as much regularity and coolness as if untouched, now and then shouting to some comrade in front of him to make room for his shot; while some scared booby, with a scratch scarce deep enough to draw the blood, would run bellowing out of range." Even a stalwart officer like John William DeForest temporarily lost control of himself when, during the May 27 assault at Port Hudson, he saw a sergeant faint while helping a wounded man to the rear. DeForest began to faint too but managed to catch himself by taking deep breaths. He thus avoided "such a ridiculous and contemptible" experience as swooning on the battlefield.[14]

Fainting and wildly firing a musket into the air were breakdowns of self-control, but they were the result of physiological rather than moral failings. Soldiers could not always control their reactions to the shock of battle. A regiment could be thrown into confusion if the first enemy volley took deadly effect in the ranks; conversely, the men could be buoyed up to steadiness if that first volley sailed harmlessly over their heads. Soldiers often responded to battle without thought. The connection between the sounds of combat and the reactions of soldiers was reduced to its essence for David Hunter Strother, a staff officer at the first battle of Winchester. As the Federal column moved along, Rebel artillery projectiles whistled as they passed overhead. "At every report, the living mass started and quickened its motion as if shocked by electricity."[15]

Of course, this innate reaction could work to the benefit of whichever army took the tactical defensive. Soldiers needed more nerve to attack a position then to defend one, and if the terrain or man-made obstacles offered them a convenient opportunity to break their forward motion and take cover, they usually did so. The 13th Indiana Infantry, for example, launched an attack on Rebel earthworks only to find a gully that ran roughly parallel to the Confederate trench. The men instinctively dove into it for cover. "They knew that in [the] economy of God's provi-[de]nce that ditch was put right there for the protection and preservation of the 13th Indiana." Other soldiers noted that Confederate troops acted the same way on many battlefields. The men of Pickett's charge halted at the famous stone fence; many of them hesitated just enough, according to Alexander Webb, Federal brigade commander at that part of the line, for the Unionists to counterattack and save the day. Charles S. Wainwright, the artillery chief of the 1st Corps, concluded that such halts in the middle of attacks were always fatal. But "so natural is it for men to seek cover that it is almost impossible to get them to pass it under such circumstances."[16]

The impulse to dive behind some convenient cover was prompted by nervous reactions to battle; the instinct of self-preservation took over, and nothing the line officers did or said could counter it. As one Federal veteran put it after the war, a "hidden hole" offered the nervous soldier a good solution to the conflict between "the physical fear of going forward and the moral fear of turning back." There was no stigma attached to this tendency; it occurred many times on many battlefields and was widely recognized by both officers and privates, and no one was prepared to criticize the men for this natural act.[17]

The soldier's nervous reaction to battle often continued after the engagement ended. Staff officer Horace Porter found it "curious" that for some time after a battle the men "would start at the slightest sound, and dodge at the flight of a bird or a pebble tossed at them." Less nervous soldiers found great fun in deliberately throwing small objects past the heads of these men to make them wince.[18]

That some men could jest about other soldiers' reflexive responses to combat is another indication that individuals went through the process of responding to battle differently. Some adapted at a more accelerated pace than others. They defined themselves as soldiers more rapidly and learned the limits of bravery more easily.

THE LIMITS OF BRAVERY

Experience became the best teacher of soldiers. After learning how reflexes and instincts could influence their reactions to battle, they calmed down into a pragmatic acceptance of their new lives as soldiers. One of the most important lessons they learned was that all men had limits. They were not expected to be foolishly brave under fire or to throw their lives away in hopeless attacks. Running away from the battlefield might be acceptable if it was done without panic and was immediately followed by reorganizing the battle line and continuing to fight. If William Ketcham was right, 80 percent of the Union army needed to exercise some degree of judgment about whether they could withstand a particular moment in battle. As long as they had a safety valve, an opportunity to temporarily take themselves out of an unbearable situation, they could return quickly to their duty without endangering the war effort or their images as good soldiers.

On many battlefields, thousands of good men hesitated at critical moments, deliberately stopping assaults when it became apparent to them that there was no reasonable chance of success. Their decisions

were rarely interpreted by officers as mutiny or cowardice. Captain
Joseph J. Scroggs of the 5th U.S. Colored Troops (USCT) witnessed a
demonstration of this on September 29, 1864, when his unit attacked
Confederate fortifications on the Petersburg line. His men were unsupported and had to contend with natural obstacles to close with the
enemy, but they pushed on. Scroggs had decided that he was going to
die and grimly went forward with his men. But one hundred yards from
the works, his people "instinctively halted as if to take breath and that
moment saved the remnant of the battalion." Given a few seconds to
think and take in the situation, Scroggs's men fully realized the "utter
hopelessness of succeeding." They began to run back, but after rushing
a few yards, they slowed down and walked out of Confederate range.[19]

The experience that Scroggs so carefully recorded in his diary demonstrated that black troops reacted under fire much the same as white
troops; the equation of fear and dedication to duty crossed ethnic lines.
An even better illustration of how soldiers chose their own limitations
on courage occurred at the battle of Pickett's Mill during the Atlanta
campaign. On May 27, 1864, in an effort to quickly outflank the Confederate army's position at nearby New Hope Church, Sherman sent
several brigades through the rough, tangled woods to roll up the flank
of Johnston's army. The Confederates stayed one small step ahead of
them. Major General Patrick Cleburne's division positioned itself on a
small ridge and just had time to cut down a few trees to create a field of
fire before the Federals attacked. It was a blind push up a deep ravine.
Ambrose Bierce, a staff officer with Hazen's brigade, watched as the
well-dressed ranks quickly broke apart and each regiment became "simply a swarm of men" surging through the undergrowth. "The front was
irregularly serrated, the strongest and bravest in advance, the others following in fan-like formations, variable and inconstant, ever defining
themselves anew." Even the color-bearers wormed their way through
the brush, closely furling their flags and holding them at an angle over
their shoulders so they would not be shredded by the vegetation.
Finally, the Federals came up to the Rebel line and instinctively formed
a tightly packed firing line without rank formation. The "edge of our
swarm grew dense and clearly defined as the foremost halted, and the
rest pressed forward to align themselves beside them, all firing."

As both sides began to open heavy fire on the other, Bierce stood near
the right of Hazen's brigade and watched in awe. He had always

wondered how men who still possessed courage could retreat, and now he saw that no matter how determined these veterans were, they would go so far and no farther. There existed an invisible "dead-line," Bierce thought, beyond which no one could force himself to step. Hazen's men stood in the open or crouched behind trees and stones while firing. Now and then, groups tried to go forward, only to be shot down before they got very far ahead of the main firing line. Even individuals tried to do this, with no better result. Bierce estimated that at least one-third of the fallen Federals lay within fifteen paces of the Confederate line, but not a single one lay within ten paces. Here was a frontier of courage beyond which no soldier was able to push. "He sees, or feels, that he *cannot*. His bayonet is a useless weapon for slaughter; its purpose is a moral one. Its mandate exhausted, he sheathes it and trusts to the bullet. That failing, he retreats. He has done all that he could do with such appliances as he has." Hazen's brigade fell back, leaving about seven hundred of its fifteen hundred men dead or wounded in an attack that lasted only about thirty minutes.[20]

This kind of self-imposed limitation on courage was acceptable. Officers believed that their men had tried their best but realized that further effort would cost more than it could possibly gain. This ability to sense an unwise attack was much more common among veteran troops, such as Hazen's men, than among green regiments. They had the confidence to make the decision to call off an unwise assault and get away with it. The line officers seldom if ever complained or tried to administer punishment, for they were on the firing line with their men and were subject to the same uneven chances of death and failure as the rank and file.

Giving up an assault without orders was possible only if it was done as a group; if individual soldiers turned and retreated, that would be defined as straggling in the best case, mutiny in the worst. Northern soldiers had many advantages and disadvantages in operating within linear tactical formations. The line became their protection and, in some ways, their curse. If most of the soldiers in the battle line decided to retreat, every individual within it had a ready excuse for saving himself. Yet the tightly packed nature of that formation meant that it was difficult for an individual to slip away. Unlike soldiers of the twentieth century, who fought in loosely ordered formations, there was less opportunity to take singular leave of duty under fire. There were just as many rocks, trees, and ravines for the Northern soldier to slip behind or into, but it was almost inevitable that someone would notice his absence from the shoulder-to-shoulder formations that carried Civil War armies into combat. Although forced to stay and fight, many soldiers were too excited or frightened to fire accurately. They popped off their muskets in the air or misloaded their pieces so that they jammed and became useless. These men, who probably would have taken French leave of the battle line if given the chance, were of little immediate use to the regiment.[21]

Soldiers learned that if they wanted to take themselves out of battle as individuals, not as part of a group, they had to do it before the battle lines were formed. Any soldier who questioned his ability to withstand combat could resort to straggling, a practice that irritated officers. Many soldiers left the ranks during hard marches because of exhaustion, but others simply pretended to be too tired to keep up with their regiments. It was difficult to distinguish the truly lame from the faker, for line officers were busy keeping the remaining men in column and preparing for battle. A moving army was hard to keep together on a forced march, especially when combat seemed imminent.

Private Wilbur Fisk of the 2d Vermont deliberately hid among the stragglers during the Wilderness campaign. He was a good soldier who had deep pride in his unit, but he had slept little for two successive nights before the battle. When his unit attacked the Confederate lines on May 6, 1864, units from the 2d Corps to his left broke and fled, leaving the Vermonters unsupported. Rebel battle lines moved forward and began to outflank Fisk's brigade as he joined his comrades in a headlong race to the rear. Fisk became separated from his regiment and found himself among the 2d Corps troops that had broken, "decidedly bad company to be in," he thought. These men paid no attention to their officers, who drew their swords and pistols in futile threats. Fisk was carried along with a crowd of men who had no intention of fighting anymore that day, and he decided to give in to temptation and become one of them.

Fisk joined the stragglers because he had lost his regiment and was among strangers. He was too exhausted and hungry to leave them and try to rejoin his unit. "I had been fighting to the best of my ability for Uncle Sam's Constitution, and now I thought it of about as much importance to me individually, to pay a little attention to my own." When officers tried to rally these men to stand at a crude breastwork, Fisk saw fresh troops coming from the army's rear and concluded that they could hold the line better than he. Fisk and the others went on. "My object was to find a safe place in the rear, and in spite of revolvers, or swords, entreaties, or persuasions, I found it." Even though an officer's horse stepped on him, causing him to lose a shoe and walk with a limp, Fisk made it to a safe place in the rear with the other stragglers. "I should have been ashamed of such conduct at any other time, but just then all I thought of was a cup of coffee, and a dinner of hard tack. The regiment might have been ordered into another battle, and every man of them been killed, and I shouldn't have been ashamed that I wasn't with them. My patriotism was well nigh used up, and so was I, till I had had some refreshments." After a meal, Fisk made his way back to the 2d Vermont and played the part of a dependable soldier for the rest of the campaign.[22]

Fisk's experience at the Wilderness illustrated how even a reliable soldier could lose grace in one battle. The breakup of unit cohesion and the loss of nourishment and sleep obviously had a role in turning men into runaway warriors. Fisk was not a professional straggler—they were a minority of the Union army—but he took from his officers the responsibility for deciding when to fight. His experience was typical of most soldiers. Because he did this only once in his war career, it did not damage his self-image. Good soldiers occasionally waffled toward the darker margins of courage and then corrected themselves.

Like straggling, helping the wounded to the safety of the rear areas also offered the anxious soldier an opportunity to get out of the battle line. Regimental officers tried to prevent men from doing this, but there were always too few hospital attendants and stretcher-bearers to handle the large numbers of wounded men in a timely fashion. The temptation to use this as an excuse was great.[23]

John R. Rankin of the 27th Indiana Infantry fell prey to this temptation at Antietam. He was impressed by the irony of a regiment moving like a machine across a fire-swept field while inside each man raged contradictory ideas and emotions. "These thoughts are private property, and are generally kept locked in each individual breast. All of us at times have thoughts we would not care to have made public, and many good soldiers would feel humiliated to have thoughts made bare which passed through their minds in certain ordeals." Long after the war ended, Rankin was ready to reveal what he called the clash "between conscience and cowardice." In his case, both were nearly equally strong, and he had to work hard to make sure that conscience won.

Rankin's problem was that he had too much time to think. Thus, he believed that privates, who had less responsibility than officers, fell prey to temptation more often. His regiment remained intact and was doing reasonably well, but the onset of heavy Confederate fire on his part of the battle line made him think deeply about his personal safety. Rankin decided to help the first wounded man to the rear, and it turned out to be the captain of his company. Unfortunately, another private had exactly the same idea and beat him to the wounded officer. Rankin had to return to his place in the line and reconsider what he had tried to do. "Gradually I lose my desire to leave the field. I now have plenty of opportunities but do not improve them." He thought less of his personal safety and more of why he had joined the army in the first place, of the consequences that a defeat in this battle might have on the cause, and he felt ready to stay and do his part for the Union. Rankin concluded that his "higher nature" had triumphed over his self-interest.[24]

If a reluctant soldier could not find a way out of battle by helping a wounded man to the rear, he certainly could find it by receiving a wound himself. Of course, it would have to be nonlethal, ideally only a slight injury, the famous "cushy" or "blighty" wound that British soldiers of World War I cherished. Elisha Stockwell of the 14th Wisconsin received such a wound at Shiloh when a spent artillery projectile glanced across his arm. Stockwell's lieutenant told him to walk to the rear and tend to his injury. He felt "as tickled as a boy let out of school" about it. Much later in the war, Pennsylvanian Frederick Pettit was wounded at Cold Harbor during Grant's horrible Overland campaign against Lee. He found that most of the wounded men he shared a general hospital with in Philadelphia could "think of nothing but staying away from the army until this fighting is over."[25]

At times, soldiers with no legitimate avenue of escape simply refused to go. This was a topic that few Northern soldiers were willing to discuss. The volunteer army did not compile cases of mutiny or publicize its occurrence, but it did happen occasionally, particularly during the grueling campaigns in Georgia and Virginia during the last year of the war. Self-mutilation, although not mutinous, was an extreme form of refusal to do one's duty. Private Martin Jones of the 19th Michigan Infantry shot himself in the foot during the battle of New Hope Church and was able to take himself out of the battle line to seek medical aid in the rear. What happened in the 47th Ohio Infantry on August 4, 1864, was much worse. The regiment had not reenlisted, and its initial three-year term of service was about to expire. The men refused to obey an order to jump out of their earthworks and recapture a line of trenches. Their major had to grab some of them "by the shoulders & lead them, drive them and shame them forward," but it did not work. These Ohioans felt they had done their share in capturing Atlanta and just wanted to go home unhurt. For much the same reason, the 11th Michigan Infantry refused to go on picket duty when ordered to do so. It happened to be exactly three years to the day since the men had been mustered in, and they were ready to return to Michigan.[26]

In Virginia, the press of operations also led some soldiers to refuse duty. During the early attacks on Petersburg, when Grant had his best chance of dealing a decisive blow to Lee and the fate of his Overland Campaign hung in the balance, many of his soldiers were too exhausted to take full advantage of their opportunities. Convinced that they could not succeed in taking the fortifications, some units in the 2d Corps simply refused to obey the order to attack. George Bowen and his comrades in the 12th New Jersey looked across the open field they were supposed to cross. Five hundred yards away, the Confederate earthworks were plainly visible and very strongly built. "[O]ur men positively refused to attempt it and no urging to get them to make even a show of going" took place. These men of the 2d Corps were right in their belief that the attack was doomed to fail. They staged the only large-scale refusal of Northern soldiers to execute an order to attack Confederate positions.[27]

Desertion was another avenue open to any man who decided that he had had enough of war. Some two hundred seventy-eight thousand Federal soldiers were identified as deserters by the army, about 9.6 percent of the total number of men who served. Yet it was impossible to determine what percentage of these men left the army because they could not stand the test of combat. Deserters did not describe their motives in letters home or write their memoirs after the war. The available evidence strongly indicates that they absconded for a wide variety of reasons ranging from homesickness to family troubles at home to a general dislike of the rigidity of army life. There was no indication of any sizable number of troops deserting directly from the battlefield. With most engagements taking place in the South, hundreds of miles from their homes, soldiers who ran from a battle simply milled around in the army's rear until it was safe to rejoin their regiments. Desertion usually took place when units happened to be near soldiers' home-towns, or at least when they were near Northern territory, rather than on the battlefield. The lure of large bounties for enlistment, which became common practice by 1862, also increased desertions by tempting unscrupulous men to enlist for gain rather than for a cause. The degree of social unity that existed in the community that organized the regiment also played a part in desertion. If recruits had strong family ties with that community, and if the town consistently offered support to its company or regiment throughout the conflict, desertions tended to be low. In short, there were many factors besides fear of combat that affected the desertion rate in the Union army.[28]

About a hundred thousand hardened Union veterans legally left the army in 1864 at the end of their three-year terms of enlistment. These men represented a valuable resource that was lost to the Northern cause. Having served in many battles, they simply decided to go home rather than to see the war to its conclusion. They did so as units, not as individuals. Their hundred and thirty-six thousand comrades in other regiments decided to reenlist for an additional three years, proudly adding the title "veteran volunteer" to their unit designation. Those who refused to reenlist often did not explain their reasons, and thus their motives remain obscure. If they were disillusioned with the war or afraid of further exposure to combat, they certainly did not express it. When they stated their reason for going home, it was always the same: a feeling that they had contributed their share toward the saving of the Union. Only eleven men of the 12th Missouri volunteered to reenlist, far fewer than the 75 percent needed to save the regiment. Lieutenant Albert Affleck was ready to go home when the regiment's term ended in August 1864. He was exhausted by the demands of the Atlanta campaign but not discouraged about the war. "I need rest and good living for a time, and then I shall be ready to go into service again if I am needed." Tragically, Affleck was mortally wounded at Ezra Church less than one month before he was to go home.[29]

The men who refused to reenlist in 1864 symbolized a major problem for those in charge of mobilizing manpower for this long, bitter war. Recruiting had been easy in 1861, with young, largely propertyless men flocking to the colors to experience adventure or to act on patriotic impulses. By 1863, it was harder for local communities to fill enlistment quotas. This was partly due to the fact that the war demanded so many men and communities had a finite supply of able-bodied recruits. It was also due to a growing awareness of the war's true cost in money and blood. Returning veterans and wounded and sick men told of the horrible bloodbaths that resulted in little strategic gain, beginning a trend toward war-weariness that would take its toll on recruiting efforts. Community leaders found themselves forced to offer money for recruits and to search outside their town limits for them. More immigrants, who were only recently arrived in America with empty pockets, were drawn into the army, and more people looking for a quick profit began to show up at recruiting stations. The Northern draft came into play as well, bringing reluctant soldiers into the service. About 6 percent of the total strength of the Northern army was draftees. By 1864, the strain on the North's ability to maintain its armies with fresh recruits was enormous, and the quality of those new soldiers was lower than it had ever been. Only in the Army of the Potomac, which had to replace half its strength lost in the first six weeks of Grant's Overland campaign, did the poor quality of recruits significantly hamper military operations, however. This was a major reason that the 2d Corps, which had repulsed Pickett's charge at Gettysburg and had fought so ferociously at Mule Shoe Salient, was only a shadow of its former self by the time it refused to attack the Confederate works at Petersburg.[30]

Finally, a tragic and extreme way for a soldier to escape the horrors of the battlefield was suicide. It was rare, but there were several well-documented cases of its occurrence. Nearly four hundred Northern soldiers were officially identified as victims of their own hand. Most of them accepted this final solution because of mental and emotional problems stemming from their civilian lives, but others did so for war-related reasons. Regular artilleryman William P. Hogarty knew of a sergeant, mortally wounded at Antietam, who shot himself in the head with a revolver when told that he had only a few hours to live. He was certain that prolonging his life such a short time was not worth the pain. Even more poignant was the sight that greeted Thomas H. Evans of the 12th U.S. Infantry when he relieved a picket on the night following the battle of Fredericksburg. He discovered a Northern soldier who had been so badly wounded that he could not move. The man was dead, his face blackened and shattered, and his rifle lay across his chest. Evans realized that the man had committed suicide and speculated that he may have believed that the regulars were Confederates and killed himself to avoid capture.[31]

It is impossible to accurately gauge the number of Northern soldiers who refused to obey orders on the battlefield, ran away from battle never to return to duty, or committed suicide rather than face a horrible wound. All the collateral evidence indicates that the numbers were small and the incidents infrequent. In contrast, there were many examples of men willingly throwing themselves into assaults that they knew were futile, accepting terrible losses to accomplish very little, and reenlisting to continue serving to the bitter end. The Northern war effort was carried by the core of highly motivated men who had enlisted in 1861 and 1862, not by those questionable patriots who were bought into the army from 1863 through 1865. Those soldiers among that core who crossed the dark margins of bravery into cowardice were a distinct minority. Others were good soldiers pressed to the breaking point. Their moral courage and the latitude granted them by officers to take themselves out of a trying spot on the battlefield carried them through the worst and allowed them to recover their composure. Nearly all men among the core of veterans who saw the war through gained some familiarity with the dark underside of courage, but few were permanently compromised by that contact. They knew, usually only briefly, what battle looked like while running away from it, but their view of it was mostly straight ahead.

What of the opposite end of the spectrum, an attraction to the excitement of battle? Many soldiers loved the exaltation of spirit, the stimulation of their senses, that battle produced. These men reveled in physical courage while ignoring moral courage altogether. No thoughts of the cause, of home, or of honor inspired them to fight, only a desire to experience all the danger that combat had to offer. They felt a passionate, yet almost clinical, response to battle.

Combat greatly sensitized the faculties of soldiers who recognized the attraction of physical courage. "My mind took note of every thing transpiring, and every incident is stamped inefficably on my memory," noted Colonel John S. Wilcox of the battle of Corinth. He "felt inclined to laugh and see every thing in a ludicrous light." The varied sounds that minié balls made while flying through the air fascinated him, and even the "ring of balls against my sword" seemed to be a matter of intense curiosity rather than of fright. Throughout the two days of bitter fighting,

Wilcox felt no fear at all, he wrote to his wife. Indeed, his description of the battle has an air of detached observation.[32]

Lieutenant William Wheeler of the 13th New York Battery felt the same kind of overriding joy during all three days of the battle of Gettysburg. He was under fire often and was pushed to the outer limits of physical excitement. Under so much threat of death, Wheeler felt that the "danger was so great and so constant that, it took away the sense of danger." Instead, he felt "joyous exaltation, a perfect indifference to circumstances," and he believed that they were three of the most enjoyable days of his life. Wheeler reexamined these feelings several months later and concluded that they were partly the result of his job as a battery commander. He had to keep all his senses at their peak in order to work his pieces to their fullest effect, and this excited his nerves and senses to an unusually elevated level. Also, he believed that much of the joy of battle resulted from the fact that he knew he was in great danger but repeatedly escaped injury. The excitement of battle lay in gambling his life in countless and repeated ways and winning every time.[33]

The "so-called joy of battle" was more often felt by troops under special tactical conditions, such as skirmishing or taking part in a particularly dangerous assault. The more individualized and fluid nature of fighting on the skirmish line allowed the soldier more freedom of movement and personal initiative. Eager soldiers took advantage of this environment to give free rein to whatever it was in battle that excited them. Attacking a battery of artillery or a heavily fortified position also inspired in many men a more intense emotional reaction to combat. They wrote of becoming so intoxicated by the excitement that a deadly assault seemed more like a dream than a reality. Impulsive reactions, "elation that lifts men above the fear of wounds or death," were common themes in their descriptions of battle.[34]

Major James A. Connolly participated in one of the few successful assaults against a fortified position during the entire war. It occurred during the battle of Jonesboro, as the end of the long campaign for Atlanta. Through hard experience, the men of Sherman's army had come to know the futility of attacking fortifications, so the tension they felt when ordered to do it once again was enormous. This time they were lucky. The Confederates had made a mistake in building an angle in this line of works the night before, and it was vulnerable. Baird's brigade of the Army of the Cumberland hit the angle, and the Rebel line collapsed. Connolly shared the elation felt by all of Baird's soldiers when he realized that this last battle of the Atlanta campaign had been an unqualified success. He was overcome, his hat was off his head, and he could not keep himself from crying.

> I could have lain down on that blood stained grass, amid the dying and the dead and wept with excess of joy. I have no language to express the rapture one feels in the moment of victory, but I do know that at such a moment one feels as if the joy were worth risking a hundred lives to attain it. Men at home will read of that battle and be glad of our success, but they can never feel as we felt, standing there quivering with excitement, amid the smoke and blood, and fresh horrors and grand trophies of that battle field.[35]

Under certain circumstances, many fields of battle became places where soldiers experienced overwhelming joy under fire. They did not love war for its own sake but were reacting to the stress of combat in ways that helped them sustain their emotions and survive it. By its very definition, physical courage is temporary and situational; it comes and goes, depending on the emotions of the moment and the kind of tactical mission the soldier has to perform. Suffering a defeat or retreating in disorder fails to elicit such reactions: "You can not make it pleasant under any circumstances," admitted John William DeForest. Another observant warrior noted how much the "excitement of success" that a soldier felt depended on "the fact that his enemy are running away from him." The men who enjoyed physical courage contrasted the exaltation of battle to the "hum-drum, quiet life of years past." Yet they knew that war was, at best, "just tolerable; you can put up with it; but you can't honestly praise it." DeForest compared it to "being in a rich cholera district in the height of the season."[36]

Defining courage was a task that all Union soldiers had to undertake. The variety of their experiences under fire was impressive, but even more impressive was the fact that so many naive young men endured it with so much success. The bulk of the Federal army passed over the threshold separating the volunteer from the veteran and went on to learn, in varied ways, how to deal with battle. Their success was the key to saving the Union.

5

Holding On

After I had got used to fighting and could appreciate my surroundings free from the tremendous excitement in the blood, of the smell of battle, I knew perfectly well all the time that if a cannon ball struck in the right place, it would kill or maim. . . . I knew it was always liable to strike somebody and therefore liable to strike me, but I always went where I was ordered to go and the others went, and when I was ordered to run and the others ran, I ran. I had a greater fear of being supposed to be as afraid as I was than I had of being seriously hurt and that is a great deal of a sustaining power in an emergency.

William A. Ketcham
13th Indiana

I saw enough to sicken the heart in the scores of blackened and bloated dead, and in the hundreds of wounded. . . . The scenes which I witnessed were enough to overthrow all imaginations concerning the glory of war; but, dreadful as they were, I hope and believe that I would be willing to suffer the worst, to die, if necessary, and leave my body to blacken on the field, rather than prove a traitor to the trust which our country reposes in all her sons. There *is* something glorious in the death of a soldier, when he dies defending principles such as our soldiers fight for.

J. Spangler Kieffer
Pennsylvania Militia

It may cost me my life, but If I cant live In a free country than I dont want to live at all. I was born & raised in a free Country & I still intend to live under the old flag of our union or die in the defense of it.

W. C. Littlefield
14th Iowa

The religious belief of the army was simple, and consisted of two articles of faith: first, that "a man will die when his time comes"; and secondly, that "a soldier who is slain in the service of his country is sure to enter the gates of heaven." The arguments of books and the sermons of divines could not undermine these ideas, in the sincere profession of which thousands fought and died upon the battle-field.

Henry N. Blake
11th Massachusetts

From present indications we will soon be in an engagement with the enemy; the extent and result of which cannot be foretold. But of one thing you may be certain—I shall do my duty to the best of my ability. I put my trust in God, keep my powder dry, and fear no evil.

David E. Beem
14th Indiana

Most Northern soldiers stayed well within the acceptable definition of courage. They stayed in line of battle, followed orders, and contributed their small part to winning the war. They did not always perform their duties with enthusiasm and conviction, but they generally avoided the appearance of disobedience. If not for this stoic attitude, the Union war effort would have collapsed at its leading edge, the battlefield.

What held these men to their work? There are as many answers to that question as there were soldiers, for each individual had his own set of reasons for carrying on even after he learned that the reality of combat did not match his romantic conceptions of it. The factors that kept men in line of battle were more complicated, multifaceted, and diverse than the factors that impelled them to support the war effort as civilians and then to join the army. It is impossible to demonstrate with "scientific" accuracy whether one factor was dominant. There are surviving letters, diaries, and memoirs from only a minority of Northern veterans. All one can do is identify the recurrent themes in these personal accounts and construct a multilayered view of the varied ways in which their authors came to grips with the emotional challenges of battle.

COURAGE, HONOR, AND SELF-CONTROL

Courage itself, enshrined by American culture as a supremely valuable ideal of action and thought, was an immensely potent factor in keeping Northern soldiers on the battlefield. They had been nurtured in a cultural environment that encouraged allegiance to a standard of public conduct few could have guessed would be applied in a conflict against fellow Americans, and they tried hard to live up to that standard. The ideal of courage, which meant to the Northern soldier "heroic action undertaken without fear," was intertwined with a range of other values such as manliness, religion, duty, and honor. Although courage was an ideal oriented toward creating useful citizens, many soldiers consciously asserted it as a factor in their willingness to fight, and large numbers of them died trying to demonstrate it in their personal conduct.[1]

Few soldiers tied together the varied meanings of courage better than Joshua Lawrence Chamberlain of the 20th Maine. College professor, self-made officer, and reflective commentator on the war experience, Chamberlain pondered the meaning of "elementary manhood, the antique virtues that made up valor: courage, fortitude, self-command." He believed that Northern men joined the army because of these things and that they were determined to safeguard what they were accustomed to viewing as a national birthright. "Individual happiness must be subordinated to the general well-being," wrote Chamberlain, "duty to country must outweigh all the narrower demands of self-interest."[2]

Other soldiers wrote less comprehensively about these values but nevertheless acknowledged their forceful influence in their lives. Many could only say, as did George W. Crosley of the 3d Iowa, that "I was eager for the fighting to begin and to have my courage put to the test." Crosley passed this test and went on to become colonel of his regiment. Other soldiers articulated their feelings even less precisely than did Crosley. Leander Stillwell dreaded battle, but he did not feel that he had the freedom to run. He had joined the 61st Illinois to do his part in saving the country, and he wanted to fulfill that commitment. Pride was an important factor keeping him on the firing line. He wanted to prove his ability to shoulder his share of the nation's burden and did so throughout the many campaigns of his regiment in the western theater.[3]

Self-control was recognized as an indispensable aspect of courage. One of the greatest fears any soldier harbored before his first battle was the fear of losing control. William A. Ketcham of the 13th Indiana was particularly worried going into his first engagement because he was a seventeen-year-old recruit in a veteran regiment. After receiving his first fire, he felt "quite triumphant—I had. . . . experienced no nervousness and no sense of fear or trepidation, and up to that time I had not known what the experience would mean to me, and I only recall the feeling of relief that my first experience under fire had not been detrimental to me or my standing with the boys." Other soldiers were bombarded with admonitions to "keep *cool* . . . dont shake in your boots, in fact think of nothing, but how you may but do your duty."[4]

Personal and public honor were so deeply involved that many men felt cheated and shamed if they were wounded in the "wrong" way or suffered an illness. Future president Rutherford B. Hayes noted that one of his men in the 23d Ohio took it hard when he was accidentally shot in the foot by a careless comrade. "'Oh, if it had only been a secession ball I wouldn't have cared," lamented the wounded soldier when he realized that this injury was not a badge of courage. Another soldier, Stephen Rogers of the 36th Massachusetts, became irritated with his enforced confinement to a hospital at the height of the fierce fighting of May 1864. "I tell you there is no *honor* in a mans *sickness*, but there is about a *wound* in the minds of most men." Like love, great ideals could produce frustration and peckishness when unrealized. This was the extent to which many Northern soldiers embraced the authority of courage, honor, and self-control.[5]

THE CAUSE

Courage and ideals of proper behavior were part of American culture and therefore transcended the particular issues involved in the Civil War. The secession crisis and the armed conflict that followed summoned a different set of cultural values and ideas more closely associated with the political history of the nation. The republican heritage of the United States, with its emphasis on the need to protect representative government, democratic practices, and public virtue, was still strong some eighty years after the American Revolution. The Northern cause, which tried to preserve this unique heritage, was a potent force in mobilizing the Northern population. It explained the Southern rebellion as a perverse revolutionary attempt to create an empire for slavery. By 1861, a widespread belief existed among Northerners that the institution of slavery had degraded white society and destroyed democracy in the South by creating an elite class of wealthy slave owners that had engineered secession for its selfish gain. In the minds of many Northerners, the Confederacy represented values and ideas that were antithetical to the national heritage. Such a dangerous entity and all that it represented had to be destroyed, not only to save the political union of the states but also to preserve the cultural foundations of national unity.

Although ideology played a huge role in motivating Northerners to support the war and to join the army, the extent to which it was a factor in helping them deal with the dangers of the battlefield is controversial. Many historians have discounted its role. Ironically, historians of combat morale in other wars have tended to give patriotism and ideology more credit than do the few historians of the Civil War who have addressed the issue. Ideology certainly played an important role in helping men endure battle. Union soldiers lived only two or three generations removed from their nearly legendary forebears who had triumphed against difficult odds in the War of Independence. They were receptive to simple patriotism, morally charged values, and inspired ideas. Ideology was taken seriously by the generation that fought the Civil War, and belief in it intensified in the wake of the unprovoked attack on Fort Sumter. Defenders of the faith readily embraced an ideologically charged interpretation of all the turmoil that fractured the nation.[6]

"Better for humanity that this and the next generation should be draped in mourning than our glorious institutions perish and freedom and Democracy bow to Slavery and despotism," wrote James Abraham, a member of the 2d West Virginia Cavalry just before his region became a state. He demonstrated that the rhetoric of the cause, and its power to influence action, was not confined to the northern tier of states; many loyalists from the upper South felt its effect. Alexis W. Tallman of the 22d Wisconsin weighed in with similar sentiments and a further demonstration that the ideology was accepted by many individuals across the nation. Writing in 1864, long after he had come to know the true nature of combat, Tallman reasserted his faith. "I do not sustain the war because I love the business, but on account of what we hope to, in the end, attain and secure by prosecuting it—the preservation of our wise and good government, and the establishment of universal liberty and justice o'er all the land."[7]

Ideology was so strongly embraced by so many soldiers because it ennobled the struggle, draped it in a mantle of transcendent significance not only for the people of the United States but also for the millions who would eventually benefit from the expansion of republican ideals throughout the Western world. Not all Northern soldiers took to this message, but its wide appeal cannot be denied, for it linked the military struggle to fundamentally important goals that justified suffering and sacrifice. John Stahl Peterson of the 20th Ohio Battery authored an essay titled "The Issues of the War" in 1864. He wrote, "If there are real issues of right and wrong involved in the contest, and we are in the right, we may rest assured that the results of a successful prosecution of the war will be worthy of all our sacrifices, and honorable to us as a people and nation."[8]

Admittedly, it was easier for the ideologically committed soldier to pen high-minded phrases of self-sacrifice before he experienced battle, but there were many such men who continued to assert their faith even after witnessing all that combat had to offer. There were men who saw, suffered, and still believed, who consciously used their principles as a shield against the horrors of the battlefield. Using ideology as a tool to maintain their sense of purpose was their way of holding on.

Joshua Lawrence Chamberlain saw this as a confrontation between the physical senses and the intellect. He knew that the instinct to survive was strong. "But men are made of mind and soul as well as body. We deal not only with exercises of the senses, but with deeper consciousness; affection, beliefs, ideals, conceptions of causes and effects, relations and analogies, and even conjectures of a possible order and organization different from what we experience in the present world of sense." Chamberlain believed in his men's ability to subordinate fear to higher ideals, a conscious assertion of ideology as a major force in the Northern soldier's ability to survive combat and triumph over it. "Their life was not merely in their own experiences," the former college professor contended, "but in larger sympathies."[9]

The depressing string of defeats in Virginia severely tested ideological faith for the soldiers of the Army of the Potomac. Time after time, they saw their sacrifices apparently wasted in pointless or mismanaged confrontations. Fredericksburg was a prime example. Ambrose Burnside ordered his men to repeatedly assault Lee's veterans, who were positioned behind a stone wall, which left this field of battle littered with bodies and soaked with blood. Walter Carter of the 22d Massachusetts survived it and managed to hold on to his faith: "My sense of right and love of country and its glorious cause would impel me forward to death, even if my poor weak nature hung back and human feelings gained control over me."[10]

Fredericksburg was followed by more than four months of rest in winter quarters and a change in army commanders. Joseph Hooker gave hope of being the tough-minded, aggressive, and persistent battlefield leader the Army of the Potomac needed. His men had time in their camps to ponder the reasons they were fighting and steel their wills for more bloodletting. Henry Henney of the 55th Ohio felt that only after several tough campaigns could a soldier begin to accept the fact that his work and sacrifice might go for naught. "It certainly is a hard experience, and I warn all grumblers to avoid it unless they have a super-abundance of patriotism to offer to their country. I've frequently had the blues myself. Still never so hard that I'd be prompted to give the battle o'er. No! What we lack in Generalship and success, let us make good by our obstinate adherence to the cause at stake. If we do this then the sacrifice can not be too great for the prize." Henney went even further and convinced himself that the suffering and wasted battles had actually deepened his commitment to the ideals of the cause rather than weakened it.[11]

Hooker planned an adroit maneuver to gain a tactical advantage over Lee and succeeded in making it work—to a point. At the critical moment in the Chancellorsville campaign of early May 1863, he hesitated and lost the advantage. Chancellorsville became a bigger, bloodier, and even more tragically lost battle than Fredericksburg had been, and coming on the heels of that earlier catastrophe, it was doubly hard to bear. Surgeon Daniel Holt of the 121st New York Infantry was drained by the broken bodies, dying men, and suppurating wounds that continued to fester for days after the battle. Writing a week later he admitted, "I am satisfied with human gore; and no one would be more willing than I to leave this spot if it could be done with honor to ourselves and justice to the nation." Yet Holt was able to continue asserting faith, refusing to let his disgust overrule his patriotism. "Sooner than recede an inch from God-inspired principle of freedom which incites to action this noble army of men, or compromise the weight of a feather with rebels in arms[,] I would still see the same scenes of bloodshed re-enacted everyday, until a perpetual and honorable peace is secured." Holt would have fully understood the reaction of Jacob Heffelfinger to the Chancellorsville debacle. An infantryman in the 36th Pennsylvania, Heffelfinger was sorely pressed by the defeat but managed to pull through. "Was not the cause of justice and right at stake, it would be enough to discourage the most stout hearted."[12]

For many Northern soldiers, the cause was the supreme motivation, impervious to setbacks and depression. Their minds and emotions were resilient enough to deal with physical pain, trauma, and the mixture of factors that resulted in victory or defeat on the battlefield. Ideology, therefore, became the most lasting justification for continuing the conflict despite the apparent lack of success.

Soldiers found something incredible about the Northern cause. Sergeant Joseph Sweney of the 27th Iowa pondered its nature for many years after the war ended and expressed his thoughts in an article about the battle of Tupelo, Mississippi, in July 1864. Sweney knew that self-preservation was the "fundamental instinct" of man, that civilian life offered few incentives to ordinary people to voluntarily set this instinct aside and willingly die for something more important. Yet Sweney claimed to have seen this at Tupelo. He encountered a mortally wounded soldier "whose abdomen was largely torn away by a shell so that his intestines were exposed, and he was suffering about all that man can suffer." When the soldier asked who had won the battle, Sweney told him that the Federals had repulsed the Rebel assaults. "Good," the wounded man replied, "I can die contented." Sweney remembered this for fifty years. "This is how love of kindred, home and native land can possess the man. This is what love of country means to the man in the hour of his country's peril. It is with this spirit and with such exaltation that in a just cause he follows his country's flag to battle."[13]

Did the wounded soldier actually die as Sweney remembered the incident so long afterward? There certainly is room to wonder. It is possible that the Iowan was influenced by nostalgia for a special period of his life. Yet the lesson of Sweney's story is not in the accuracy of his memory but in the persistent influence of the cause in his interpretation of the war and its meaning. Sweney came to fully understand that ideology was the most potent explanation for self-sacrifice in the war.[14]

The authority of ideology was so strong that it inspired comparisons between the Northern cause and Confederate motives for leaving the Union. Northern soldiers naturally concluded that there was no basis for comparison. They viewed the Southern cause as no cause at all and found it difficult to believe that anyone could willingly fight for the Confederacy. Many Northern soldiers believed that Southerners were cruelly misinformed about the nature of the conflict, having been forced into military service by a despotic government and a selfish planter class. They often viewed Rebel soldiers as poorly educated, disadvantaged victims of a social and economic structure that denied them opportunity for individual improvement. Of course, this picture of the Confederate soldier was not only ungenerous but also greatly skewed by the passions aroused by the war; it was powerful and widespread, however. The ideology of the cause added a sharp, bitter edge to the war, in addition to providing a solid foundation for motivation.[15]

Nineteen-year-old James H. Leonard, born of English immigrants, summed up the Northern view of the Southern cause while describing what he saw on the battlefield at Seven Pines. Two weeks following this early battle of the Army of the Potomac, Leonard's duties with the 5th Wisconsin permitted him to wander over the field and see what combat was like. It was an awful sight; everything on the field from fences to trees to bushes was broken, scarred, or "literally torn to pieces with Bulletts and Shell." Dozens of graves marred the landscape, with Union dead buried separately from Confederate. As Leonard looked at the Federal graves, he thought of the wives, siblings, and children of the dead men and concluded that the only consolation that would be great enough to counterbalance their grief was "that they had died in a good cause." Leonard could not come to the same conclusion when he contemplated the Rebel dead. "The sorrow of their friends must be all the sadder, because . . . posterity shall write over them, *Sincere, and self-sacrificing, but misguided victims to a causeless* and *therefore wicked rebellion.*"[16]

Patriotism became so important, passionate, and consuming to some Northern soldiers that it assumed a religious aspect. As such, it compelled even more intense devotion and self-sacrifice than a mere political ideology could command. The ideology of the Northern war effort was deeply concerned with morality and thus had a natural affinity with religion. Men such as Lieutenant William Wheeler, a Yale graduate and New York artillerist, called the war "the religion of very many of our lives." He believed that those soldiers who thought long and hard about the issues of the conflict came to "identify this cause for which we are fighting, with all of good and religion in our previous lives, and so it must be if we are to win the victory. We must have an impulse, made of patriotic fire and a deeper feeling, which takes its rise in the thinking soul." Wheeler combined intellectualism with a passion for prosecuting the conflict. The mind and the heart came together in his conception of the war and its meaning.[17]

OF GOD AND MEN

Traditional religion also was a potent force in keeping soldiers to their work. When the war came, churches all over the North answered the call to support the cause and encourage men to join the army. In Sterling, a small town in northwestern Illinois, Will C. Robinson was swept up in the excitement following the attack on Fort Sumter. He listened to a sermon in his Congregational church and found it "running over with patriotism and love to the old Union. It was quite warlike, and proved that every man who fell sustaining the government, fell in a just cause." Robinson soon joined the 34th Illinois, where he undoubtedly heard more sermons from the regimental chaplain that fortified his patriotism. Chaplains struggled to ensure that their charges—often young and impressionable men away from home for the first time— remembered their religious upbringing and behaved accordingly. Their sermons were often filled with patriotic fervor, reminding soldiers of the righteousness of the Union cause and urging them to keep the faith until the final victory.[18]

Those men who felt the tug of emotion in these sermons advanced religion to the first rank of justification for killing rebellious countrymen. *"Every man that feels that he is accountable to a just God for the deeds done in the body* should give *himself* as a willing sacrifice to his country in this, her hour of need," proclaimed Benjamin Stevens, an Iowan serving as an officer in a black regiment. Stevens used religion with a mixture of confidence and fatalism. His belief that God was on the side of the Union ennobled the conflict, invested it with a heady sense of righteousness, and endowed the suffering with meaning. If he or his compatriots fell, they were assured that God would take them in. Dying in the nation's cause, which was the Lord's cause as well, would make them martyrs. As an Illinois soldier named Jacob Behm put it, "There will be thousands inflamed with my spirit, and impatient to tread in our steps." The religiously committed soldier could take comfort in the knowledge that his death would not be unrewarded.[19]

It was one thing to be moved by thoughts of martyrdom before a battle, but quite another to maintain that belief during or after a bloody engagement. Many soldiers clung desperately to thoughts of God while bullets flew over their heads and dimly seen lines of Confederates began to appear in their front. This was the elemental role that religion played in the soldier's ability to hold on. It steadied his emotions at a critical time and provided a rock on which he based his courage.

The battle of Stones River, fought late in December 1862 near Murfreesboro, Tennessee, was one of the most cruel engagements of the western theater. Nearly one of every three Union soldiers who fought there was killed, wounded, or captured in the equivalent of one and a half days of battle. James Greenalch of the 1st Michigan Engineers and Mechanics Regiment instinctively turned to God for help. "When I saw that we were attacked . . . and bulits began to come on their erands of death, I prayd now Lord protect, and thank God I came out unhurt." Greenalch hated the thought of killing another man, but he loaded and fired his musket at the oncoming Rebels. His desire to save "the best government on earth" and the loyalty he felt toward his comrades impelled him to fight. Yet several days after the battle, he happened across several decaying corpses of Union soldiers that had not yet been buried, and the sight made him wonder. "[W]hen I think of what is religion worth to one exposed hourly to disease and death it is everything, for it is more than family or friends, and if it is my lot to share what I have described, I hope to feel it safe to cling to."[20]

A year and a half later, Frederick Pettit of the 100th Pennsylvania also clung to religion while fighting in the Wilderness. "War is a sober thing, he concluded, "and a soldier needs something more than mere courage to support him. Reading the Bible never seemed to afford me so much comfort as it does now." Pettit found special strength in his conviction that God had preordained fate. He was sustained by the fatalistic belief that whatever was meant to happen was unavoidable.[21]

Pettit's fatalism was consistent with the general view of Providence held by most people in mid-nineteenth-century America. They had no confident belief that God judged human events in ways that would lead to a better life on earth. Instead, they simply used religion as a way to accept whatever God gave them. The mass of ordinary Americans tended to associate Christianity with the gloom of Calvinism. Those soldiers who relied on God in the midst of battle were concerned with weathering the immediate storm rather than constructing a hopeful view of the postwar nation. Combat was an intensely reductionist experience. Men whose lives might be snuffed out at any instant were not inclined to ponder the future but were content to find a spiritual refuge for the moment.[22]

The sword of God had two edges. Whereas the first one provided incentives to pursue the war, the second one offered a serious obstacle to killing. The Sixth Commandment posed a problem for devout Christians who took up arms to suppress the Southern rebellion. The result was ambivalence in the minds of many Northern soldiers about the deed that all tacitly agreed was necessary to save the Union.

The most troublesome aspect of war for some was the impact of deliberate killing on the conscience. To Nelson Chapin, it seemed a "strange phase of the human mind" that men "who would not willingly wound the feeling of the most sensitive" rejoiced over the death of a Confederate "as much and more than if he were a wolf in the woods." Chapin might have been referring to an Illinois infantryman who described the "not unpleasant" sight of enemy wounded "kicking like a flock of dead partridges."[23]

Vigorous supporters of the cause considered any ambivalent attitude toward killing the enemy to be unacceptable. Nathan Webb of the 1st Maine Cavalry tried hard to convince himself that a soldier should have no "squeamishness and tenderness at heart for open-handed Rebels. They must be treated as personal enemies, seeking his individual life. . . . No gloved hands must be used in this war." Many men tried but failed to live up to Webb's standard. Chauncey Cooke was a young Wisconsin abolitionist who found it impossible to hate the Confederates or glory in their deaths. At Resaca, he fired so much that he emptied his cartridge box several times. "I saw men often drop after shooting, but didn't know that it was my bullet that did the work and really hope it was not. But you know that I am a good shot."[24]

Cooke and Webb were wrestling with the same issue that soldiers of all wars have to deal with: reconciling peacetime norms of behavior with the often contradictory demands of war. Bishops and ministers had little difficulty making exceptions to the Sixth Commandment to suit political needs, but they did not have to do the killing; those men who pulled the trigger, crouched in the trench, or walked across an open field into the face of massed musketry often found it more troublesome to come to grips with their consciences than to brave the physical dangers of the battlefield. They often had to conclude that war itself was a hateful phenomenon precisely because it forced moral dilemmas on good Christians. "The spirit of war originates in sin," believed Lieutenant Francis Riddle of the 93d U.S. Colored Infantry. The only way a good man could engage in war was if his "spirit and motive" were strong enough to "give character to his calling, dignify his manhood, exalt his deeds, and make him a factor for good or evil in society."[25]

Those soldiers who joined religious leaders in justifying killing did so by embracing the political cause. John Russell of the 21st Illinois was fully aware of the dangers attending combat but was not afraid. "I firmly believe that every Rebel deserves death yet I have no desire to kill them if it was possible to avoid it consistent with the just demand of our country." But the "present deplorable state of affairs" made him willing to shoot and kill in order to save the country. Other men, such as New Hampshireman Charles Paige, combined God's will with the patriotic demands of the nation to justify killing. A devout Christian, Paige reminded himself of "His Eternal truths and principles of justice" so that he could hold on to a God-ordained reason for shooting Rebels.[26]

Even such a man as Walter Stone Poor, a twenty-six-year-old New York infantryman who admitted to being "naturally tenderhearted, almost to being womanish" about the thought of killing another man, was able to bring himself to do it for the cause. "I confess . . . it seems impossible for me to kill, or even wound any one even in self-defense. It seems that I would rather die than do it." Yet Poor believed that a good goal had to be attained by paying a price, and the loss of his innocence was a fitting sacrifice for the Union. For deeply conscientious men like Poor, coming to such a decision could be more painful than losing a limb.[27]

When soldiers accepted killing and the possibility of being killed, they also accepted certain unwritten but widely known conventions of military conduct. Those conventions centered on the business of death as an impersonal process of chance. The battle line delivered fire en masse into often dimly seen enemy lines, with relatively little opportunity to aim at individual targets. Thus, one of these conventions was the understanding that a soldier was not personally responsible for the effect of his fire.

Behavior that violated this or other conventions was considered unfair and was often deeply resented as an atrocious act. Deliberately shooting Rebels who were on picket duty, unless there was some overpowering reason to do so, seemed "too like murder" to Major Rutherford B. Hayes of the 23d Ohio. Pickets were isolated and vulnerable sentinels, and killing them seemed more personal than firing on a battle line. Even in the middle of a battle, instances of individual killing were condemned by worried survivors. At the battle of Wauhatchie, as the enemy retired into the darkness following a failed assault, a single Confederate hid behind a tree for several minutes, then took a potshot at a Union soldier who stood up in the belief that the danger had passed. An outraged Federal called this man an "assasin," expressing the moral revulsion he felt at so personal an act.[28]

Sharpshooters generally were viewed in negative terms. Late in the war, when armies tended to be in continuous contact for months at a time, men were chosen to move from one concealed position to another, taking life on a routine basis. A skilled and determined sharpshooter could compile a long list of victims, taking as much pride in his work "as a hunter does in the chase." One observer of the Atlanta campaign noted that sharpshooters kept track of the killed by placing them in categories such as "certainly," "probably," and "possibly" dead. It seemed to be a dehumanizing way of saving the Union.[29]

Although some soldiers took to sharpshooting with diligence, even fulfillment, most detested the role of the sniper. New Englander John William DeForest noticed that some of his fellow officers tried sharpshooting while their units were on duty in the trenches outside Port Hudson, but he refused to do so. "I could never bring myself to what seemed like taking human life in pure gayety." As much as most soldiers disliked being snipers, they hated being targets even more. When a Rebel sharpshooter targeted Theodore Lyman, a member of George Meade's staff, he hated the experience; "it is so personal," he stated. Imagine how personal it felt when soldiers were shot at while relieving themselves. Most soldiers obeyed what one man called "an unwritten code of honor" that forbade killing a man who was answering nature's call, but sharpshooters did not let this code interfere with their tallies. They often took advantage of a man when he was in this vulnerable position.[30]

Skirmishing was a different form of combat than sharpshooting, and it elicited varied reactions from soldiers. Skirmish lines were commonly used to develop enemy positions, harass opposing infantry lines and artillery units, probe for weaknesses, and scout terrain. Skirmishing was a military necessity, and most Union soldiers spent some time performing this duty. Skirmishing demanded different qualities of the warrior than did the battle line. Men had to be able to work in loose-order formations, taking advantage of natural cover, sniping at the enemy, and generally becoming the gnat that hounds the elephant. This type of warfare did not suit everyone.

Benjamin Thompson of New York thought that fighting on battle lines was "barbarous," but skirmishing was nothing less than "savage—nay, devilish. To juke and hide and skulk for men and deliberately aim at and murder them one by one is far too bloodthirsty business for Christian men." Those who took to the business did so precisely because the juking, hiding, and skulking tested their personal abilities. They enjoyed the "individuality in the effort," the opportunity to display their acute vision, their wits, their agility, and their marksmanship. Some units that were regularly sent out to skirmish came to like it much better than serving in the battle line. The men of the 190th Pennsylvania grew to enjoy skirmishing so much that they became irritated when other regiments were given the job.[31]

These attitudes toward killing and being killed mirrored an ambivalence in American attitudes toward the soldier and his craft. The warrior hero embodied all that was good in the nation, but he was engaged in a business that inspired violent passion. Deliberate killing, although done in the name of the nation, posed a threat to social order. Was the warrior a patriot, or only an executioner? At what point did his killing cross the line between culturally acceptable violence and outrageous barbarism? Northern society had a responsibility for these men, and it fulfilled that charge by convincing most of them that they fought a morally justifiable war. Only then could soldiers hope to reconcile their religious teachings with the call to arms.[32]

Furthermore, many Northerners came to see the killing of their young men as strengthening the cause. It became something of a ritual purification, a symbol of the regeneration of American society. The war was widely viewed as clearing away political issues that had clouded the country's vision for decades, and the emancipation policy of Lincoln's administration added a revolutionary aspect to the Northern war effort. To view the soldier's sacrifice in the conflict as symbolic of a new life tapped into a deep cultural phenomenon that has been common to all societies from ancient history to the present. It may well have been even stronger in America because of the country's experience at carving Western civilization out of a hostile wilderness and its birth in the midst of a bloody war with England. The regenerative potential of the warrior hero's death soothed the loss of brave young men and ennobled even the most painful and sordid form of death.[33]

Howard Stevens of Illinois lost a brother at the battle of Raymond, Mississippi, during Grant's Vicksburg campaign. More than two months later, he wrestled with his loss in a consolatory letter to an uncle back home. It bothered Stevens that his brother's body still lay buried in what he considered "a traitorous land," but he wondered whether that might not be the most appropriate place after all. Perhaps "the blood of our fallen heroes will purify and place an indellible stamp of true patriotism upon this curssed soil and every hero that falls will be as a nail driven in a sure place rendering the Union one and inseparable forever hereafter." The image of a dead soldier physically bonding the Union together again was striking. It represented a deep willingness to believe that the violent death of a soldier could regenerate the nation.[34]

Northern soldiers had to craft a meaning for their war. With a variety of cultural tools at their disposal—ranging from the ideals of courage, honor, and self-control to the ideology of the cause and to religion— many men became convinced of the transcendent significance of the Civil War. Other soldiers resorted to other ideas or themes to deal with combat. In a costly and seemingly endless conflict, the variety of supports for morale was impressive. The supports discussed here were external to the soldier. He drew them from the cultural life that surrounded him and incorporated them as a meaningful part of his philosophy, his thoughts, and his dreams. These supports connected the fate of the individual soldier to that of thousands of other soldiers in Union service and to the fate of the nation itself. The Northern soldier believed that he was fighting for a universal cause, and this enabled him to hold on.

6

The Psychology of the Battle Line

The man who can go out alone and fight against overwhelming odds is very rare, and for every one such there are thousands who can "touch the elbow" and go forward to what seems almost certain death.

E. L. Marsh
Iowa Volunteers

Any correct picture of this charge would represent a V-shaped crowd of men with the colors at the advance point, moving firmly and hurriedly forward, while the whole field behind is streaming with men who had been shot, and who are struggling to the rear or sinking in death upon the ground. The only commands I gave, as we advanced, were, "Align on the colors! Close up on that color! Close up on that color!" The regiment was being broken up so that this order alone could hold the body together.

Rufus R. Dawes
6th Wisconsin

From a house on a hill I watched the advance of our troops in successive lines, listened to their deafening cheers as they double-quicked upon the batteries, and saw the brave hosts melt away before the terrible tempest of iron hurled against them, till nothing but poor weak remnants remained, scattered in the advance, unsupported, and their valor uselessly thrown away. The quick wasting of the Union troops, who disappeared suddenly, as if the earth had yawned and swallowed them, was awful to gaze upon. Yet they still recklessly pounded on, cheering and keeping up a continuous fire of musketry.

Edward King Wightman
9th New York

The fragment of my old company, in its last bloody fight with a gallant enemy, made charge after charge under a corporal. "You don't go into such a hole because you like it," explained a trooper, describing a dash through a cannon-swept valley, "you go in because you are ashamed to go back on the boys."

John W. DeForest
12th Connecticut

. . . tumbling over dead & dying, in mud and gore, among agonizing groans, execrations, oaths & prayers, witnessing scenes that angels weep over if they ever weep, and as I lay there contemplating the misery of that battle, my eyes resting upon the scene of its occurrence, I could not but feel a shudder at the thought that we will most likely soon bear another, severer even than that, and none knew who may suffer in the next. But then the thoughts of home came again, and again I thought of your good kind letter, and I felt willing to endure the privations, hardships and dangers of this life so long as it may be necessary to secure the safety and comfort of our friends at home, in return for their encouragement to us.

A. Stokes Jones
72d Pennsylvania

Much of what kept men going in the challenging environment of the battlefield was the mutually supportive interaction among the members of the small, tight, intimate community of the regiment. Its members often were residents of the same town or county who had joined as a community response to the war effort. Once in uniform, they forged bonds of trust and affection that went far beyond civilian acquaintanceships. Developed during hard marches in all types of weather and long nights spent in tented camps under the stars, these bonds knitted the regiment into a military family and endured the ultimate test of the soldier on the battlefield. The regiments were what Shakespeare called a "band of brothers," enjoying nearly inexpressible ties of comradeship and respect that enabled the individual members to function during the worst trials combat had to offer. The military family had a psychology of its own.

TOUCH OF ELBOW

Every group of soldiers in every war develops a special relationship that transcends explanation. It ties the individuals together with invisible cords forged by their common experiences under extreme conditions of death and suffering. The near presence of these special companions enabled soldiers to endure much. The linear tactical formations used in the Civil War grouped them together on the battlefield in intimate ways. They stood next to their comrades, shoulder touching shoulder, forming an unbroken chain across the contested and deadly field. They shared the same dangers, stood the same chances of getting hit, fired their muskets in unison or at least as individuals supporting one another's fire. They accepted the task of helping one another through the most exciting, demanding, and passionate experience of their lives.

The soldiers found, for example, that shouting was a great way to relieve stress, and with several hundred willing voices packed into an area small enough for nearly all to hear, a regiment could let loose a deafening sound. The men shouted to keep up their spirits; observers noted that it was a deep, guttural intonation. They often used foul language to keep their minds from dwelling on danger or to encourage greater exertion. "The swearing mania was irrepressible," recalled Captain John William DeForest of his unit's first battle. "In the excitement of the charge it seemed as if every extremity of language was excusable, providing it would help towards victory." It worked not only in pulling the Connecticut infantrymen through the ordeal of a frontal assault but also in disconcerting the enemy. Captured Confederates told DeForest that they were not hurt much by the fact that his men fired as they advanced, but they certainly were scared by the wild yelling and cursing. This assault was one small example of how vocalization could aid military success more decisively than firepower.[1]

It is possible that DeForest's regiment used shouting so effectively because it was a green unit. Other soldiers noted that new regiments often displayed a "wild *elan*" that carried them through battle and enabled them to achieve battlefield successes that more seasoned and cautious regiments would not have attempted. Shouting was more common among green troops than among veterans, although it certainly occurred in all regiments at one time or another.[2]

Music also played a large role in steadying nerves that were strained by the excitement of the battlefield. It could have a powerful effect in helping to stem the retreat of nervous troops. The band of the 14th Connecticut played songs such as "Yankee Doodle," "The Star Spangled Banner," and "Red, White, and Blue" during the retreat of the 11th Corps at Chancellorsville. At a much smaller engagement, Samuel Cormany found singing to be an effective way to help rally his squadron of the 16th Pennsylvania Cavalry. He and several of his comrades "lustily sang the song 'We'll rally round the flag Boys.' Others, who had fallen back without orders, rallied to us, and soon order was restored, and we presented a solid front."[3]

One of the most touching incidents of the war involved music and the comforting effect it could have on the minds of men preparing to enter battle. On the night of December 30, 1862, some forty-four thousand Federal soldiers nervously camped within a few hundred yards of the Confederate Army of Tennessee outside Murfreesboro, Tennessee. These men of the Army of the Cumberland, many of whom were about to enter their first engagement, enjoyed the music of their regimental bands that night as they rested for what would be the bloody battle of Stones River. Across the cold, wintry landscape came the sounds of patriotic songs designed to reinforce devotion to the cause. The Confederates, as well, could hear these tunes and began to retaliate. Rebel bands started up their own patriotic songs, and an impromptu musical contest developed, with both sides trying to drown out the other. "Yankee Doodle" contended with "Dixie," and "Hail Columbia" was answered by "The Bonnie Blue Flag." Near the end, a Federal band began "Home, Sweet Home," and no one could resist it. A Confederate band also began playing it, and before long its soft, gentle melody was all that could be heard in either army. This neutral song bridged the gap, and men who would be killing each other the next day joined in an unusual example of emotional reinforcement—not just among members of the same regiment but among members of opposing field armies. It was one of the most poignant moments in a war filled with bitterness and pain.[4]

The battle line was a venue not only for the musical stimulation of the spirit but also for the physical reinforcement of morale. The closeness that each soldier felt to his comrades on either side gave him strength. Horace Porter, who served on Grant's staff and dwelled at length on the nature of bravery in his postwar writings, called this the "strength which comes from union, the confidence which lies in comradeship, the support derived from a familiar 'touch of the elbow.'" Other soldiers spoke of a "curious electric thrill" that merged their self-awareness into a "composite consciousness" on the battlefield. This bound all regimental members into a collective will that enabled the regiment to act as a united whole. Jonathan P. Stowe of the 15th Massachusetts was moved beyond measure by the cheering of his regiment and many others during an engagement of the Seven Days campaign. Along a battle line that stretched four miles, one unit after another took up the shout. "*I assure you* the effect is electric," he wrote to friends. "It thrills the senses to feel assured by enthusiastic shouts that plenty of friends are present to back you, and you go forward with a *rush* lest *your pride taunt you of cowardice.*"[5]

This feeling of togetherness went far beyond the immediate confines of the battlefield for some soldiers. Charles Mackenzie believed that the electric thrill was felt by all Federal soldiers in every theater of operation. There was an invisible line stretching two thousand miles, with hundreds of thousands of men united by a common objective. These men "felt that they were all in touch, elbow to elbow, as it were, although hundreds of miles intervened." If they lost a battle, there was always the assurance that other links in this nationwide chain would step forward to carry on the war for the Union. There would always be others ready to take their places in the ranks if they fell. "Along the entire line was an invisible cord, binding all hearts in the immortal faith that the free institutions of the United States were not born to die," concluded Mackenzie. He had conceptualized the entire Union war effort as a macroversion of regimental cohesion.[6]

Massed tactical formations certainly gave the Northern soldier something that future soldiers, who employed loose-order formations, did not have: the comfort of feeling his comrades physically near him, sharing his danger, seeing him fall and making sure that someone cared for him. But if shoulder-to-shoulder formations could inspire a regiment to go on, the breakup of those formations could ruin an attack. Of course, from a purely technical viewpoint, the breakup of a linear formation was the breakup of an assault; Civil War armies maneuvered in those formations and could not be managed effectively without them. But from another equally important viewpoint, it also represented the breaking of that electric bond that molded the soldiers into a truly cohesive unit. The collective will dissipated, and soldiers became individuals again, more concerned with survival than with the objective of the moment.

"Men fight in masses," observed William Thompson Lusk, an officer in the 79th New York. "To be brave they must be inspired by the feeling of fellowship. Shoulder must touch shoulder. As gaps are opened the men close together, and remain formidable." But Lusk saw what happened at the battle of Fredericksburg when Confederate musketry tore the life out of massed Union assault formations. Division after division moved doggedly across an open, ascending slope toward Rebel forces firmly positioned behind a stone wall. The slaughter was enormous, and all the bravery these Federals mustered could not overcome the massed fire, the terrain, and the bad luck that the Army of the Potomac seemed doomed to endure. Lusk watched as the neatly dressed ranks were torn and then began to disappear. Many of the individuals drifted toward the rear; others lay dead or injured on the ground. "A few men struggle along together, but the whole mass has become diluent. Little streams of men pour in various directions. They no longer are amenable to command." Of course the regiments were capable of reforming. When the colors were repositioned to the rear, the men gathered around them and began the process of regaining touch with their comrades, rebuilding the bonds that knitted the battle line into a formidable force. Flexibility and resiliency made regiments into successful military units.[7]

This kind of resiliency had to be learned. Although maintaining physical closeness was important to all soldiers at every stage of their war careers, it was a matter of degree. Experienced warriors could maintain a looser battle line than green troops. The latter seemed obsessed with keeping the ranks and files dressed and tightly packed. They possessed what Thomas L. Livermore called "that anxious effort to preserve the alignment" because they were not yet familiar enough with battle or with one another to feel comfortable about losing physical contact with their comrades.[8]

Captain John William DeForest of the 12th Connecticut recalled his unit's first battle, a small engagement in October 1862 in Louisiana. The regiment advanced over a cluttered landscape. It had to burrow through a patch of tall reeds, knock down a post-and-rail fence, and then maneuver through an area littered with thorny thickets. "We might have met bayonets in good order, but we were thrown into confusion by this host of briars." Company officers exhorted the men to "Centre dress! Close up those gaps! Centre dress!" They tried hard to obey. "In our inexperience we believed that everything was lost if the men did not march shoulder to shoulder; and all through the battle we labored to keep a straight line with a single-mindedness which greatly supported our courage." The regiment was forced to deploy into columns in order to work its way through the thickets, but it successfully re-formed its battle line and moved on.[9]

A more telling example of a new regiment's need for constant realignment under fire occurred at Chancellorsville. The 26th New Jersey participated in the successful assaults that captured Marye's Heights at

Fredericksburg on May 3, 1863. This was the same position against which the Army of the Potomac had wasted itself the previous December. Now, with most of Lee's army battling Hooker in the vicinity of the Chancellor House, the Federals assigned to this sector had a real chance of success. The New Jersey unit advanced across plowed fields under artillery fire and lost its alignment. Colonel Andrew J. Morrison ordered it to halt, instructed the men to lie on the ground, and then told the guides to stand up. The three men who had been assigned these positions raised themselves, one on the right, one in the center, and one on the left. Their job was to form a straight line so that the regiment could redress its alignment. Ira Seymour Dodd was the left guide. "There we stood," he recalled many years later, "while the regiment crawled up and 'dressed' by us." Shells burst all around Dodd and the other two guides as their comrades tried to perform a parade-ground maneuver under fire. They could not have moved fast enough to suit Dodd, who found it bizarre to be one of only three men standing erect in this storm of bursting shellfire. He was not exactly afraid but "wondered whether I was actually myself and whether my head was really on or off my shoulders." It took only a few minutes, which seemed like hours to Dodd, for the regiment to finish its alignment. Then the other men stood up and they all marched forward to help capture the heights.[10]

Unlike Dodd's comrades, experienced soldiers were capable of flexibility and often worked effectively in more loosely controlled formations. Yet they always operated in close physical contact with one another, even if they did not "touch elbow." Frank Wilkeson saw his first battle in May 1864, when Grant met Lee in the Wilderness. He was surprised at the degree of disorder in the ranks of veteran regiments; the men "moved to and fro—now a few feet to the right, now a few feet to the left." The battle line became more like a writhing, dangerous snake than a rigid architecture of tense men.[11]

A greater degree of flexibility was seen in several battles during the latter half of the war. At Opequon, one of Sheridan's victories in the Shenandoah Valley, John William DeForest described the appearance of a line of Federal troops as it rushed at the double-quick for a quarter of a mile across a meadow. "Of course there was soon no such thing as a battalion line; we were a loose swarm, the strongest in front and the feeble in rear." It was quite a comparison for DeForest; only two years before, during his first battle in Louisiana, he had observed his 12th

Connecticut awkwardly stumble its way around natural obstacles, trying desperately not to let a dent appear in the alignment of rank and file.
Now, while moving over a cleared field, it was able to loosen into a
"swarm" without losing its cohesiveness or sense of purpose. Ambrose
Bierce saw the same thing at Pickett's Mill. Hazen's brigade advanced
over rough terrain with considerable tree cover. It lost its rank formation but did not lose cohesiveness. The men advanced individually and
in clusters and then gathered to form a solid line without rank or file to
deliver fire at short range. The attack was unsuccessful, but not because
of the men's failure to maintain alignment. Whether in tightly dressed
ranks or in loosely related clusters, soldiers needed to be physically near
one another. Becoming a veteran did not exempt a man from feeling the
basic human need for the comfort of closeness in times of danger.[12]

COMRADES

This need for closeness helped foster a relationship among soldiers that
was uniquely their own. It was a spirit of comradeship that suffused
their lives. This feeling of belonging to a special group of men grounded
them, providing a sense of stability, security, and trust. It created a working environment in the field that was essential for their survival, and it
created lifelong memories that would deepen in their significance as
time shadowed the recollection of their suffering and anxiety. If it were
possible to pinpoint one factor as most important in enabling the soldier
to endure battle, it would be the security of comradeship.

   "I always found comforting in battle the companionship of a friend,
one in whom you had confidence, one you felt assured would stand by
you until the last." Thousands of Union soldiers would have found
these sentiments, expressed by Captain Frank Holsinger of the 19th U.S.
Colored Infantry, resonant with meaning. They knew that numbers
counted for more than mere arithmetic in the equation of battle, that
trusted colleagues marching shoulder to shoulder could perform mira-
cles, and that engagements were won by units, not by individuals. Illinoisan Onley Andrus did not believe that any men in his regiment were
cowardly, but he also knew that none of them were likely to "rush into
a fight alone on account of their patriotism." Knowing that thousands
were sharing his own fate gave a sense of confidence to the soldier. It

spread the anxiety and fear, made it shallow and manageable, and took the lonely burden of personal responsibility for the fate of the Union off his shoulders. As General John Logan put it, in the "grim play of battle," the soldier needed to know that his comrades were doing their part, or else he would be crippled by the knowledge that his own possible sacrifice could be wasted.[13]

The spirit of comradeship created a sense of belonging in the regiment that resembled the sense of family but went beyond it as well. The members were tied together by something different from blood, by unique common experiences. They depended on one another for survival in an environment that was much more deadly and demanding than most civilian occupations. In war, danger was the central characteristic of life, not a vicarious part of it. As Glenn Gray, a philosopher and veteran of World War II expressed it, sharing common experiences freed the soldier from his "individual impotence" and led him to become "drunk with the power that union with our fellows brings." Other twentieth-century commentators have noted that the spiritual union of soldiers is different from that which develops in other occupations. It is universal as well, characterizing the soldiers of all wars and nations.[14]

Alva C. Griest of the 72d Indiana admitted that the soldier's real home, the one he left behind, remained uppermost in his mind. But beyond that, his "object of interest" was "first in his company, next in his regiment, next in his Brigade and division and outside of this he has no interest other than the general one, which unites all Union Soldiers in one holy determination to crush the Rebellion." During his service in the army, the soldier's "interest" was drawn to his military family, for it was the group that he worked and lived with on a daily basis. He did not forget his civilian family or the cause, but it was natural for him to build and maintain good relations with his brothers in arms while he needed their support to survive the war.[15]

Overwhelmingly, the sense of togetherness created by the military family had a positive effect, but there was always a certain danger in it. The loss of close comrades distressed the soldier, sometimes resulting in depression, guilt, or a frenzied, almost animalistic desire for revenge. Different soldiers experienced different reactions to the loss of their comrades.

Captain Alexander B. Pattison of the 7th Indiana went through a juggernaut during the Virginia campaigns of 1864. His regiment, part of the famed Iron Brigade of the Army of the Potomac, suffered draining losses. On the evening of May 12, after his unit supported the crushing assault on Mule Shoe Salient, Pattison relieved some of his stress in a diary. "Father spare us from more sorrows. For our griefs are more than we can bear. My best men are falling around me and I am untouched. I am not better than they." He felt the guilt known by many soldiers whose friends fell while they survived. Several days later, when he was feeling less strain, Pattison reassured himself with the thought that even if he was not more deserving of life than those who had fallen, at least he had the satisfaction of risking his life just as they had done. He found this to be more of a tribute to his dead comrades than staying at home, as some of his acquaintances were doing.[16]

Soldiers were so loyal to their military family that they felt guilty at the thought of leaving it before the war ended. They often preferred to remain in the army rather than seek safety at home. One Indianan assured his sister that living safely on the home front would only be "a source of annoyance to me." Men who had no desire to see the elephant still could not bring themselves to stay at home. "I should feel ashamed of myself," admitted James A. Connolly of Illinois. Another soldier named Albinus R. Fell firmly resolved to share the fate of all others who served the Union. "I am here to stand my chances and am willing to do it and will till we conquer or die."[17]

The deaths of comrades also infuriated survivors, often leading them to fight more ferociously. This emotional transition sometimes took them to new levels of bitterness. Lieutenant Colonel John S. Wilcox of the 52d Illinois conducted himself coolly through the first half of the fighting at the battle of Corinth, Mississippi. Despite the extreme heat and the pressure of fierce Confederate attacks, he had no unpleasant thoughts until word was passed along that his regimental adjutant had been killed and that General Pleasant A. Hackleman, his brigade commander, had also fallen. "And then I felt malice & hatred—I did not swear but I shouted & screamed 'damn them, boys give them hell.'" Members of the 25th Wisconsin felt the same emotions as a result of their participation in a fight on July 4, 1864, during the Atlanta campaign. The regiment supported two Ohio units that were launching an attack against strongly built Rebel earthworks and losing a considerable number of men in the process. The Wisconsinites could do little to ease the loss. After the Confederates retired and the men had an opportunity to move forward to see how their Ohio comrades had fared, they were angered by the sight of dead and dying Federals. The frustration of being unable to prevent these heavy losses hit home, and many men of the Wisconsin unit began "crying like children, running back and forth without hats or guns and cursing the rebels for killing their comrades." Many other soldiers on other battlefields reported the same reaction. They described it as becoming "maddened" at the sight of their friends being shot down.[18]

In these cases, the maddening process temporarily turned the soldiers into more efficient killers. They reported renewed enthusiasm for fighting that lasted for the duration of the engagement. Other soldiers took more lasting heart when they recalled their feelings about the deaths of comrades in battles such as Antietam and Chancellorsville. Sometimes long after the engagements were over, they renewed their devotion to the cause and vowed to avenge lost friends. William P. Barker of the 6th New York Heavy Artillery took this to the extreme, but he had good reason for doing so. His son, who had served in a different unit, had been killed. In February 1865, Barker was recovering from a wound and had just been told that he would soon be sent back to his regiment. He was sorry that the war seemed about to end. "I Ache for a little more Revenge for my poor Son and also 4 times wounded myself i hate To give it up so." In Barker's case, his motives for continuing to press the war were bound up with a desire to avenge one who had been a member of his civilian family as well as a member of his extended military family.[19]

If the rank and file of a regiment were the siblings of that military family, the officers were the fathers. If they were good fathers, they guided their men through the process of becoming soldiers, looked out for their well-being, and inspired them with enthusiasm for duty. The men often developed attachments to their favorite officers, which played a significant role in their ability to sustain the rigors of war. For some, these attachments were first developed in camp, long before battle. Colonel John M. Palmer of the 14th Illinois, later to become a corps commander in the Army of the Cumberland, certainly inspired George H. Barker early in the war. Barker described Palmer as "good and kind hearted" and thought that anyone was "bound to love him—fight for him—yea die for him if it is necessary."[20]

The quality of officers has always been recognized as important in the general morale of troops. Officers could reinforce the attachment the men felt for them, or begin to develop it, through conspicuous acts of bravery in battle. Adoniram Judson Warner, colonel of the 39th Pennsylvania, recalled how he and some of his subordinate officers "forced a cheerful mood" and walked among the enlisted men before the battle at Antietam, trying to display a pride and confidence that, according to Warner, worked to inspire them. "The effect of this elan upon others is magical. Such a fire in an officer touches wonderfully the spirit of his men. At such a time when nerves are stretched to their fullest tension it takes but little to lighten or to darken." Even more dramatic acts could inspire even more enthusiastic responses. Victor Comte, a Swiss immigrant in the 5th Michigan Cavalry, saw brigade commander George Armstrong Custer in action at Gettysburg. Comte watched with pride and excitement as Custer managed to "plunge his saber into the belly of a rebel who was trying to kill him. You can guess how bravely soldiers fight for such a general."[21]

By far the best example of how a charismatic officer could infuse spirit into soldiers on the battlefield occurred at Cedar Creek on October 19, 1864. Major General Philip Sheridan almost single-handedly turned an embarrassing defeat into a major Union victory. He was absent from his Army of the Shenandoah when a Confederate force under Jubal Early struck it, took the Federals by surprise, and sent the entire army fleeing. Some Union units retired in good order, but others dissolved into confused masses of disoriented men. Regimental officers tried to re-form them, but James Franklin Fitts of the 114th New York believed that it was impossible. "The face of every man in the ranks was clouded with disaster. That we had been beaten, and severely beaten, nobody could deny; and I think the prevalent idea of the situation was that there was a long and a quick march down the Valley before us."[22]

Then Sheridan came. He had started from Winchester that morning on his return from Washington, D.C. Learning that a battle was on, he spurred his horse and reached the field by midmorning. He rode among as many of the scattered men as possible, telling them not to worry, that he would turn everything around, and they believed him. The news that Sheridan was back ran "like an electric shock" among the men. "I heard no more talk of retreating to Harper's Ferry," recalled Fitts. "Every man understood that the presence of Sheridan meant fighting, and with another result than that of the morning." Staff officers rode about, regimental officers found it easier to manage their men, and soon a battle line was formed. Sheridan was advised to show himself again to this line, for many men had been unable to see him earlier, so he rode in front of it, flamboyantly waving his hat. The Army of the Shenandoah counterattacked and drove Early's regiments off the field. Cedar Creek helped ensure Lincoln's reelection to the presidency some two weeks later.[23]

Overwhelmingly, the affection that many enlisted men felt toward their commanders had a positive effect on their ability to withstand the rigors of battle. There were times, however, when it posed a real threat to their stamina. Henry Elijah Alvord's attachment to his superior was too deep to be healthy. He served on the staff of Colonel Charles Russell Lowell, commander of a cavalry brigade at Cedar Creek, and he was utterly devastated when Lowell was killed. "I loved, I honored and admired—I *almost* worshipped him, and now he is no longer at Head Quarters with the command. I feel there is no longer any interest there for me." Alvord felt lost and believed that his "army home" had been broken apart. He could see no prospect of it being reconstructed. His spirit and enthusiasm for the war had been dealt a nearly fatal blow by the loss of a favored commander. Affection could certainly cut both ways; it could demoralize some and inspire others.[24]

The military family was a vessel in which hundreds of thousands of Northern men survived the storm of war. For those whose intellectual devotion to the cause was weak or who could not figure out what had motivated them to join the army, there was the devotion to beloved comrades to give them a reason to fight. This was probably the most pervasive and most deeply felt source of battlefield morale for the Northern soldier.

HOME

The military experience took the soldier out of his domestic environment, which Victorian culture believed was essential for moralistic education and civic indoctrination. The environment of the home, with mother or wife as influence, civilized men and made them productive members of society.

In many people's minds, the military family threatened these virtues that were so slowly created in the hearts of civilians. Americans had always distrusted military service, partly because of the potential threat that a professional army posed to a democratic government. But just as important, they distrusted it because the army took impressionable young men into a world without women (or at least the right kind of women). It was an environment where harsh discipline and rough manners were the norm and learning how to kill was the ultimate lesson. There was no opportunity for education or for learning a trade or a profession. There was no civilizing influence, no opportunity to find a suitable wife or raise children on the pitiful pay of a professional soldier. The men could not vote because they had no permanent residence. Only officers could hope to find some kind of social acceptance; enlisted men were given little consideration by a society that looked on the regular army as a necessary evil.[25]

The vast majority of Northern men who fought in the Civil War were volunteers, separated from the regulars and enlisting only for the war. Yet they were in many cases commanded by regular officers and were under similar constraints as those who served in the professional army. The separation of hundreds of thousands of men from their civilian families was no small matter, and it became important that the volunteer not be lost to the military family. Maintaining contact with the domestic family and its values made it easier for the soldier to become a civilian again after the war.[26]

Most soldiers maintained their ties to the domestic family, although the intensity and extent of these ties varied. Married men with children tended to be much more faithful in their emotional and mental devotion to the home front, for obvious reasons. Colonel John S. Wilcox thought of his wife "often, very often" while under fire during the first day of fighting at Corinth. He had no fear or "unpleasant thought or feeling," at least until he received word of the deaths of respected superior officers. Other soldiers reported the same thing. Thinking of family members seemed to create a feeling of peace and composure amid the noise and chaos of battle. Captain Nelson Chapin of the 85th New York described it as an "almost entirely dreamlike state—without any realization of fear." For those soldiers who did not have wives or children, there was always the beloved parent. Unmarried Oliver Wendell Holmes, Jr., went through the Seven Days battles in the 20th Massachusetts and admitted to his parents that "the thought of you dear ones sustained me in terrible trials."[27]

These thoughts were the result not only of the soldier's memories but also of letters from home, which constituted a paper tether that kept the

soldier from sinking irretrievably into the military environment. Each
missive from an adoring wife or doting parent reminded him of his true
family and his future. It also could spur him to do his duty. That certainly was the intention of Elizabeth Stevens of Oskaloosa, Iowa, whose
letters both encouraged her husband to fight and assured him of her
concern for his welfare. This seemed to be the best combination, for
other men also responded well to it. Massachusetts infantryman Walter
Carter thanked his father for what he called "a model of a letter to a soldier," received when his unit was in the middle of Grant's horrific campaign against Lee in 1864. It was encouraging and sympathetic, yet
subdued in its expressions of concern for his safety. A more worrisome
tone would have made him feel blue, but this letter created "excellent
morale and *esprit de corps*, and makes me a solid, substantial man, upon
a firm footing."[28]

Thoughts of home could sustain the soldier in another way as well,
by creating a visual image of something real for him to fight for. Many
men convinced themselves that saving the Union was necessary to safeguard their domestic bliss. This was not illogical if the soldier believed
that the slave empire of the South meant to spread the institution to all
parts of the United States, destroying democratic government and other
free institutions in the process. The Confederacy's aggressive intent, they
believed, was evidenced by its unprovoked attack on Fort Sumter.
Everything that contributed to a peaceful domestic development—from
public-school education to representative politics to free labor—seemed
threatened, and many soldiers wanted their children to grow up with
these advantages.[29]

In short, many soldiers keenly felt the necessity of saving the home
environment from the threat of an independent, aggressive slave nation
in the South. Their very way of life, domestically, politically, economi-
cally, and culturally, was threatened, and they believed that they were
fighting a defensive war. W. H. L. Wallace, who would become a division commander and die at Shiloh, wrote openly to his wife about it. "I
feel that in this war business I am engaged in the holy cause of defending & preserving a home made dear by your love." Wallace wrote this
in April 1861, when the passions aroused by Sumter were running high.
But long after the war ended, other soldiers repeated this sentiment in
their speeches and writings. "Above the smoke of battle," wrote Iowan
Charles Mackenzie in 1892, "in the clear empyrean, arose the vision of

the American soldier's home, secure to him and his loved ones only in the continuance of the government of his country."[30]

For the harried, exhausted soldier, the home became exactly as Victorian culture pictured it: a haven of comfort, security, and love. It posed a stark contrast to the military environment, particularly for soldiers like Claiborne J. Walton, whose medical duties with the 21st Kentucky Infantry brought him nearly to the point of emotional breakdown. He was ready to leave the army and *"come under Petticoat rule,"* he informed his wife. "We were once so happy as we well could be upon Earth. We were not wealthy but what little we had was neat and tidy and done up in good style. . . . How I long to be permitted to see her as in the days past seated at the head of the table pouring out my coffee and doing the honors of the table generally." There was no brave posturing in Walton's attitude, but an almost desperate longing for peace and pampering. Memories of home became bittersweet for him, but they certainly counterbalanced the string of wounded men he had been treating for days before writing home.[31]

Walton used his vision of the home environment to help sustain his faltering morale. But visions of home and family could hurt morale as well. The fate of loved ones who would be left without companionship or income if their husbands, siblings, or sons died occupied the minds of some soldiers to the point of distraction. Colonel James W. Monroe of the 123d Illinois told one of his officers that "getting married was the worst thing I could do as a soldier." He always thought of his wife during battle and had a strong desire to protect himself so that he could go back to her. This added another factor to the mix of concerns that every soldier felt while under fire.[32]

Many other men worried about their brothers. They were concerned that with too many siblings in the army, the family might be devastated. Lysander Wheeler and his brother both served in the same regiment. It bothered him to know that one or both could die, leaving their parents brokenhearted and facing old age with no doting son to care for them. Wheeler's concern was so great that he thought it interfered with his duties. When his brother was discharged, he felt a great sense of relief. "Now I will have no one to take thought of but myself and perhaps would tend to my business better."[33]

Wheeler's fear of losing a family member in the war was never realized, but Iowan Joseph H. Sweney was not so fortunate. His brother, a member of his own regiment, was severely wounded at the battle of Tupelo. "Then it all came to me," he wrote years later, "all of my anxiety and fears for his safety were realized; all that I had been dreading had come to pass, and all or the worst of disaster which could come to a brother on the battle field had come to me and I was completely overwhelmed." Sweney took the wounding of other comrades in stride, but his brother's fall temporarily took the power to be a soldier out of him. The home could be a double-edged sword, offering support on one side and a cutting danger to morale on the other.[34]

For the most part, images of home, like the lure of comradeship and the comfort of fighting in closely ordered formations, supported battlefield morale. They loomed large in the Northern soldier's ability to keep his emotions under control while leaden sheets sailed over his head. Yet by creating an element of security, these factors could also threaten morale. Through the death of a brother, the killing of a favored commander, or the breaking up of a battle line, the sense of support could quickly be destroyed. Normally, this was a temporary loss; one could renew the sense of security by resorting to any number of other lifelines the military experience offered to soldiers. The multifaceted nature of battlefield morale, the fact that there was a variety of factors working to support the soldier's resolve, meant that one support could quickly be replaced by another. The psychology of the battle line was the psychology of survival.

7

Shaping the Battle Experience

I know of no horror so terrible as the period just preceding the shock of battle. When engaged, that feeling has given way to the excitement of action. The mind being engaged by a thousand circumstances, fear has been dissipated, and a sense of relief has taken its place. I think I can truthfully say I was most comfortable under a most galling fire. The thud, the groans of the wounded, no longer salute the ear. The desire to get in your best licks is all you care for. You yell, you swing your cap, you load and fire as long as the battle goes your way. The enemy falling back, you follow, cheering as you advance. It is a supreme minute to you; you are in ecstasies. Should the battle be against you and you have to retreat, there is no triumphant shout on your part. You are scared. Your only desire to get under cover, to increase the distance between you and the foe.

Frank Holsinger
Pennsylvania Reserves

The first shot I fired seemed to take all my fear away and gave me courage enough to calmly load my musket and fire it forty times.

Samuel H. M. Byers
5th Iowa

I did not feel anything strange on first going into battle[;] we were drawn up in line of battle [and] I was looking as anxious for the secesh as ever I did for a squirrel.

Edgar Embley
61st Illinois

As they became familiar with the nature of combat, soldiers also began to realize that they did not have to be passive victims of war. Each of them had the chance to deal with battle by shaping their perception of it. They gained a handle on the experience by using models or metaphors. It was a conscious effort to make battle familiar by comparing it to experiences in their civilian lives. Through this process, soldiers

127

tamed battle. They relied on romantic literary conceptions of war, on nature, and on the familiar habits of their working-class lives to serve as models of behavior and thought. This was a workable strategy for mastering a unique, unprecedented part of their lives.

ROMANCE AND WAR

One of the models used in this procedure came from the popular culture industry, a romantic vision of reality that had been inspired by artistic and literary developments in Europe and America since the turn of the nineteenth century. Romanticism, as filtered through the popular media, offered Civil War soldiers a device to soften the experience of combat by reconciling it with an artistic vision of reality they already knew. Romanticism took the horrific and turned it into the awesome; death became bittersweet, and the ugly became the poignant. To a degree, this was a process of denying the reality of war. Viewed more generously, it became an essential survival mechanism for men trying to impose order on a volatile experience. They had to make sense of battle in order to survive it.

One of the better examples of using romantic visions to impose order on combat was offered by Daniel McCook, a member of an Ohio family that contributed several generals to the Union cause. He was serving as a staff officer in the Army of the Ohio at Shiloh and found the body of a former classmate leaning against a tree. His friend had been a Confederate, killed in the fighting at the Peach Orchard the previous day, but McCook's closeness to him meant he had to use the same softening devices that would have been needed to face the killing of a comrade. McCook wrote of the incident in an article published two years later in one of the leading popular literary magazines of the North, *Harper's New Monthly Magazine*. In carefully selected phrases, McCook painted a nearly perfect romantic vision of death on the battlefield: "The pitiless rain had fallen on his upturned face all night. A smile beautified his features, while his eyes seemed gazing far to the southward, as if there an anxious mother were waiting for words of hope from that war-swept field. A cannon-ball had partly severed a branch of the tree. Flower laden, it fell in scarlet festoons about his head—a fitting pall for his gallant, pure-hearted, yet erring nature." McCook arranged to have his friend buried under an oak tree, and a picture of a woman with "a fair, girlish face" was placed on his breast.[1]

McCook thoroughly gilded death's visage on the battlefield. He wrote the article for public consumption and was eager to use the romantic model to reach readers who were more used to its images than to the reality of battle. Yet even when soldiers wrote only for themselves, not for the media, they often used romanticism to soften and ennoble war. Consider the case of William Camm, the twenty-five-year-old lieutenant colonel of the 14th Illinois Infantry. His regiment, like so much of the Federal army at Shiloh, had been battered and forced to retreat on the first day of fighting. Camm had time to contemplate the day's occurrences when night fell. "Everything seemed very unpleasant but very real, and very far from exciting or romantic. We had been whipped; all our camp and stores were in the hands of the enemy." Yet despite this hard lesson in the brutal reality of war, Camm's thoughts immediately turned to poetry. In the diary entry that described the fighting, he later inserted a popular verse:

> Night closed around the conqueror's way,
>   But lightnings show'd the distant hill,
> Where those who lost that dreadful day
>   Stood few and faint but fearless still,
> The soldier's hope, the Patriot's zeal,
>   Forever dimm'd, forever crost—
> O! who can say what hero's feel,
>   When all but life and honour's lost?

Camm testified to the power and stamina of the romantic vision of war. Even though he recognized its inadequacy as a description of combat, he felt comfortable with its lack of realism. It enabled him to order a threatening, chaotic experience and make it meaningful.[2]

The artificial nature of the romantic vision did not make it less important in helping the soldier emotionally survive battle. He gilded the harshness of combat in an effort to support the cause or simply as a way to soften the psychological impact of battle. As Camm seemed to indicate, the soldier knew all too well that battle was an unromantic affair with far too much bloodshed and suffering. The soldier who adopted coping mechanisms, who consciously tried to shape the battle experience, also recognized the need to go beyond the harsh reality of that experience in a psychological sense rather than simply be dominated by it.

Ironically, the relationship between romanticism and war could be turned on its head. The Federal assault up Missionary Ridge, part of the pivotal Chattanooga campaign, was a triumph of the human spirit over hard terrain and the bitter legacy of defeat. After their disastrous beating at Chickamauga, the men of the Army of the Cumberland were besieged at Chattanooga and needed reinforcements from the Union's two other major field armies. The main Confederate position seemed well entrenched atop Missionary Ridge, several hundred feet high. On November 25, 1863, the Army of the Cumberland launched what was to have been a limited assault to capture trenches at the foot of the ridge, but the men could not stop there and raced up the steep slope. They were impelled by the danger of remaining in the Confederate first line, exposed to fire from atop the ridge, and by their desire to make up for Chickamauga. To nearly everyone's surprise, they topped the ridge, captured it, and sent the Confederates reeling in retreat. This was an unusually dramatic battle that resulted in an unexpected and clear tactical victory. For Major James A. Connolly, it seemed almost unrealistic. "Indeed the plain unvarnished facts of the storming of Mission Ridge are more like romance to me now than any I have ever read in Dumas, Scott or Cooper." In this case, reality out-romanced literature.[3]

NATURE

Nature played a major role in shaping the battle experience. In a nation that was still heavily oriented toward agricultural pursuits, where much of the territory was still undeveloped, and where even portions of the settled regions were sparsely occupied, nature was an intimate part of everyone's life. It was a nearly universal metaphor.

Not surprisingly, many soldiers could not help but recall the sounds of nature when they heard the roar of battle. A charge of canister striking a stone wall behind which soldiers took shelter at Antietam sounded like hailstones striking window glass. Minié balls flying through the air made a sound resembling "a swarm of bees running away in the hot summer air overhead."[4]

Comparing flying balls to bees not only gave the soldier something familiar to associate with the experience of battle but also helped soften the fear of combat. The effect could be even more pronounced if the visual scene of battle could be associated with some pastoral image from the soldier's rural background. John K. Ely of the 88th Illinois Infantry was on the picket line between the Federal and Confederate positions outside Chattanooga one morning in October 1863. A month before the assault up Missionary Ridge, Ely was one of many soldiers who had to maintain a vigilant watch between Orchard Knob and the ridge. Rebel pickets were so close that he could hear them cough as the sun began to rise, and then he dimly saw them in the growing light. "They all had their long white blankets over their Shoulders, and while I was laying flat on the ground watching them, I could not but help thinking how much they resembled the Cranes, on our Pararies in the fall of the year."[5]

Wedged between two great armies, lying in the cold dawn only yards from the enemy, Ely found comfort in recalling his boyhood prairie farm and making the connection between that heartwarming image and the threatening view of blanket-clad warriors who might try to kill him. Even for soldiers who were much farther from danger, there was comfort in connecting battle with pastoral imagery. George Claflin Parker of the 21st Massachusetts Infantry witnessed a Confederate attack on a battery at Second Bull Run in the darkening shadows of evening. He was so far away that he could not distinctly hear the guns, but he could see the flash of artillery fire. "I could only think of a meadow full of fire flies on a Summer evening." John William DeForest also gazed upon a faraway field of battle at Cedar Creek. The sound of the guns did not carry to his position, but the "long ripple of smoke" arising from volley fire was plainly visible, "like waves breaking on a distant shore." The simile in DeForest's case sprang from his New England seashore upbringing.[6]

Many soldiers of World War I stressed the pastoral imagery of their conflict as an attractive alternative to the industrializing culture of the early twentieth century. For them, at least at the beginning of the war, it seemed to be an escape from the tensions of rapid, far-ranging modernization. Civil War soldiers felt none of this. Their use of pastoral imagery was an effort to control the battle experience through the use of familiar, comforting metaphors that allowed them to get a handle on their reactions to it. They expressed few misgivings about economic and social progress; indeed, many of them firmly believed that they were fighting for progress. Pastoralism became a tool to help control their reactions to the experience of combat.[7]

Other men were so tried by combat that pastoral images became ironic, bittersweet contrasts to the ugly reality of war. There was an attitude of desperation in some soldiers' use of this contrast as they tried to cope with the emotional strain.

Colonel Robert McAllister of the 11th New Jersey Infantry was haunted by a sound during the battle of Chancellorsville, but it was not the whiz of a minié ball or the thump of a twelve-pounder Napoleon. "I shall never forget the screams of the poor Whippoorwills . . . on Saturday night, May 2. Amidst the lightning flash and roar of our artillery and musketry, and the storm of lead and iron, the screams of the poor bird could be heard mingled in distress with the groans of dying and wounded." The same feeling of desperate contrast was felt by Frederick M. Woodruff, a trooper in the 2d Missouri Cavalry. His regiment participated in a fight at Prairie d'Ann during Frederick Steele's expedition into southern Arkansas in April 1864. His regiment paused on the battlefield, an open prairie surrounded by thick woods. Lines of enemy troops and booming artillery formed the background of Woodruff's view, but vibrant, blooming prairie flowers formed the foreground. A hummingbird, oblivious to the coming battle, hovered and flitted near Woodruff, feeding on the brightly colored flowers. "I contrasted strongly in my mind the peace of this near picture, the picture of the flitting bird, with the angry scene in our front!"[8]

For both McAllister and Woodruff, the contrast between the beauty and charm of nature and the ugly reality of combat was incomprehensible. These sensitive men understood the absurdity of killing in the benign environment of a wood or a prairie bursting with new and delicate life, but neither articulated this knowledge. They recorded their feelings and pressed on, wondering at the nature of war. Other men went a step farther and openly questioned the philosophy of the warrior. To them, nature was so overwhelmingly beautiful that man's political quarrels seemed foolish by comparison. Captain George F. Noyes slept on the battlefield of Antietam amid corpses and material debris and was so impressed by the magnificence of the night sky that he thought "how utterly absurd in the face of high Heaven is this whole game of war."[9]

Some soldiers' appreciation of nature was so strong and refined that it sometimes overpowered their awareness of the war itself. Oliver Willcox Norton of Pennsylvania could not keep his eyes off the beautiful scenery of western Maryland during the Antietam campaign. "I almost forgot the war and the fact that I was a soldier as I gained the summit of the first range of mountains, and the Cumberland valley was spread out before me. I was in love with the 'Sunny South.' The brightest, warmest, richest landscape I ever saw lay sleeping in the mellow sunlight of a September afternoon." Numerous other men were kindred spirits of Norton's; they had a sensibility soft and refractive enough to temporarily shake off thoughts of war and carve out moments of repose amid blood and thunder.[10]

In many ways, nature figured prominently in the soldier's perception of combat and his confrontation with fear. It could be an easy, even superficial relationship, with natural images used as metaphors for gaining a handle on battle. Or it could be ambivalent, unresolved, and poignant. The war was fought by a generation familiar with the natural environment, and quite naturally, it used that environment to come to terms with the experience of battle.

WAR AND WORK

A soldier's most important source of models for coping with battle was the civilian life he had lived before the war. The vast majority of Union soldiers came from working-class backgrounds. Their habits of thought, their experience with manual labor, and their philosophy of life all contributed to their emotional ability to survive battle. On one level, they consciously used coping devices from their civilian lives to deal with the challenges of their military lives. On a deeper level, they simply survived without much thought or reflection at all. Living hard lives of never-ending labor, they had developed a pragmatic acceptance that helped carry them through the dangers of combat, much as it had helped them endure the less lethal dangers of years spent on isolated farms or in claustrophobic workshops.

Descriptive rolls reveal that most Yankees made a living with calloused hands and strong backs rather than with professional training or intellectual finesse. Nearly half of all Federal soldiers were farmers, and about a tenth of them were common laborers. Most of the rest were skilled artisans. The percentages could vary from one unit to the next. The

154th New York Infantry had a much higher proportion of farmers, 73 percent, than the national average; only twenty-three men, 0.02 percent of those who gave an occupation, made their living by means other than manual labor. Even an urban regiment such as the 12th Missouri Infantry, recruited principally from St. Louis, was filled with members of the working class. Only 28 percent of that regiment were farmers, but the number of men listing unskilled and skilled labor as their occupation was much higher than in the rural 154th New York. The number of 12th Missourians classified as other than manual laborers was comparable to the number in the New York unit.[11]

The educational level of the Union's defenders reflected their working-class origins. In a massive study of over ten thousand Federal soldiers, Benjamin Gould found that only 47 out of 1,000 had any education or professional training beyond grammar school. The fact that 881 out of 1,000 had either a limited or good grammar school education was a testament to the progress of basic learning in America. The impressively high literacy rate, over 90 percent, also meant that the average Union soldier was adept at describing his war experiences. But basic education was just that—imparting a fundamental ability to read, write, and be familiar with history. It prepared the individual to become an effective citizen at whatever task life assigned him, with little opportunity to use specialized training to achieve social mobility.[12]

Its working-class character did not make the Northern army unique in the history of warfare. Laboring classes have constituted the major portion of all armies, making the impact of class culture on attitudes toward battle significant and enduring. For example, there was a real difference between upper-class and working-class soldiers in the German army of World War I, according to Eric J. Leed. The former saw the war as an opportunity to add value to lives that had become enervated and passionless; they hoped that the common experience of battle would unify society and give it common purpose. Workers, in contrast, viewed the battle experience as labor, a job that had to be done as efficiently as possible. Leed wrote of the disillusionment of the upper-class volunteer—his "realization that war was work and that the comradeship of soldiers was little different than common subjection to the necessity of labor." There is no reason to believe that Leed's analysis of German class consciousness in the kaiser's army is directly analogous to that of the Northern volunteer. America's essentially preindustrial society and the far different issues involved in the Civil War made Billy Yank's thinking less like that of the industrial proletariat and more like that of the agrarian laborer. Yet class attitudes toward battle have been pervasive in all wars.[13]

Lord Moran, a medical officer in the British army of World War I, identified what he called the "yokel" soldier as the backbone of that army. Moran specifically referred to a category of men not only used to physical labor but also still mostly untouched by modern, industrialized society—a rural worker of the land and the lathe. He was particularly impressed by the blankness of the yokel's consciousness. "Their courage seems to have had its roots in a vacant mind. Their imagination played no tricks. They drew no picture of danger for their own undoing." Moran's admiration for the endurance of the yokel was real, even though he was bothered by the yokel's lack of sensitivity and distrust of intellectualism. The yokel possessed another quality that Moran admired; he defined it as phlegm, "a supreme imperturbability in the face of death which half amused them and half dominated them—the ultimate gift in war."[14]

There was every reason to believe that the rural workers who made up such a large proportion of the Union army shared much the same qualities that Moran identified among England's yeomanry. Many Federal soldiers developed a phlegmatic insensitivity toward danger and a pragmatic acceptance of whatever the battle experience had to offer its participants. Those attitudes were partly learned through exposure to combat and were partly the result of preconditioning by exposure to the rough life of a man of labor before the war. Certainly, David Hunter Strother, a staff officer in the Shenandoah Valley campaigns of 1864, would have completely agreed with Lord Moran about the importance of phlegm. "The greatest cause of cowardice is the imagination," he confided to his diary. "Men will coolly face a visible danger, who will stampede and disgrace themselves on some false report or fancied terror. A lively imagination is therefore a disadvantage in war and the greatest courage is that which is proof against imaginary terror. Characteristic incredulity and a contempt for the enemy has always been my safeguard against stampede."[15]

The phlegmatic soldier was the mainstay of the Northern army. A task assigned to him was a job to be done, not thought about, and demonstrations of concern were taboo. Leander Stillwell of the 61st Illinois

Infantry grew up among farmers and admired their stoic nature in the face of war's uncertainties. When he left for his regiment after a furlough home in November 1863, his father accompanied him to the train station. As they waited for the train to arrive, Stillwell faced his father to say farewell. The elder Stillwell responded, "'Good-bye, Leander, take care of yourself.' We shook hands, then he instantly turned and walked away, and I boarded the train." The two knew by this time the terrible cost of the war; they knew that this could well have been their final farewell, but there was no demonstration of anxiety, no tears or hugging, not a word of affection or care. "Nor did this manner spring from indifference, or lack of sensibility," Stillwell knew. "It was simply the way of the plain unlettered backwoods people of those days."[16]

On an open, conscious level many Northern soldiers used work as a model to shape the battle experience and make it familiar. The period immediately preceding a battle, when the men knew with certainty that combat was approaching, became no more than the necessary preparation for a job they had voluntarily agreed to do. "The preparations for battle, to the civilian, seem terrible," reasoned James A. Connolly, "but the tried soldier regards them as the farmer does his preparation for harvest." This was such a widespread view that Joseph H. Sweney, who served in a different field army than Connolly, described the moments just before the battle of Tupelo in exactly the same way. His comrades in the 27th Iowa Infantry had been relaxing—some of them were gathering berries—when the long roll sounded to prepare them for battle. They fell in line matter-of-factly, "with very little more confusion than men in a big thrashing crew would resume their work at and around the machine, upon an energetic call to return to their work."[17]

Across the breadth of the sprawling Union war effort, soldier after soldier reiterated the work motif. They compared building breastworks to logging bees back home. They compared standing up to enemy fire to hoeing corn or digging potatoes. Indeed, Hugh C. Perkins of the 7th Wisconsin Infantry did this even after balls flew so close to him at Antietam that it made his "face smart." The motif went much deeper than mere comparisons. Major General John M. Schofield marveled at the pragmatic attitude of his volunteer soldiers. They gauged the prospects of success or failure in any upcoming action as if it were a business venture. Schofield attributed this to their intelligence, not to a lack of enthusiasm for the cause. "The veteran American soldier fights very much as he has been accustomed to work his farm or run his sawmill: he wants to see a fair prospect that it is 'going to pay.'"[18]

Work was more than just a model. Many soldiers actually went about the duty of loading and firing their muskets as if it were a real day job. Like any other occupation, combat demanded a certain level of training. The soldier had to learn how to properly use the tools of the trade—learning the nine steps of loading a musket, mastering the complicated movements of linear formations, and getting used to obeying orders without hesitation. When it was time to put these vocational lessons to the test, the soldier often was so involved in doing the job right that his mind had no room for thoughts about the horrors of combat.

No matter how nervous or apprehensive a man was just before the first shot of an engagement was fired, he could become very workman-like when he realized that it was now time to be a soldier. Lewis M. Hosea of the 16th U.S. Infantry heard the sound of firing on the second day at Shiloh. Then his officers shouted, "Attention!" His comrades obeyed that command quickly, but the key word was "Load!" This order meant that fighting was at hand, and it brought Hosea's frightened thoughts to a precisely defined sense of purpose. "That order, like the jarring touch upon the chemist's glass, crystalized the wild turmoil of thoughts and focalized all upon the actual business of war. I can realize now how important a thing in war is the musket as a steadying factor for overwrought nerves; and how that first order to 'load!' brought the panicky thoughts of men back with a sudden shock to the realization that they were then upon equal terms with the enemy to do and not alone to suffer." The sound of rifle butts hitting the ground and ramrods driving home the charges encouraged Hosea's comrades, and the regulars went into the fight.[19]

Ebenezer Hannaford of the 6th Ohio had the same experience at Stones River. Although he was excited in the midst of this "terribly deadly earnest work," he had no fear as he labored. "I never had more perfect or readier command of every faculty in my life. All thoughts of personal danger was over with the firing of the first shot. There was no time for fear. Every power of body and mind was bent to the work; every eye strained forward on that line of dingy gray." The concentration Hannaford described could turn men into efficient killing machines. In fact, New Jerseyan James O. Smith characterized himself that way when recalling Antietam. "Like an automaton, I kept loading and firing, oblivious of everything about me except that musket and my duty to load and fire it in the direction where the enemy was supposed to be." He could not even see the Rebels, but he knew they were firing at him, so he "kept pegging away."[20]

This single-minded attitude toward the labor involved in fighting a battle played an important role in steadying men. It gave them something to think about other than the danger of getting hit. Many soldiers were surprised at the calmness with which they endured combat, but they came to realize that "battle seems more dangerous in thinking it over afterwards than it does right in the midst of it." Preoccupied with the mechanics of fighting, they could view a corpse as "a bundle of old clothes" and "pass the most fearful wounds with a mere glance and without a thought."[21]

Officers had an easier time of ignoring the dangers of battle than did enlisted men, for they had more responsibilities. Their workload was heavier and more complicated. William Wheeler, commander of the 13th New York Battery, was surprised at how little thought he gave to death at Second Bull Run. Even when in the greatest danger, he was so busy supervising his guns that he "hardly noticed the bullets whistling and shells exploding around." Infantry officers had even more to do while under fire, for they were responsible for many more men and hundreds of weapons. Enlisted men had to look out only for themselves and therefore thought only of themselves, reasoned John W. DeForest, but officers had to constantly think about and control many others. "His whole soul is occupied with the task of keeping his ranks in order, and it is only now and then that he takes serious note of the bullets and shells." DeForest and other company officers, such as James A. Connolly of the 123d Illinois, so preoccupied themselves with trimming ranks and encouraging the men to fire steadily that they had no time to think of "the other world, which was so near." With responsibility came a welcome excuse to ignore suffering, at least while the battle was on.[22]

Approaching battle as if it were a job went to the heart of the working-class experience of the Northern soldier. But it was impossible for the work model to block out all thoughts of death all the time for all men. It was inevitable that, either during combat or between battles, the soldier would have to think about and come to grips with the real possibility of losing his life. Religion, patriotism, and a wide range of other factors could help him. One such factor also came from the working-class culture of the North. Common Americans, according to historian Lewis O. Saum, had an intimate acquaintance with death in the mid-nineteenth century. "Theirs was an immediate, not a derivative or vicarious, awareness. . . . Little in the shape of an institutional shield stood between the lay person and the untidy details of disease and dying." They approached it with practicality, mourned, and then went on with their lives. There was less of the elaborate ritual and prolonged mourning associated with middle- and upper-class Victorian ways, and more of an emphasis on death as an escape from "whatever had plagued" the deceased and as an opportunity for a better life with God. Working-class Americans felt the agony of loss as much as anyone, but they hardly allowed themselves the luxury of indulging that feeling. Stoicism and acceptance, not ostentation or affectation, characterized the common man's attitude toward death.[23]

Soldiers simply could not afford to dwell too long on dying, for it was a darkly seductive feature of their military lives. Regiments could lose one-third or more of their number in a single engagement, and over the course of their three-year enlistments, only a fraction of the original complement would be alive when it was time to go home. With the primitive state of medical care, life as a civilian before the war had been precarious, but in the army, death came with even more suddenness and trauma. For both the soldier and his loved ones, this was an odd situation. "You say in your letter that you wrote with strange feelings not knowing whether I would ever read what you wrote or not," noted James K. Newton to his mother. "I also while I write am thinking of the uncertainty of human life. How can I think otherwise, with the sound of battle all round me."[24]

Some soldiers simply refused to think much about dying. They assumed that all volunteers knew the dangers of army service and had accepted them when signing the enlistment forms. Thomas F. Miller of the 29th Illinois Infantry saw plenty of men "fall lifeless on the ground by my Side" at Shiloh, "but we need not murmer or Complain at all this for a Soldiers Duties and Ententions are to kill or get killed."[25]

Other soldiers refused to place too high a value on life. Theirs was a pragmatic rationalization of a natural process over which they had no control. In some cases, this resulted from the accumulation of losses as the war progressed. Pennsylvania cavalryman Charles Weller, while standing guard at the Chickamauga battlefield several months after the engagement, pondered the falling of so many men in so many battles and exclaimed, "what at the present time is a man's life worth! Comparatively nothing[;] he falls and is forgotten except by his immediate friends." W. H. Clune of the 6th Iowa Infantry went much farther than Weller, refusing to give his wife details of the death of friends because "we must deal with the living." Clune went on to wonder how important was the life of a soldier. If he died, "a few tears are shed, the hearth stone for a few days is desolate, then smiles return, mirth and festivity are guests, and in the brief period of a decade, even his family have forgotten him." This was not only practical but "wisely ordained," Clune thought, leading him to "estimate life at its true value—nothing."[26]

Few soldiers would have agreed with Clune's extreme views. He tried overly hard to rationalize death and minimize the loss of comrades. Yet many men certainly joined in his effort to rationalize death in some way. One of the oddest and least believable methods was to assert that death was no more common in the army than in civilian life. Disease, it was thought, took as many lives on the home front as bullets did on the battlefield. That may have made sense to men who were used to losing family members to the many illnesses that nineteenth-century medicine could not control, but statistically, there was no validity to Thomas H. Benton's claim that "life is no more uncertain here than at the home fireside."[27]

A much more impressive and effective approach to the subject of death was to adopt an attitude of fatalistic acceptance. "I do not expect to dy till my time comes." announced Illinoisan Jacob Behm to his brother and sister just after the battle of Shiloh. There was nothing to be done; if a soldier's time was up, he would die whether on the battlefield, in the hospital, or home on furlough. Many soldiers understood the futility of worrying about death and refused to be bothered. The fact that they were one small part of a vast war effort minimized the loss, for the war would continue without them. Onley Andrus of the 95th Illinois had been worried about his wife if he should die, but through some means he had been able to prepare her financially, and in the spring of 1863, he no longer concerned himself with her possible widowhood. She then had enough money for "quite a sitting out," and he had only his own fate to think about. He wasted no time worrying about himself, however. "I dont think we shall go into danger very soon," he reasoned only a few weeks before the Vicksburg campaign began, "and if we should go into a fight I dont calculate to get killed. But if I should it wont kill anybody else but me & I am of no great consequence."[28]

Another aspect of working-class culture that played a role in the soldier's ability to face combat was a dedication to the ideal of patriotism. This arose from the political and social conservatism that was typical of working-class Northerners. Many soldiers took patriotic jargon and ideals seriously, readily identified with the symbols of American nationalism, and easily made the connection between self-sacrifice and love of country. They were genuinely ready to die for the cause.

Of course, it was easier for these men to espouse the value of the cause before they experienced battle. Innocence paved the way for self-sacrifice. The members of a volunteer company from Canonsburg, Pennsylvania, gathered in camp by mid-May 1861 and inscribed mottoes on the walls of their barracks. "We ask no better death than to die for our country, no better winding sheet than the stars & stripes." These Easterners were as enthusiastic as Dietrich C. Smith of Illinois. Only six days after the fall of Sumter, just after he joined a volunteer company from Pekin, he assured his sweetheart that "when we fight we will fight victoriously & when we die we die gloriously for we have the cause of truth & justice on our side."[29]

Those men who could continue to make the connection between death and patriotism even after they had experienced battle became the solid foundation of the war effort. Dietrich C. Smith saw his first dead comrade at Fort Donelson, yet he refused to give up his idealism. His dead comrades were "no more," he informed his girlfriend. "We must see them shot down by our side[,] victims to this unnatural rebellion, [but] they died bravely & for a good cause[;] silent & blessed be their rest in the soldiers grave." Throughout the following three years, Smith's reassuring sentiments would be repeated by thousands of other soldiers who continued to view the Union as a "glorious cause" and reiterated their willingness to fall for it. Iowan James H. Bradd's assertion of faith was typical of a large segment of the Federal army: "if it is my fate to fall in defence of Country So be it. I will die a true man."[30]

Their dedication to the cause was so strong that many soldiers felt bitter at the thought of dying as the result of anything but a Rebel bullet. That kind of death would sanctify the act, making it a sacrifice rather than merely the loss of a life. As Indianan Alva C. Griest put it, if he was to die, "Oh God, let it be upon the battlefield in the full performance of my duty, fighting for our glorious stars and stripes." Soldiers were horrified at the thought of succumbing to an illness or drowning while crossing a turbulent river. Likewise, many soldiers were willing to give up their lives to a shell fragment on the battlefield but were upset by the thought that their remains might be left as debris to be cleaned up by anyone unlucky enough to be assigned to a burial detail. Their bodies would be heaped into communal and temporary plots, "where no loving hand can strew flowers and shed tears of love over my grave." Death was not the most fearful thing about battle, these men thought. Its horrors could be managed, and the patriotic fervor felt by so many working-class soldiers was a major component of that managing.[31]

Attitudes toward death illustrated many soldiers' commitment to the cause and demonstrated an important aspect of their civilian lives. Whether working a farm or trying to assault a Rebel fortification, they had a job to do that involved some kind of risk to life and limb. Feeling that they had no choice but to continue to do it in order to survive, they suppressed thoughts of danger and death as much as possible and kept trying to succeed.

As in their efforts to take control of their lives and careers in the civilian world, soldiers came to understand that they did not have to be passive victims of battle. They had the opportunity to take hold of the experience and mold it into familiar and manageable forms. Individual soldiers used a variety of tools, ranging from romantic literature to pastoralism to the intimate workings of their common lives, but the result was similar. The unique horror of combat was softened and domesticated, and battle was turned into an experience that could be understood. Soldiers not only survived it but emotionally triumphed over it as well.

8

Knowing War

During my service in the volunteer army from April '61, to May '66 I do not remember that I swelled up with pride at every glimpse of "Old Glory floating in the breeze" for our regimental colors kept one man from using a gun and disclosed our position to the enemy. The screeching of the fifes, and the beatings of drums did not thrill me with determination to do and die for my country, but only with the disposition to make a bonfire of those instruments of torture and soldiers of the torturers. And I readily overcame that feeling of dependence upon the commissioned officers that I had brought into the service with me, for a better acquaintance taught me that many of them were in all respects inferior to some of the privates in the ranks. Also I could see no use of a chaplain wearing an officers uniform and drawing the pay of an half dozen soldiers boring us with his dull sermons for I couldn't imagine the soul of a soldier who had died in the defense of his country being consigned to an orthodox hell, whatever his opinion might be of the plan of salvation. One can scarcely respect a man who voluntarily enlists in a war, and then persistently sends up petitions to the throne of grace for protection from the dangers incident thereto.

In war it is the duty of a soldier to kill as many of the enemy as possible, and take every practical precaution against the enemy killing him and his comrades. Every soldier killed is a dead loss to himself, and a large money loss to the government.

David Cornwell
8th Illinois

The troops in their private thoughts make the thrashing of the Rebs a matter of pride, as well as of patriotism.

Theodore Lyman
Staff officer, Army of the Potomac

The soldier of '61 was full of life and patriotism, his ardor undampened by the stern discipline and reverses of the war. The soldier of '65 was inured to hardship and adversity, and hoped less, but fought and accomplished more. The period of romance had changed to a period of system and endurance. Individuality had given place to mechanical action, and what was lost in

143

enthusiasm and animation, was made up in concert of action and confidence in method. The military machine ran more smoothly and with less friction, and inspired greater confidence. The history of these four years of war has its counterpart in our own lives. In our youth, we acted upon impulse regardless of consequences, now we think before we act.

Henry F. Lyster
2d and 5th Michigan

The mass of Union soldiers who survived their initiation into combat began a long journey through their nation's history and their personal development as citizens. They began as innocents at war, naive about the role of the warrior, enthusiastic about the prospect of glory, and impatient to experience the ultimate test of the soldier. As they gained exposure to battle, they lost the naiveté, enthusiasm, and impatience but did not necessarily lose their devotion to the cause. Those who carried the war through to its conclusion developed into efficient fighting men and saved the Union. They became men of war, individuals who had gained an intimate knowledge not only of the techniques of soldiering but also of the psychology of the warrior. They no longer were dilettantes but were skilled, seasoned veterans who could soldier as effectively as they could swing an ax or guide a plow. They became experts at marching without wasted motion, constructing fortifications in the blink of an eye, making their meals under atrocious conditions, and killing Rebel soldiers. Making war was not just their job; it was their life and the fundamental justification for the existence of the military family.

GETTING USED TO BATTLE

Becoming a seasoned soldier was a conscious learning process, willingly undertaken. It was aided a great deal if the soldier was flexible and possessed a willingness to persist and to adapt. Young men were better equipped to handle combat than older men, because they were more pliable and could be molded more easily. The Federal army was filled with them. By 1863, three-fourths of all Union soldiers were under thirty years of age; more than half of them were less than twenty-five years old. Historian Bell Wiley noted in his social history of the Union soldier that morale was much stronger, more vibrant, and more persistent among the young than among the old. Men who were in their middle twenties or younger tended to be unmarried and thus less worried about families at home. Physically, they endured the stress of campaigning more successfully than their older counterparts and "recovered more quickly from the shock of combat."[1]

Many soldiers would have agreed with Wiley's point. They often commented on the value of having young men in the army and consistently cited qualities such as adaptability and eagerness. "Easy to manage, relying upon his officers for guidance and example instead of his own discretion, less conscious of danger, too young to be bound by any habits, the boy will generally out-march, out-work, and out-fight the older man; and you may be sure that in a tight place he will stick to you gallantly, and if you will only *lead*, he will *follow* through thick and thin."[2]

Young soldiers like these were better equipped to deal with the physical and emotional challenges of combat. Through experience, they quickly adapted to it and became veteran warriors. But the process of becoming a man of war was greatly accelerated if the individual could endure his first battle without excessive nervousness or fear. Many Union soldiers found to their surprise that this was the case. They saw the elephant for the first time with as much ease as they had approached any civilian experience before the war, and their ability to cope with battle deepened as they continued to fight.

"I now know myself better than I did before," proudly proclaimed one man, who, like many others, had wondered whether he would fight or run in his first battle. There was an overriding sense of discovery, even surprise, to find that they could stand and fight well. Some of them admitted to being nervous. Indeed, Harvey Reid of the 22d Wisconsin decided that he was too excited to trust his aim as he fired over his comrades' heads. Yet he was not afraid; his nervousness was that which normally accompanies a new and exciting experience. Most strikingly, men like Reid claimed to have had no reaction to seeing their comrades killed. Charles S. Wainwright, an artillery officer in the Army of the Potomac, wrote of his first battle: "As to seeing men shot, dead or dying, I had no feeling but one of perfect indifference. When Lieutenant Eakin fell against me, and cried out that he was 'a dead man,' I had no more feeling for him, than if he had tripped over a stump and fallen; nor do I think it would have been different had he been my brother."[3]

Some soldiers were more amazed at growing callous toward death than about any other part of the process of becoming a veteran. Yet it made sense to them. Illinoisan William Ward Orme, a regimental commander, theorized that this was simply a normal part of adaptive behavior. "We easily fall into regular channels of habit. And when a man goes to war as a soldier he soon finds that the duties of war come upon him easily." Familiarity bred indifference for many soldiers; they learned to pay little attention to the balls and shells flying about them during a battle. Indifferent to their own personal danger, they naturally grew indifferent to the wounding and death of those around them as well. "I am getting so used to this thing that I dont mind it at all anymore," wrote Daniel Faust of Pennsylvania about the many men who fell at the battle of Gettysburg. Indeed, except when "them blue pills wizzes round your ears," Faust could think of no better occupation than soldiering. Death had become less fearful because it had become an ordinary part of his life. Another soldier admitted that he and his comrades did not think about *whether* they would die but *how* they would die. "We have death so constantly before our eyes that it loses its terrors." He only hoped that his demise would be honorable and result in some tactical advantage for the army.[4]

The process of getting used to battle seemed simple to the men who went through it. Langhorne Wister, who was a veteran of the Peninsula campaign and a friend of prominent Philadelphian Sidney George Fisher, described it in detail. He told Fisher that the only time he felt fear was during the few minutes immediately preceding an engagement. That feeling turned to relief as soon as the first shot was fired. It took only one battle for Wister to become so inured to the sight of wounded and dying men that he could thereafter look upon it "with perfect indifference." After the initial trial, everything fell into place with remarkable ease and rapidity. "Habit & circumstances then develop qualities of our nature otherwise unsuspected. But for this, war would be impossible."[5]

LIVING WITH WAR

As they adapted to a life of conflict, soldiers reached a point at which they could function normally. They learned to enjoy schoolboy pranks while under fire, to laugh at the sight of a man who had been shot in an unusual way, to coldly calculate their chances of being hit or of surviving a number of different kinds of wounds, to mingle with the enemy in peace during impromptu truces, or to retreat from a lost battle with calm indifference and a readiness to fight another day. Even the most horrible aspects of their military lives had become minutiae. They had grown used to living with war.

"It was wonderful how quickly our soldier fitted himself to the new conditions that now shaped his life," recalled Abner Small, "and accepted all the good and bad surroundings that to him had become living facts." It then became possible to incorporate parts of their civilian lives into their military lives and to give free rein to the playfulness that was a gift of their youth. Some members of the 136th New York teased their comrades during the battle of Lookout Mountain. While the regiment took shelter in a depression with enemy fire overhead, they tossed pebbles onto those men who were too frightened to look up, trying to make them think that balls were falling much closer than they expected. Other Federal soldiers in other regiments took up the habit of chewing bits of paper cartridges mixed with a few grains of powder while under fire. Iowan James Samuel Clark found that the odd combination of the "tough brown paper" and the "coarse black powder" tasted "pleasant," and his comrades calmly chewed while loading and firing "as a school girl would chew gum." The pets that a regiment accumulated during its service also provided the men with amusement during battle. Three greyhounds became excited by the noise during the capture of Orchard Knob and flushed out several rabbits. Although the men of the 88th Illinois Infantry were under fire and pushing forward their skirmish line, they could not help but pay more attention to the hunt than to the Rebels, shouting, laughing, and encouraging the hounds to their work. The "sharp quick yelps" of the dogs sounded strange in contrast to the roar of musketry, admitted John K. Ely, but that did not dim his enjoyment of this playful, happy scene.[6]

If they were in continual contact with the enemy, Federal soldiers had an extended opportunity to live with war. Jacob C. Switzer of the 22d Iowa Infantry had gotten so used to sleeping with the sound of artillery during the Vicksburg siege that he found himself unable to rest properly without it. He had spent a month on the front lines before being assigned to guard wagon trains to the rear. Miles away from the trenches, with only the sounds of insects and the wind, Switzer could not sleep until he returned to his regiment and bedded down next to an artillery battery. During the Petersburg campaign, the opposing armies were in continual contact for eleven months. There were many periods of inaction between short and bloody offensives. The members of one Federal regiment became so bored at one point that they gathered the guns of the dead and deliberately fired ramrods from them toward the Rebel lines. The Confederates were intrigued by the strange whine, discovered its cause, and returned the playful gesture. This ended after "both sides became tired of the novelty." Soldiers refused to allow the horrors of war to rob them of the opportunity to create a bit of innocent fun.[7]

Arthur B. Carpenter, a volunteer in the 19th U.S. Infantry, documented his progress from being awed by the sight of blood to laughing at death. At Shiloh, his first battle, Carpenter was stunned by the wounded who lay immobile on the ground, "with their pale & haggard faces, and dangling limbs, with *blood running off in streams*." He hoped afterward for a speedy end to the war. Nearly a year later, at Stones River, Carpenter had a change of heart. Experience had taught him not to worry about things over which he had no control. "Not withstanding the horrors of a battle, there is a good deal of fun, and a great many jokes made. A man who was wounded in the nose by a passing bullet which just carried away the bridge of his nose, met another soldier who was wounded in the arm. 'Hallo,' says he. 'They tried to get your arm off did they.' 'Yes but they didn't make it, but I see they come pretty near getting into your cranium.' 'Yes and they come dam near missing me too.'"[8]

Carpenter was by no means the only Federal soldier to find amusement in wounds. Sometimes the men laughed at what were truly horrible injuries. Chesley Mosman and his comrades of the 59th Illinois Infantry had become so callous by the time of the Atlanta campaign that they could crack jokes about almost any kind of wound. Charley Brown was struck by several pieces of shell on July 4, 1864, and one gouged a hole in his buttock. "Charley straightened up as well as he could and placing both hands on his back said to Mennent, 'Captain, they have shot the ass off me this time.'" Three weeks later another regimental member was killed during an artillery exchange. A solid shot struck his head, and it "disappeared." Mosman penned a gruesome joke, writing that the "poor fellow 'lost his head.' . . . Someone said he had no further use for it anyway. That sounds rather heartless and so it would be if the balmy pinions of peace were spread over this region, but they are not."

Neither Mosman nor his comrades were heartless men (nor were they good comedians), but their jokes revealed the state of soldiering in 1864. They were comfortable enough with battle to make fun of even its most awful aspect.[9]

When members of the Army of the Potomac bivouacked on the corpse-strewn battlefield of Antietam, they were literally living with death. David Hunter Strother, a member of George McClellan's staff, recorded an amazing scene that night in Miller's cornfield. Some two hundred to three hundred Rebel dead littered the field. "Many were black as Negroes, heads and faces hideously swelled, covered with dust until they looked like clods. Killed during the charge and flight, their attitudes were wild and frightful. One hung upon a fence killed as he was climbing it. One lay with hands wildly clasped as if in prayer. From among these loathsome earthsoiled vestiges of humanity, the soldiers were still picking out some that had life left and carrying them in on stretchers to our surgeons." None of this seemed to bother the Federal troops, who settled down for dinner and rest. "In the midst of all this carrion our troops sat cooking, eating, jabbering, and smoking; sleeping among the corpses so that but for the color of the skin it was difficult to distinguish the living from the dead."[10]

Perhaps these Union soldiers took the concept of living with war to its logical extreme. During Vietnam, many Americans talked of the living-room war, the transfer of combat into the domestic scene of the civilian home. Strother saw that soldiers could transfer domesticity to the battlefield, which symbolized an acceptance that was intimate and profound. It was as profound as the famous incident at Cold Harbor in June 1864, where men were seen pinning their names and addresses on their backs just before launching what they knew would be a bloody assault on well-prepared Confederate defenses. Horace Porter, one of Grant's staff officers, initially thought that these men were mending their coats but soon found that they were preparing for death as calmly as if they had indeed been tending to their wardrobe. There could be no more poignant image of the Civil War soldier than this stoic and pragmatic acceptance of fate.[11]

Also pragmatic was the soldier's frank acceptance of chance on the battlefield. He knew that he could become a casualty but worried little about it. At first, many soldiers naturally did worry; they supposed, as Frank Holsinger of Pennsylvania put it, "that if a gun is discharged, he or some one is sure to be hit." But after the first battle, they usually realized that most men survived, no matter how high the casualty rate, and they knew that "of the hundreds of thousands of bullets that are fired, but very few hit anybody." It was a source of wonderment to many men that so much lead could be expended to kill so comparatively few soldiers. The common rumor was that it took a man's weight in lead to kill him. Whether or not that was true, the fact that most engagements were eminently survivable for most men strengthened them. They no longer felt "as large as a good-sized barn, and consequently very likely to take in all the balls, shells, grape, and canister, and such odds and ends, coming in his direction." They were convinced that they were "not so large, after all," and could walk "amid a storm of missiles unharmed."[12]

This realization naturally led to an even more comforting conclusion: if a soldier survived one horrible battle unharmed, maybe it was a sign that he could survive the war. "Now I believe, by God, that no bullet is for me," boldly asserted Henry A. Kircher of the 12th Missouri after surviving Grant's May 22 assault at Vicksburg, where his unit lost a third of its number in one attack. It was a presumptuous thought, but Kircher and many other soldiers embraced it for the emotional comfort it provided. In Kircher's case, however, it was misplaced. At the battle of Ringgold, Georgia, on November 27, 1863, he was hit three times and lost an arm and a leg as a result. In a way, he had tempted fate with his belief in invincibility, for every soldier had a chance at death whenever he came under fire.[13]

The soldier needed to know that he had a chance to win the game of survival if he were to function properly as a warrior. "Men will enlist for their country when there are ninety-nine chances for dying and one for living," mused Iowan William W. Belknap after the war. Eliminate that one chance in a hundred, he thought, and wars would become impossible. Most soldiers accepted the odds, which they knew were considerably better than one in a hundred, without falling into the trap of believing themselves invulnerable.[14]

Indeed, they became so good at calculating the odds of survival that they could often predict the chances of dying from a wound better than their surgeons. After observing the fate of hundreds of their comrades, they developed a remarkable judgment about medical matters. This judgment applied to their own injuries as well. In the hottest part of the battle of Chickamauga, William Joyce of the 96th Illinois Infantry was hit by a musket ball that cut his foot. With Rebel balls continuing to fall around him, Joyce "deliberately removed his shoe, examined the wound, and then, as if disgusted with himself at having spent so much time with so trivial a matter, replaced the shoe and resumed firing." He knew it was a light wound that would not keep him from his work, and he even resented the few minutes it took to find this out.[15]

Joyce's experience at Chickamauga was a marvelous illustration of the aplomb of a veteran soldier, treating a wound much like he would react to an injury on a civilian job. Veteran soldiers demonstrated their comfortableness in the world of combat in other ways as well. On July 4, 1864, Thomas White Stephens of the 20th Indiana watched as many of his comrades joined with their Rebel counterparts in an impromptu truce to celebrate Independence Day. Such truces were not uncommon for the purposes of trading tobacco, coffee, and news. They also were useful as temporary, self-created breaks in the soldier's long exposure to death and wounds. As Stephens noted in his diary, they were important as recreation too. The pickets, who had agreed not to fire unless a general engagement began, met and frolicked in the no-man's-land between the Petersburg siege lines. "They both are out running around, throw clods of dirt at each other, halloo at each other &c."[16]

Truces demonstrated how comfortable soldiers could become when facing the enemy not with a rifle but with coffee or a newspaper in hand. Another way to gauge the comfort level of veteran soldiers was to examine how they retreated under fire. The Northern people had never really gotten over the sting of their humiliation at First Bull Run, where so many green Federals had run in panic. They had recovered from the strategic setback and gone on to win many victories, but the memory of a mass, uncontrolled exodus from a significant field of battle wore at their self-respect. Later, smaller retreats, such as the flood of stragglers on the first day at Shiloh, the breakup of Nelson's army at Richmond, Kentucky, and the retreat of much of the Army of the Cumberland on the second day at Chickamauga, would bring back painful memories of that first black day of battle for the Union war effort in Virginia.

As they became veterans, Union soldiers were able to retreat without panic. They realized that leaving the scene of battle in a hurry was not a sign of moral degradation but of military necessity. It was a fact of military life for Confederate and Federal alike and was no longer seen by the soldiers as a source of shame. This was not so clear to civilians or new recruits, who still felt queasy at the news of yet another battlefield exodus. The latter had to be taught to retreat properly when they joined their veteran comrades in battle. It was as important a lesson as learning the drill or the proper sequence of steps involved in loading and firing a musket.[17]

Learning to retreat began with a realization that, as John William DeForest put it, "the terror of battle is not an abiding impression, but comes and goes like throbs of pain." Repeated experience with combat led the veteran soldier to "know when there is pressing danger and when not; the moment a peril has passed they are as tranquil as if it had never come near." The art of retreating involved a narrowing of the imagination. As soon as the soldier was out of the range of danger, even if he had moved only a few yards from the enemy, he could rally his nerves and immediately prepare himself for further duty. Repetitions of this act made it familiar, and soldiers often did not even bother to run to get away from danger. Staff officer Horace Porter found it "provoking" to see soldiers walk away from a situation they found too dangerous. Apparently, he would have preferred a frenzied retreat, for that would have indicated equally fierce efforts to accomplish the goals their field commander had set for them. The calmly retreating soldier was not a slacker but a hardened pragmatist who found the odds prohibitively against him. He could hardly be persuaded by cajolery, threats, or exhortations from a staff officer to turn around and try again against his better judgment. Porter, in frustration, contended that one might as well "try to reason with lobsters when they scramble out of a basket and start for the water" as try to talk such a veteran back into an unequal contest.[18]

Soon after their initial battle, soldiers found the composure to handle tactical setbacks more calmly than they had at First Bull Run. Units of all sizes found it necessary to fall back under fire many times in the fluid environment of battle. The presence of fresh troops a short distance behind the lines helped steady and restore their stamina, and retreats became short tactical maneuvers instead of strategic routs. After Second Bull Run, Captain Henry Pearson of the 6th New Hampshire Infantry characterized the battle as a defeat "as complete as that of the old Bull Run. The difference was that in this battle when a regiment was defeated it was not panic stricken, but rallied on its colors the moment it got behind the reserves." The same was true on many other battlefields. At Champion's Hill, the 5th Iowa Infantry retired rapidly when a Confederate force outflanked its position. Several men tried to shame the regiment into stopping, but they "might as well have yelled to a Kansas cyclone" for all the good it did. Not until the regiment found Union artillery in position did it regain its composure, re-form its battle line, and successfully counterattack.[19]

To a large degree, men retreated in a disorganized fashion because their unit cohesion had been broken by the shock and fire of combat. They had lost contact with their military family and felt alone and vulnerable. Colonel Adoniram Judson Warner of the 39th Pennsylvania Infantry saw this vividly illustrated at Antietam when he was injured and made his way to the rear through a stream of retreating soldiers. Many of them were walking wounded; others were physically fit but emotionally lost. They "felt powerless" because "their companies and regiments had been broken up." Yet they did not panic. "It was a great pouring back—not running, not wild confusion, and the fire still kept up against the rebels [by those who remained on the firing line] was heavy."[20]

Once men like these had an opportunity to re-form their military families, they became useful soldiers again. Perhaps the ultimate example of veterans who regained their ability to fight after retreating from a seemingly lost battle occurred at Cedar Creek, where Philip Sheridan's army was the victim of a surprise attack by Jubal Early's Confederates. The massed retirement of the Federals was an unusual sight, for despite their numbers, there was no panic. They were disorganized, and many were disarmed, but they were "just trudging tranquilly rearward like a crowd hastening home from a circus." They looked out for their safety with remarkable aplomb, "discreetly selecting the best cover, slipping through hollows and woods, halting for rest and discourse behind buildings, and in short taking care of themselves with provoking intelligence." When confronted by a strange officer, they refused to stand and reorganize, but they responded well when provided the opportunity to re-form with other members of their own company. Officers reacted much the same way, except that they could sometimes be prevailed on to create a new, impromptu military family by a superior. Given orders to take a few rallied men from different units, "his morale restored by the authority and responsibility which have been thrust upon him," the officer would lead them back into battle. Thus a soldier went from longing to belonging in a fluid environment, seemingly able to regain his composure and fighting ability in an instant. At Cedar

Creek, the work of re-forming nearly the whole army occurred rapidly after Sheridan arrived and his veterans settled down for further work. While waiting, they calmly smoked their pipes, chatted, and read newspapers as if they had never seen or ran from the enemy that day.[21]

The soldier who had learned to retreat, to bounce back quickly, and to prepare for further fighting had become enough of a veteran to live with war. This was a sign that those men who made up the backbone of the Federal army had gone through a comprehensive learning experience and had fitted themselves to battle. They had tested their fears and resolution, adjusted their expectations, and, without ignoring the dangers and horrors of combat, had pragmatically made themselves into men of war.

SHAPED BY THE BATTLE EXPERIENCE

But to what extend did the men adjust themselves to battle, and to what extent did battle shape the men? It was more than a semantic difference, for there was a danger that in becoming men of war, Federal soldiers could lose their civilian identities altogether. They went through a learning process that forced them to change their self-images and become players in a drama very different from that of their civilian lives. Many observers worried about the dangers inherent in molding an effective army. Would the process produce hardened men who were indifferent to civilian concepts of moral behavior? Would the Federal army become an unstable, lawless element in society when the war was over? Would Northern families lose their sons and fathers to the brutal world of the battlefield even if those men survived the war? Clearly there was some cause for concern that physical survival might not be enough, that emotional and moral degradation could be as serious a problem in the postwar world as amputated limbs.

The soldiers had to answer these questions by defining for themselves the meaning of the war and assessing their role in it. Federal veterans quickly rejected the more unrealistic images of combat and the soldier that were handed to them by the media and the educational system. History books, pictures from the illustrated newspapers, and poetic descriptions of combat paled in comparison to the unadorned reality they saw in their first engagements. "This contest exploded all my notions derived from histories and pictures, of the way men stand up in the presence of the enemy," declared Warren Olney about Shiloh. Other soldiers felt a tinge of bitterness when they noticed the great gulf between civilian conceptions of battle and the reality of combat. Welsh-born Sergeant Thomas H. Evans of the 12th U.S. Infantry recalled that poets could clothe battle in romantic images but could not change its reality. "Rain is almost certain to follow a heavy artillery engagement in a few hours. A poet might say, such are Heaven's tears over the dead and wounded, but there is no poetry in the fact."[22]

They also realized that the novelist's conception of the soldier's feelings on the night before an expected engagement was entirely wrong. Veterans went through many such nights and took them in stride rather than agonizing in a Gethsemane-like mixture of fear for personal safety and faith in the cause. Many times the expected battle did not occur, causing them to realize how wasteful it was to work up their emotions beforehand. Normally, the experienced soldier slept the night before combat, knowing that he would need all the stamina he could muster the next day.[23]

Soldiers so firmly rejected the romantic images of battle that they were taken aback when, now and then, combat presented them with scenes that actually resembled those descriptions. Theodore Lyman, an aide on George Meade's staff during the Petersburg campaign, found it "curious" that a Federal attack seemed so reminiscent of "one of those stiff but faithful engravings of Napoleon's battles." Another member of the Army of the Potomac noted that historians "draw largely on the imagination when they talk of heaps of slain, and rivers of blood." Yet he actually saw this before the stone wall on Cemetery Ridge after Pickett's charge. The dead lay so thick in one area that it was impossible to avoid stepping over bodies, and in about a dozen spots, corpses were piled atop one another.[24]

There was every danger that the experience of battle, which was so jarring, so confusing, and nearly overwhelming, could destroy a soldier's faith in the war effort. It was a powerful force, made more stunning by the sharp contrast it presented to the man's prewar conception of battle as a glorious romp through the history books. "Of course, we laughed at the romance and grumbled at the reality," asserted Abner R. Small of the 16th Maine Infantry. The soldiers knew, according to Small, that "they stood with one foot in the grave all the while." Indeed, he believed they were better soldiers because of this knowledge.[25]

But knowing this fact too well could turn a good soldier into a bitter man. Constant exposure to death in its most disgusting forms affected many Federals. Massachusetts infantryman Robert G. Carter recalled his feelings at Antietam: "A kind of hardness crept over us during the long, wakeful night we passed in that blood-stained, death-strewn spot by the Burnside Bridge, and we grew older in thought and feeling by having come in contact with such misery and suffering." This hardness surfaced in many ways. Federals who were assigned the task of burying the dead at Antietam ignored prayer and ceremony. They simply shoveled the corpses into holes and told "ribald" jokes to pass the time while doing so. Having lost what John William DeForest called the "innocent, pacific air" of the volunteer, his men waited with a "strong, indifferent stare and an expression of surly patience, reminding me of bulldogs and bloodhounds held in leash," as they waited for the order to assault the Confederate defenses at Port Hudson. Or it could manifest itself in depressive broodings, as Lieutenant Colonel William Camm of the 14th Illinois found out. Three days after Fort Donelson surrendered and after he had ridden over the battlefield, Camm marveled at his feelings. "How soon one grows calloused to the sight of mangled and contorted human bodies. We are only clods at best, clods to be broken." Lying in his tent all day with rain pelting the canvas, Camm wondered "what sort of a riddle humanity is, and where the glory comes into such scenes as I have just witnessed."[26]

The soldier's knowledge of war could produce bitterness toward civilians, who were isolated from combat and still retained unrealistic conceptions of it. There was a danger that this could cause a widening gulf between the warrior and those he volunteered to fight for—who were also the people he would rejoin as fellow citizens after the war ended. Illinoisan Amos W. Hostetler, an officer, vented his frustration with home-front busybodies right after the battle of Stones River. "If you folks at home would send us more men and aid us in finishing what has been commenced instead of sitting around your fires croaking about the horrors of war and things you know nothing about you would accomplish more."[27]

Most Federal soldiers did not allow frustration, bitterness, or callousness to permanently alter their character or their faith in the war effort. The surest proof of that was the tone and content of their memoirs and public speeches to veterans' groups, in which they evaluated and reaffirmed their war experiences. It certainly was true that the experience of battle took whatever glory there was out of the war. The expectations of combat held by most volunteers of 1861 were so naive that any exposure to battle would have destroyed them. But becoming men of war did not necessarily destroy the soldier's commitment to the issues of the conflict or his willingness to temporarily embrace the deadly game of the warrior to achieve the war's goals. The conflict became a dirty job to be finished as expeditiously as possible, not a ruined crusade or a cruel joke played by manipulative politicians. It was possible for the average Union soldier to recognize the folly of liking war without rejecting the need to use war as a legitimate method of settling important issues.

They developed a sense of professionalism that was based not on the models offered by the media or by politicians but on their own personal experiences with combat. They did not need the harsh discipline or the long training that was the basis of professionalism in the regular army; they needed only enough time to learn the technique of war and develop a guarded familiarity with its dark side. The transformation of these new men from volunteers to a kind of military professional was the subject of many writings by the veterans themselves. It was a source of pride, awe, and satisfaction that they could give up the naive enthusiasm of 1861, mature into effective soldiers, and then leave the hatred, bitterness, and cold professionalism behind in 1865. The national policy of relying on a vast army of citizen-soldiers to meet a crisis such as the Civil War was obviously fraught with weaknesses—some of them nearly fatal—but the truth was that the system worked. As New Jerseyan Ira Seymour Dodd put it, "The process was not ideal; it was in many ways illogical, unmilitary, and wasteful; yet its results have seldom been surpassed."[28]

9

Memories

Believing war to be a concentration of all that is wicked; and the most cruel invention of the worst enemy of the human race. And believing that were the real truth with regard to its extreme cruelty known, much would be done at least to soften its horrors if not to eradicate it from the worlds history. And knowing that the truth will never be known unless those who have witnessed its heart-s[ic]kening scenes record the same. I have written this Journal with a view to telling some truths that will not be recorded in its histories.

Daniel Bond
1st Minnesota

But when a man has spent a week in toilsome marches toward battle, and then faced the enemy when death was hovering in the air, it is not easy for him to forget the fatigue, the hunger and thirst, the blanket-bed by the roadside, the hot skirmish on the picket-line, the gallop of the battery into position, the steady advance in line of battle, or the fierce charge at a turning-point in the engagement. Though these scenes make but little impression on his mind at the moment, they all come back to him in after years, and he is surprised to find how clearly he can recall each little incident. It is this faculty that leads the veteran, whether he wore the blue or the gray, to talk lovingly of the days when he carried the musket or the sword.

George F. Williams
5th and 146th New York

Life, nor liberty was of little value without a country and let us hope when time has softened the feelings and experience has shown the folly of our misguided countrymen who fought against their own best interests that they will realize that it has been best for them that they were defeated, and the old flag restored and is again the only emblem of authority from ocean to ocean and from the gulf to the great lakes.

Lemuel Adams
22d Illinois

For you must know that *then*, the War, to all of us, was *everything*, it was all in all. The past was forgotten; the future we scarcely dared to think of; it was all then the grim present.

John H. Brinton
Surgeon, U.S. Regulars

War, when you are at it, is horrible and dull. It is only when time has passed that you see that its message was divine.

Oliver Wendell Holmes, Jr.
20th Massachusetts

For that brief period, at least, we lived over again the memories of days of war and battle; of the days when the destinies of our Country trembled in the balance, and where the terrible stake was the future of a Great Nation. We, who were of that party, have lived upon the heights—have breathed anew the air of patriotic service, suffering and devotion, and have returned better men, better citizens, truers of our Country than we have ever been before. I can hardly yet adapt myself to Boston and to the duties of today. I have lived over the days of forty-six and forty-seven years ago.

Henry M. Rogers
Massachusetts Volunteers

Wars do not end when the shooting stops. When young men are taken from their homes and civilian lives and taught new and terrible lessons of war, the impact stays with them for the remainder of their lives. Increasingly, they find it necessary to deal with the experience, to reinterpret its significance and reevaluate its impact on their self-image. The ways in which they do this can mean a great deal for their sense of self-worth. It can also delineate the place of that war in the culture of their nation.

As time went by, veterans were drawn to reliving the war through their written memories. Those writings reveal a great deal about how the war affected the rest of their lives. Reminiscences can be useful in understanding how the soldier felt during the war, but they are even more valuable in revealing how he felt about the war long after the last shot had been fired. They are a reflection of his attitude, enriched by the perspective of time, as he entered middle age. Did he still believe that the war had been worth fighting? Had the experience of battle changed him? Was America a better place without slavery in the South? What kind of memories did he choose to write about? Why was he writing, and who was he writing for?

At first, it was understandable that the Northern soldier had no interest in telling about the war. It was too hard to think about it for several years after Appomattox. Too full of "raw facts," they wanted to heal, not evaluate. Many of them consciously made vows not to speak a word of their experiences, at least for the time being, and the fact that few memoirs were published for at least fifteen years after the end of the war indicated that they were men of their word. As J. T. Holmes of Ohio put it: "In those days the great interest lay rather in what was before than in what was behind us. The time to look backward either at the war, or at life, in the general sense, had not come to us. We were young men yet and the war was not two years old."[1]

As time went by, these attitudes changed. Hard memories softened, and distance lent perspective to the veteran. He found it possible to deal with the war as a conscious memory and to ponder it as a significant experience in his life. By the 1880s, more and more Northern veterans were taking pen in hand to explore their personal past. By the 1890s, what had started as a tentative trickle became a deluge. The Northern book and periodical market was awash in a sea of memoirs, reminiscences, and diaries written by everyone from cooks, privates, and chaplains to colonels, generals, and political leaders. Many other men chose not to publish their memories, preferring only to write them down and file them among family papers. Still others only spoke of the war to friends and relatives, perhaps to have their experiences remembered and passed down secondhand to succeeding generations. By whatever means, the Union veteran dramatically broke his silence after the passage of nearly a generation, and the war became real once again.

They created one of the most remarkable bodies of literature in American history. No other event inspired so many books, articles, and unpublished texts as did the Civil War. The Northern veteran needed only some impetus to set him to writing. Many were pushed into it by requests from sons, daughters, nieces, and nephews for information about their role in the great war. Family friends, usually youngsters, also cajoled veterans for stories about their experiences.[2]

Even more important than family and friends were the former comrades of the veteran; they inspired one another to write. At veterans' reunions, the call repeatedly rang out to record what had happened before time took its toll on the graying army that had saved the Union. As they had supported one another on the battle line, these aging men now sought to reinforce the bonds of the military family by telling of their time in the army. Their purposes were entertainment, commemoration, and the recording of factual information to keep the story straight. Many also wanted the nation's memory of the war to be well-balanced; they were afraid that the many memoirs written by generals would give the country the impression that the rank and file had had nothing to do with winning the war. Justice had to be served for the common soldier, civilians had to be informed about the facts of the army and the war, and young men had to be made to "realize what war really is." The Union veteran took his role as a citizen-soldier seriously; he also took his role as a historian seriously, but above all, he wrote for himself and for his comrades. Nixon B. Stewart of the 52d Ohio was typical of the veteran-author. For years he had wanted to write the history of his regiment but was not prompted to take action until he gazed at a flag standing in the corner of the assembly hall where his comrades were holding a reunion. "And instantly some strong nerve of mine felt down its way at last to that period point, and almost before I knew it, I was writing my heart out in admiration and love for the courage and fortitude of those comrades of mine, who were splendid in doing, and grand in suffering."[3]

These amateur authors had to grope their way through the writing process, much as they had had to struggle to learn the art of the warrior in 1861. The fighting on this literary field of battle was less deadly. The great majority of memoirists had no experience in writing for publication, and some of them openly apologized for what they were certain would be texts "devoid of literary flavor." Whatever they lacked in terms of accepted style these books, articles, and essays made up for in candor and sincerity. The authors experimented with format, some of them believing that a diary would be more personal and therefore more interesting to the casual reader. Others based their narratives solidly on a rereading of letters or diary entries long since buried in trunks and forgotten in attics. Several veterans were surprised at how difficult it was to write for publication, and they devoted much time and energy to learning how to do it properly. Melvin Grigsby, for example, had been asked to tell his story to so many acquaintances after the war that he decided to write a book to save himself from having to repeat the narrative over and over. Yet he found it so difficult that he postponed the writing until "through reading and education" he acquired "a better command of language." Other veterans regretted confining themselves to the written form alone and longed for the opportunity to embellish their stories with gestures, eye contact, and sound. A few recognized that when they wrote for a wider audience than their immediate circle of family and friends, their language, style, and even the content of their narratives changed. Yet they all attacked the role of author with the same kind of perseverance they had used to take Vicksburg or Richmond.[4]

Not all veteran memoirists apologized for their lack of sophisticated literary style; some were proud of their rough-hewn writing. Far from "well rounded sentences, or flights of eloquence," they presented the reader with blunt words, stubby sentences, and stark images. "Those were rugged times," asserted Charles O. Brown. "The words which would recall them, even briefly, must not be too smooth." Oddly, numerous soldier-authors felt it necessary to apologize for writing a book about their own experiences, afraid that readers would view them as egotistical. With a charming modesty, these authors graciously acknowledged that other soldiers had shared and exceeded their own experiences. They had no intention of aping the self-serving puffing that characterized so much of the writing produced by generals. They were humble, self-giving men in the war, and they continued to be self-effacing in peace. Some of them even played with this theme. Charles Morton cleverly wrote of his reminiscences of Shiloh:

> I desire it to be understood that I am not fully persuaded that I fought that great battle all alone on our side, nor that I can convince you now that it is to be greatly regretted that I was not in supreme command at the time. And I further trust that I will be exempt from any accusation of an egotistical desire to parade my personal prowess in the battle, when I tell you frankly in advance that the most prominent feature of my conduct was the tall running I did; and if the pronouns *I* and *we* seem conspicuous, let it be understood that it is merely for convenience of brief expression.[5]

As they struggled with writing, the soldier-authors also began to deal with memory itself. They were fascinated by the process of remembering events, emotions, and images that they had suppressed for so many years. J. T. Holmes had completed his book on the 52d Ohio; it was 1898, and he spent most of the night reading proof sheets. It mattered not to him whether the reading public found an interest in his words, for the personal experience of reliving the war had been overwhelming for him. "I have lived over again these thrilling years," he wrote. "No others in my three score can begin to compare with them in depth of interests and feelings, involved and evoked; in the burns and scars from the war that scorched and withered by many a touch; in the profound and moving tragedy that passed like a horrid dream, with its lights and shadows, before my youthful eyes." Writing obviously was therapeutic for Holmes, but it also reminded him of his age and mortality. The war was over, and with the passing of the veterans all would "soon be history, memory, silence, only."[6]

Holmes realized, as did many other memoirists, that memory lay in the subconsciousness of the veteran to be called upon when he was ready to relive the war. James R. Carnahan of Indiana compared it to a painting, except that the soldier's vision of war was imprinted by fear, suddenness, and harsh sensual experiences rather than the calm repose of an artist working in his studio. Although vivid, the war vision inevitably grew a bit dull over time and was partially replaced in the veteran's consciousness by his civil preoccupations. Then, at some point, it came back with something like its old clarity. The sight of a face or the sound of a voice could trigger this process for Carnahan. The connection between sound and memory was so strong for New Jerseyan Ira Seymour Dodd that he crafted an entire essay about his experiences at Chancellorsville around it. Entitled "The Song of the Rappahannock," it deftly wove together several variations on the theme of sound, silence, and battle. "The Song has been silent for more than thirty years. In another thirty years it will cease to be a living memory save to a handful of very old men. But those who once heard can never forget its weird, fantastic, sinister tones." At the end, Dodd had heard whippoorwills singing at night after the sound of the firing had ceased on the corpse-strewn field. He still could not hear the song of that bird, more than thirty years later, without thinking of Chancellorsville.[7]

Not only sound, but also smell, served the veteran as a trigger for memory. James O. Smith had wandered over the field of Antietam to satisfy his morbid curiosity about death. The smoke from the fighting had not yet dissipated, but the smell of rotting flesh had already begun to fill the air. It mingled with the odor of pennyroyal, an aromatic plant with small blue flowers. The contrast of the smell of the wildflower and the smell of death was so vivid for Smith that it "added horror upon horror to the scene. The smell of pennyroyal will to this day bring vividly to my mind all the terrible sights and events of that afternoon."[8]

After familiarizing themselves with the mechanics of writing and calling up the stored memories of their youth, Northern veterans turned their attention to the content of their memoirs. These writings fell into four broad categories. First and most significantly, authors recalled and reasserted their faith in the cause that had impelled them to enlist in 1861. Second, a small number of veteran-authors completely rejected the cause. They became something of a "lost generation" of the Civil War era, believing that ideology and patriotism were hollow incentives for war and that their own lives had been warped by their battle experiences. Viewing their sacrifice as useless and their youthful enthusiasm for service as naive, they had clearly lost their faith in the cause. A third group of authors held somewhat similar views but came to a different conclusion. They avoided any expressions of faith in the cause but found new faiths to believe in. Instead of ideology, they used devotion to comrades or to a philosophy of personal development as valuable concepts around which to build a satisfying view of their war experiences. Finally, a fourth and more complicated group of authors avoided the dark side of their war experiences as much as possible in their memoirs, preferring to concentrate on the "good" aspects such as amusing camp stories, the excitement of living outdoors, the comradeship of good friends, and the novelty of military life. These men did not dwell on the cause or paint war as a horrible experience or search for new faiths to believe in, yet they were not necessarily antipatriotic, disillusioned about the war, or insensitive to battle's true nature. A variety of factors explained why they refused to either denounce war or praise it as a useful endeavor.

The proportion of men who fell into each of these four categories was uneven. Of the fifty-eight memoirists consulted on this topic, nineteen were overtly ideological in their judgments of the war experience. Three were "lost" soldiers, and four searched for new faiths to believe in. Twelve veterans were careful to avoid describing the horrors of war, and twenty men frankly described death and battle but made no judgment on it. Overwhelmingly, these memoirists asserted faith in the cause, chose to avoid negative reporting on the war, or displayed no difficulty in dealing with its memory.

REMEMBERING THE CAUSE

The first group of authors, those who vigorously reasserted their faith in the cause, was the most prominent. Together with the last group, whose members concentrated on the comradeship of the war experience, these men represented the overwhelming majority of Northern veterans. The ideologically committed ex-soldier made his views known in reunion speeches as well as in books and other publications. His opinions were strong, eloquently expressed, and often rather sophisticated and broad in their implications. He was the thinking veteran, highly concerned with making ideological sense of the most disruptive experience in the history of his nation.

The ideological veteran also could be rather shrill in his concern for the future of the nation. He often couched his views in the form of a warning, for he feared that the country was forgetting why the war had been fought in the first place. Decades of peace and prosperity, the onset of rapid industrialization, and a modern consumer economy had dulled the people's sensitivity to the moralistically charged issue of slavery that he believed was involved in the war of secession. If America forgot the ideas that underlay the conflict, it would lose the most important lessons learned from it, such as the need for an ever-vigilant population to safeguard liberty. These veterans thought that there had to be a higher, transcendent meaning and result coming from this war or else their sacrifice was rendered useless.[9]

R. L. Ashhurst of the 150th Pennsylvania spoke of these things at a regimental reunion held in 1896 on the field of Gettysburg. He reminded his audience of Stephen Crane's novel *The Red Badge of Courage* and the author's vivid re-creation of the life and fears of a soldier in camp and in battle. Ashhurst thought Crane had captured that subject, but he was irritated, even frightened, by Crane's avoidance of ideology. The novel said nothing "of the great and glorious object of the sacrifice, nor of the noble glow of true patriotic fervor which, as we know, was the governing note and tone of the chords of the soldier's heart, and without which the story of the American soldier's deeds and endurings is but as a tale told by an idiot—full of sound and fury, signifying nothing. On the contrary, if we knew not better we would arise from its perusal with the feeling that nothing could justify or compensate the horror and suffering undergone." For Ashhurst, as for so many other veterans, it was not sufficient to describe the true nature of battle. One also had to endow it with meaning and significance. The war had not been a mere conflict of opinion, as another veteran pointed out, but a conflict of right versus wrong, and the postwar public had to be reminded by those who had fought it which side had been right. It had been not only a war to save the Union, as William P. Hogarty asserted when he reminded his reunion audience of the abolition of slavery, but a war "to make the Union worth saving."[10]

After reminding readers of the cause, veterans went on to reassert their conviction that ideas had been the basis for their motivation to fight. Even after the war was over and victory was assured, they continued to believe that any level of personal sacrifice would have been a price worth paying for the cause. When speaking of the deaths of others, not surprisingly, they had no difficulty asserting this theme. Accepting the general principle of sacrifice for the greater common good was easy, and it was repeatedly done by many veterans in reunion speeches as well as in published and unpublished memoirs. The authors often noted that an individual life was "but a mere pittance compared to and with the value of the results that we hoped" to gain through winning the war. Indeed, Ira Seymour Dodd crafted an essay entitled "Sacrifice" in which he movingly wrote of the deaths of the best and the brightest that the North had to offer. He firmly argued that the result of the conflict was worth the price in suffering. In a much less poignant, more pragmatic way, another veteran listed all the benefits he believed that his fellow soldiers had achieved for the nation through their defeat of the Confederacy. He also listed the cumulative costs of the war—statistics regarding money spent, soldiers killed and wounded—and came to the predictable conclusion (he was speaking to a veterans' group) that it was all worth it.[11]

Parading dry numbers before an audience that was already committed to the conclusion was one way to reaffirm the satisfying image of a good war justly won. But an even more significant and meaningful way was for a veteran who had suffered personally to speak mainly to himself. In an unpublished autobiography, Lemuel Adams of Illinois addressed this theme. He had been medically discharged from the service near the end of 1862 after enduring "severe" hardships, but he "never regretted the part I took in that great struggle[;] many lives must be sacrificed and much blood was necessary to be shed, and my life and my blood was no more precious nor my life more valuable than thousands of others." Jacob C. Switzer of Iowa was even more seriously affected by his war experience but even more eloquent in his assertion of continued faith in the cause. Having lost a leg because of wounds received at the battle of Winchester in September 1864, he was disabled for the traditional occupations his fellow veterans adopted after the war. Switzer felt "at sea" in civilian life, yet he was not disheartened. "I came home fully satisfied with the results of my service with regards to its effects upon myself; glad that I could say I served until the cause for which I gave so little, compared with the sacrifice made by so many, was won honorably, the Union saved, slavery dead, and treason made odious."[12]

There obviously was a strong self-interest operating in the minds of veterans who so strongly proclaimed their faith in the war experience. To deny its worth would be to deny a huge and important part of their lives. It was a self-assurance that they had played a significant role in great events and had helped shape the contours of a growing society. Ohioan Levi Wagner admitted that he was proud to have served in the Union army. "Why should I not be? Is it not a pleasure to us old landmarks of today, who are now old, feeble and gray, that in looking back over lifes way, we can, with some degree of pride, feel that somewhere in the past we have not been altogether useless; that our lives have not been spent in vain, as we through our valor and patriotism can today show the whole civilized world one of the greatest, best and undivided governments that exists on the face of this earth."[13]

Besides the sense of personal fulfillment that Wagner noted, veterans cited a number of other themes when arguing that the results of the war were worth the cost. Some argued that army service had improved the character of the Northern soldier, giving him "a better physical and mental manhood. The discipline of battle purified them; suffering taught them humanity and self-reliance; dangers and hardships, endured together, bound them to their comrades by a type of friendship that was ennobling. Of many it can be said; 'The war made men of them.'" Other veterans noted the explosion of material progress that followed the war, resulting in factories, growing economies, and new inventions. Charles Robinson left service in the 2d Michigan and moved to Chicago, where he helped build the first packing house that would help turn this modest lake town into a world-class city. "Looking back since then," he wrote, "I have felt that I helped initiate the new era—the great industrial and expansion movement that followed the war. That era was to bring great changes to our home community, which had supported the war so faithfully."[14]

The impact of the North's victory became headier the more veterans dwelled on it. Many were convinced that it had spurred the progress of democratic institutions in other nations. The destruction of slavery was uppermost in these men's minds, for it eradicated what they now saw, in the postwar atmosphere, as a fundamental weakness in the American nation. "We now know that the glorious result of universal freedom is worth the price we paid," asserted George E. Sutherland before a veterans' reunion in 1888. This view even led to a devaluation of the accomplishments of the Founding Fathers. Before the war, the generation of George Washington, Thomas Jefferson, and John Adams had always been viewed with reverence by a public awed by the sufferings of the Revolution and the apparent majesty of the Constitution. Now, many Northern veterans saw flaws in those accomplishments. Compromises on the existence of slavery had set the stage for the Civil War nearly a century later. The men who had risked their lives on the fields of Bull Run and Peach Tree Creek could now claim to have corrected those errors and saved from destruction the nation that the Founding Fathers had only imperfectly created. This was an awesome revision of what had been a fundamental article of political religious faith in a nation that was still undergoing the pains of adolescence.[15]

Ideologically committed Northern veterans sought to clothe the memory of the war with nobility. They were frightened by the growing tendency to ignore the fervency that had moved so many Northerners in 1861. As the sections grew closer together by the 1880s, and as the bitterness of the war subsided, they grew more apprehensive that their 1865 victory would be robbed of its meaning. The "lost-cause" mythology was taking root. Created by Southern writers, many of them former Confederates, this interpretation of the meaning of the war deemphasized slavery as a cause of the conflict, highlighted constitutional issues rather than moralistic concerns as the impetus for secession, and portrayed the Confederates as noble champions of a charming, high-minded, yet tragically doomed way of life. Even the Northern public found this romantic legend irresistible, as novels, essays, and Confederate memoirs refocused the nation's understanding of the war. Calls to remember the true nature of the Confederacy rang out at veterans' reunions and suffused the pages of many Union veterans' memoirs. They sought to remind people that one should support the reconciliation of North and South, that the Confederate soldier deserved respect for the sacrifices he endured, but that there was just no way to compare the Southern and Northern causes. As George R. Skinner of Iowa noted in a reunion speech, it would be impossible to argue that a Confederate victory in 1865 would have had the same benefit for the nation as a Union triumph. Do not apologize for being a Yankee, he told his fellow veterans; boldly admit that the Northern cause was right and the Southern cause was wrong. Teach America the "truth" of the war's real issues. There certainly was a poignant sense of loss in the urgings of veterans like Skinner, as they clearly began to sense that although they had won the military conflict, they were fast losing the battle to shape the nation's memory of it.[16]

The vast majority of ideological veterans expressed themselves in factual writings, but a tiny minority tried to write fiction as well. John William DeForest, the Connecticut captain who produced so many valuable descriptions of combat in his memoirlike essays, also produced one of the most widely read novels of the war, *Miss Ravenel's Conversion from Secession to Loyalty*. Published in 1867, before the lost-cause mythology took root, the story had a cast a characters who represented different types: the ideologically committed New England volunteer, the educated Southerner ostracized with his beautiful daughter to the North for his antislavery views, the former slave owner who remained loyal to the Union. Throughout this long narrative, DeForest vividly and accurately described battle for what he knew it to be. He portrayed Southern culture as degraded by the existence of slavery. He reminded his readers of the shrill bitterness of the conflict, the unforgiving nature of convictions on both sides, and the demand to be all one thing or all the other—to take sides and believe in the transcendent importance of values and ideas.

The novel was more than this as well. DeForest deftly portrayed the two kinds of Unionism. New Englander Colburne was righteous, abolitionist, serious about the moralistic implications of the war, a vigorous prosecutor willing to accept nearly any policy to destroy the Confederacy. John Carter, the Southern Unionist, refused to see any moralistic component to the war. A sentimental sense of duty to American nationhood impelled him to fight for the North, but he did not condone abolition or the self-righteousness of his comrade Colburne. Carter's degeneracy, his indulgence in debauchery and lechery, was portrayed by DeForest as typically Southern. His amorality mirrored the conservative Unionist's attitude toward Lincoln's emancipation policy: that it was only an incident, not an essential part of the war's meaning. Lillie Ravenel, the exiled daughter, gravitated from one man to the other, thus converting from one extreme of Unionism to the other. She initially shared Carter's views but suffered because of his infidelity. Lillie became a more serious and politically aware person as she turned her affections toward Colburne. Her political conversion was symptomatic of a moral conversion. DeForest took joy at the triumph of emancipation and the Union together, and he expressed that jubilation with the personal transformation of Lillie, the eventual death of Carter, and the success of Colburne. Written at the beginning of Radical Reconstruction, this novel sent out a strong, resonant call for ideological purity.[17]

Veterans who remained committed to the cause used a wide range of forms, from the novel to unpublished memoirs, to express their faith. Public speaking, especially before veterans' groups, was the venue for the most strident assertions of ideology. The style and passion of those speeches struck at least one modern historian as suspicious, possibly indicating that the veteran felt compelled to deny the horrible reality of war in order to perpetuate jingoistic attitudes toward the conflict. But there is no reason to assume that veterans changed their views to suit their audiences. The speeches they delivered to regimental reunions were not false or exaggerated simply because they were patriotic. If veterans did not dwell on the horrors of war, it was because they had a resilient faith in the results of the conflict and a recognition that, despite its horrors, it had been essential to save the Union and destroy slavery. Veterans reiterated the same ideological faith in all forms, including unpublished memoirs, which they assumed would be read only by members of their families.[18]

It was hardly surprising that these veterans were particularly strong in their assertions when speaking to fellow veterans or to the public at large, for they considered themselves guardians of the cause. The convictions that moved them began to lose much of their power and clarity as the decades passed. By the twentieth century, new generations were much more interested in the romantic images of the South that the lost-cause writers were producing than in the moralistic political sermons of Union veterans. The men who had saved the Union and retained faith in the cause had to be content with their own self-assurance that right had been on their side, even if society as a whole did not always recognize it.

LOST SOLDIERS

In stark contrast to the ideological veterans was a small group of Northerners who could find no self-assurances of any kind about the war. These men were unique among veterans, refusing to attend reunions or to dwell on the adventure of military life or the value of the cause. In a real sense, they were lost soldiers, men who had served well during the war and survived the terrible battles only to go home empty and embittered by their experiences. They could find no redeeming consequences of the war, no personal sense of accomplishment. Their lives were warped in some way by the conflict. Theirs was a particularly dark field of battle, made all the more lonely by their scarcity.

It was possible that the lost soldier simply could not bring himself to write a memoir and that the number of people who agreed with this dark interpretation of the meaning of the war was greater than is apparent. When he did write of his feelings, the message was clear, however, for it lacked any positive conclusion. The lost soldier wrote of the cost of the war, expressed his view of it as a bloody horror, yet he refused to round out his account with an assurance that the cost had been worth the gain. What made these men even more intriguing was that they had been good soldiers and were willing to buck the trend among veteran-authors. None of them gained much publicity among their more positive ex-comrades, but they had the courage to offer a different perspective on their war experiences.

Abner Small rose through the commissioned ranks to command the 16th Maine by the end of the war. His regiment saw hard service, particularly on the first day at Gettysburg, where it was decimated by overpowering numbers of Confederate troops. Small had served well, and he admitted in his memoir that he remained loyal to his government. At times after the war, Small wished that it were possible to erase the war from his memory; at other times, he was glad it had been "indelibly stamped into my being," for he could pass on some of his observations to his sons and teach them the cost of patriotism. Thus Small was torn between loyalty to the cause and a dark, bitter lesson learned from battle. He tottered on the fence, unable to firmly plant himself in the camp of the ideological veteran and afraid to allow himself to fall irretrievably into despair. Judging from his memoir, which was published long after his death in 1910, he never came to a satisfactory conclusion.

The shock of battle was the origin of Small's dilemma. It upset his ideological faith in the war. "The bravest front, bolstered by pride and heroic resolution, will crumble in the presence of the agony of wounds. Wading through bloody fields and among the distorted dead bodies of comrades, dodging shells, and posing as a target to hissing bullets that whisper of eternity, is not conducive to continuity of action, much less of thought. The shock from a bursting shell will scatter a man's thoughts as the iron fragments will scatter the leaves overhead." This dissonance between the mental world of ideology and the physical world of the battlefield created doubt and the possibility of disillusionment for Small. Then, when he was captured during the Petersburg campaign, a Rebel soldier offered him half of his own meager rations. "In all my life I was never more deeply touched, never more conscious of the brotherhood of man, and from that moment war was hateful to me." Small found it impossible to view his Confederate counterpart as an enemy. Indeed, he came to find more affinity with him than with the civilian population at home in the North.

Even though Small could not espouse the self-satisfying conclusions of the ideological soldier, he did find therapeutic value in writing. It offered him the opportunity to express his feelings, although his work was never published in his lifetime. Few other lost soldiers summed up their agonized questions better than Small. Writing of the soldier who became used to seeing horror, the Maine veteran stated: "He resented it all, and at times his resentment grew into a hatred for those who forced the whirlpool of war. . . . He hated his surroundings and all that war implied," yet he "forced himself to resist whatever was inimical to the interests of a hated service. If he had at times any longing to lay down his arms, he carefully concealed it. . . . He might have the courage of his convictions, yet behind his bravery there lay something that mystified and repelled him. He didn't know what it was, so inevitably he went to find out. I don't know that he ever got an answer. I didn't."[19]

By far the most famous, prolific, and embittered lost soldier of the Civil War was Ambrose Bierce. An officer in the 9th Indiana Infantry, veteran of Shiloh, Chickamauga, and much of the Atlanta campaign, Bierce served faithfully through some of the worst combat the war had to offer. He saw much and conscientiously analyzed and absorbed it. After the conflict, Bierce wrote a remarkable body of work. His "Bits of Autobiography" are just what the title implies, fragments of memories of his war experiences, valuable as insights into how the conflict affected his life. However, he became much better known for his fictional writings, a series of short stories that expose one of the most bitter indictments of war ever produced by an American veteran. Bierce was relentless in his macabre irony; his refusal to see anything noble, heroic, or redeeming in the war experience; his hard-edged narrative style; and his detailed knowledge of the reality of warfare. He wandered through life after the war, participating in the failed experiment of Radical Reconstruction, rejecting ideological interpretations of the war's significance, and finally losing himself in the turbulence of the Mexican Revolution early in the twentieth century. His fate in Mexico is still a mystery today, but Bierce's literary legacy and what that legacy tells us about this lost soldier of the war to save the Union remain.[20]

One would have to look beyond "Bits of Autobiography" and the short stories to gain another important insight into Ambrose Bierce. In a set of miscellaneous poems and stories, he revealed his utter disgust with the failure of Radical Reconstruction. The South was reenslaving African Americans, Bierce wrote, and the North was doing nothing to prevent it. In a poem entitled "The Hesitating Veteran," Bierce depicted a wounded ex-soldier of the Union who contrasts the exhilaration and faith of the war years with the seeming lack of morality in the postwar world of graft, industrialization, sharecropping, and Jim Crow. "I know what uniform I wore—O, that I knew which side I fought for!" bitterly laments the veteran. In another poem, "A Year's 'Casualties,'" Bierce sarcastically tells us that two score thousand veterans die each year, mourned only by pension agents and "orphaned statesmen." Their work during the war has been forgotten, and the North has lost the peace it sacrificed so much to gain. "O Father of Battles, pray give us release / From the horrors of peace, the horrors of peace!" There is no doubt from Bierce's other work that he felt the shock of battle, that it set the stage for disillusionment. But there is also no doubt that he left the war still hopeful and tried to secure the Northern victory by working for the Radicals to reform the prostrate South. His real disillusionment became apparent when that reformation failed. Bierce's major writings—produced in the 1880s, the decade following the collapse of Reconstruction—depict the war experience itself as a failure. What had been a horrible but necessary experience could have been redeemed if the effort to reconstruct the nation in a progressive fashion had succeeded. Without that necessary work, the war became a hollow, cruel lie.[21]

Bierce wrote differently of the war experience in "Bits of Autobiography" compared to his short stories. In several of the "Bits," he wrote much like the typical veteran, concentrating on the beauty of the landscape in West Virginia, the scene of his earliest service with the 9th Indiana Infantry, or describing his capture and escape in Alabama in the fall of 1864, or describing "What Occurred at Franklin" in much the same matter-of-fact way that any veteran related the occurrences within his own line of vision in a great, seething battle. The only difference lay in Bierce's style—his lucid, detailed, evocative language tinged with irony even when he meant only to describe the vision of one soldier among many. The piece entitled "A Little of Chickamauga" was most like the reminiscences produced by thousands of other veterans. It is a straightforward telling of his experiences at the battle without the bitterness that would characterize his fiction.[22]

The two "Bits of Autobiography" that step away from the model of the soldier memoir and point the way toward Bierce's fiction are "What I Saw of Shiloh" and "The Crime at Pickett's Mill." Shiloh was Bierce's first battle, and by the 1880s, he had come to view it as a turning point in his life. He began the piece by imitating the soldier memoir, apologetically telling the reader that this would be "a simple story of a battle; such a tale as may be told by a soldier who is no writer to a reader who is no soldier." He also summarized the strategic context of the battle. Yet in his description of the litter on the battlefield and the sight of dead, charred bodies, Bierce's vivid prose transcended the writings of his fellow veterans. He had gone into line at night, into unfamiliar woods, with the possibility of enemy troops only yards away who would try to kill him. Nature had always seemed comforting to him before the war, a physical arena demonstrating harmony, beauty, and beneficence. Now it was the arena for hatred and brutality. Bierce turned the title of his piece on its head. Whereas most other veterans literally described what they saw at a battle, he pointed out the characteristics that a man was capable of assuming in battle. What Bierce saw at Shiloh was not just death and conflict but man's ability to be brutalized. He saw the lack of harmony in life, the incomprehensibility of human nature, and the complementary evil in the natural world as well. All this changed him. Bierce plaintively lamented the loss of his innocence at Shiloh. "O days when all the world was beautiful and strange; when unfamiliar constellations burned in the Southern midnights, and the mocking-bird poured out his heart in the moon-gilded magnolia." This innocent at war lost his comforting sense of coherence on his first field of battle; at least that was how he viewed it twenty years later.[23]

"The Crime at Pickett's Mill" is one of the most evocative descriptions of combat ever written by a Northern veteran. It reads rather like a typical soldier memoir except for the Biercian style—sharp clarity, tinged with irony. The biggest and most important departure from the memoir model is Bierce's characterization of the attack as a "crime." No other veteran wrote of a failed campaign in that way. They often described terrible tactical mistakes committed by their superiors but never went so far as to indict their officers as criminals. Remembering how he had stood on the far right flank of Hazen's brigade when his comrades came upon the waiting Confederates at the head of that long, torturous march up the ravine, Bierce decided that losing half the brigade for no gain had been a crime, not just another example of the fortunes of war.[24]

Bierce also crafted his fictional stories in such a way as to show continuity and contrast with the typical soldier memoir. Two remarkable features stand out. First, Bierce, like his fellow veteran-authors, accurately described the experience of battle. He wrote of the difficulties of seeing and hearing while under fire, of battle's ability to deafen and mask the senses. He wrote of the imperative of doing one's duty, of a wounded man committing suicide, of the fear of failing to do one's duty while under fire, of soldiers falling asleep while on guard duty, of the impact that a beloved officer's death could have on the battle spirit of his men, of soldiers who deliberately exposed themselves to danger to prove their bravery. These fictional works were obviously written by one who knew battle intimately.

The other prominent feature of the stories is the slant Bierce gave to all these themes. Unlike the "Bits of Autobiography," the short stories are consistently ruthless. Bierce refused to let up in any of them, treating the themes with the most bitter irony possible. In "Chickamauga," he described a six-year-old boy, a deaf-mute, who wanders through the rear areas of a great battle, unable to comprehend what is happening or to ask questions or communicate in any way with the wounded soldiers he encounters. The boy, who began the story assuming that this was a game, is turned into something inhuman at the sight of his mother's body, mutilated by a shell. "The child moved his little hands, making wild, uncertain gestures. he uttered a series of inarticulate and indescribable cries—something between the chattering of an ape and the gobbling of a turkey—a startling, soulless, unholy sound, the language of a devil."

Bierce's treatment of the other themes is nearly as startling in their unrelieved tragedy. Soldiers unknowingly kill their fathers or brothers in the line of duty, wounded soldiers commit suicide only minutes before comrades arrive to help them, men anxious about their bravery under fire kill themselves rather than put their courage to the test, men maddened by the death of an officer rush into a foolish assault that gains nothing but litters the battlefield with the fallen, soldiers foolishly expose themselves and die because loved ones at home taunt them about cowardice.[25]

Throughout all the stories is the common theme of perception. Characters perceive the possibility of danger or failure so strongly that they react in illogical or unreasonable ways. Or characters fail to perceive reality as it is and commit acts that have unintended consequences. Bierce knew that the environment of battle is one of reduced visibility, not just in terms of visual seeing but also in terms of emotionally and psychologically comprehending what is happening. He knew that the physical environment of the battlefield is threatening, that nature can no longer be considered an eternal, knowable truth, and that on any field of battle, comforting assumptions are no longer valid. Thus he created a fictional field of battle in his short stories where reality was skewed to its most unpredictable, surrealistic margins. It was a cry of anguish, a profound comment that this horrible experience might have been endured and considered worthy if the North had done a more successful job of winning the peace through Radical Reconstruction. Without that success, the suffering could not be justified.

Bierce was not alone in his attitude toward Reconstruction. Other veterans who had served faithfully during the war and participated in the effort to reform Southern society came away from that experiment disturbed by the complacency of the Northern people. Albion W. Tourgee of Ohio was one such man. He had served as an officer during the war and worked diligently to make Reconstruction work. By the 1880s, he too began to write voluminously about it. In both fictional and factual works, Tourgee thoroughly laid out his plea for a raising of the Northern consciousness regarding the postwar South. He urged people to recall the war not just as a series of campaigns and battles but as a crusade for freedom. He reminded the Northern people of what they had felt about the war, not just what they remembered seeing or doing in it, and he reminded the North that good men had died to set other men free. The war had changed nothing in Southern society, Tourgee argued. Unlike Bierce, he never interpreted the sacrifice of the war as wasted foolishness, but Tourgee certainly warned that the sacrifice was in jeopardy.[26]

Unfortunately for Tourgee, most Northern veterans did not pay much attention to the outcome of Reconstruction. Most of them did not share Bierce's disillusionment or connect the failure of Reconstruction with a negative view of the war. While glorifying what they had done in the conflict, they ignored the reality that the power structure of Southern society was still intact, that blacks were still oppressed under a different but equally unjustified system of racial control, and that the ex-Confederates were winning the battle to interpret the conflict as a "war between the states" rather than a "war for freedom."

PRAGMATISTS

A larger group of veterans would easily have understood the grim depiction of battle in Bierce's writings, and they might well have agreed that Reconstruction was a tragic failure, but they were not lost soldiers. They found new faiths to justify and ennoble the horrors of war. Rejecting ideology—which was an old and tainted faith, in their view—they looked inward to a creed that portrayed war as a crucible of inner strength and character development. Or they looked to war as a larger crucible for the development of a more efficient, scientifically oriented society, a catalyst for modernization. These veterans did not look to the past, as did the ideological soldier, or into nothingness, as did Bierce, but into the future. They were the ultimately pragmatic realists, accepting the necessity for war and making the best of a hard reality.

In short, the pragmatic soldier invested his interpretation of the war experience in a creed of self-development and scientific efficiency.

Prominent among these men were Oliver Wendell Holmes, Jr., and
Charles Francis Adams, Jr., both of them young, well-educated New
Englanders of high upbringing. They accepted war and all its frustra-
tions, hardships, and terror without needing an ideology to justify it.
The experience itself and how the soldier dealt with it were the crucial
things to consider.[27]

Holmes stands out as ready-made spokesman for the modernist soldier. Son of a famous physician and essayist, he served as an officer in
the 20th Massachusetts Infantry, was wounded several times, and survived horrible battles, including Antietam. As one of America's most emi-
nent legal theorists and Supreme Court judges, Holmes was called upon
after the war to speak at many ceremonies. Before veterans' groups and
graduating classes, he presented a number of addresses in which he
mused on the meaning of the war. The overriding message he tried to
convey was that fighting the war well had been its own justification.
Holmes paid little attention to the political, social, or economic results of
the conflict. Instead, he concentrated on whatever measure of self-giving
the war had drawn out of each individual. He knew as well as any other
veteran that this war had demanded much of its soldiers, that a man
could give his all in a single battle, only to see nothing of strategic importance result from its outcome. In a much larger sense, Holmes did not
seem surprised that the conflict had failed to result in a transformation
of Southern society. He found comfort simply in having fought without
fear. To a veterans' group meeting on Memorial Day in 1884, he said,
"you must be willing to commit yourself to a course, perhaps a long and
hard one, without being able to foresee exactly where you will come out.
All that is required of you is that you should go somewhither as hard as
ever you can. The rest belongs to faith." Holmes consistently spoke out
against the calculating, moneymaking tenor of the postwar era and contrasted the self-giving attitude of the Civil War soldier as its preferred
antithesis. What was important was to give everything of oneself for a
cause that was good in a contest whose outcome was uncertain. As he
put it in another address, "to be enduring and disciplined and brave is
not less an end of life than to shine in the stock market and to be rich."[28]

Holmes summed up his view of the martial experience best in his
most noted work, an address to the graduating class of Harvard in 1895
entitled "The Soldier's Faith." He first established his credentials for the
young graduates by assuring them that anyone who had been in battle

would instantly know what the soldier's faith was: "If you have advanced in line and have seen ahead of you the spot which you must pass where the rifle bullets are striking; . . . have heard the bullets splashing in the mud and earth about you; if you have been on the picket-line at night in a black and unknown wood, have heard the spat of the bullets upon the trees, and as you moved have felt your foot slip upon a dead man's body." Yet in that suffering lay nobility. Holmes warned the Harvard class not to be seduced "by a rootless self-seeking search for a place where the most enjoyment may be had at the least cost." Instead, he urged them to commit themselves to an inner-directed lifestyle, a way of thinking that, for Holmes himself, had resulted from his postwar ruminations on the meaning of battle. Remember, he told the students, "that the joy of life is living, is to put out all one's powers as far as they will go; . . . to pray, not for comfort, but for combat; to keep the soldier's faith against the doubts of civil life, . . . to love glory more than the temptations of wallowing ease, but to know that one's final judge and only rival is oneself." This inner-directedness was at the heart of one of the most often-quoted thoughts in this speech. Referring to the burial of his regimental commander three years before, which had been attended by a small group of family and remaining veterans, he said: "It is as the colonel would have had it. This also is part of the soldier's faith: Having known great things, to be content with silence." Holmes was not referring to the silence of the soldier, for he and so many others spoke out repeatedly about the war. He meant that a soldier, having served well and learned what was important about war, had no need for praise from society. He could be content to die quietly, without thanks.[29]

Holmes was not an apologist for war, nor was he a jingoist or a militarist. His was at first a grudging acceptance of the necessity of conflict. Later in life, by the 1880s and 1890s, he came to embrace war not just as a horrible necessity but as a potentially positive influence on the life of a soldier. Although not an ideologue, he had come as far as the ideological soldier in triumphing over the horrors of battle. He could say that man's "destiny is battle" without eliciting winces from his audience, for they knew his war service gave him the right to make such judgments. If nothing was true, Holmes argued, "there is one thing I do not doubt . . . and that is that the faith is true and adorable which leads a soldier to throw away his life in obedience to a blindly accepted duty, in a cause which he little understands, in a plan of campaign of which he has no notion, under tactics of which he does not see the use." Holmes had embraced the war experience so intimately that it had become a foundation of his being; it was the benchmark for the rest of his life. He felt blessed, in an important way, by the suffering he had endured in the war. "Through our great good fortune, in our youth our hearts were touched with fire. It was given to us to learn at the outset that life is a profound and passionate thing."[30]

Joseph Kirkland was another realist veteran. Born in New York State but serving as an officer in the 12th Illinois Infantry, he wrote of the war experience in one of the better novels produced by a soldier, *The Captain of Company K*. It is the story of Will Fargeon, a well-intentioned volunteer soldier who finds himself in command of a company. Neither he nor any other volunteer in the book speaks of ideology or the political issues of the war. Kirkland graphically describes combat and avoids romantic images, but this is far from a tragic story. The hardworking, suffering, but optimistic common soldier, never entirely reconciled to the difficulties of war but willing to do his part, is the true hero of this book.

Kirkland went to great lengths to describe the life of a soldier accurately. Many of the small but authentic facets of the war experience appear, such as the reality of friendly fire on the battlefield, details about skirmishing and how a company is led in battle, the difficulty that newspaper reporters had understanding the experience of combat, and the appearance of dead bodies. Battle itself had become industrialized and impersonal. "To such simple, mechanical, dull, dogged machine-work has the old art of war come down . . . no more of the exhilarating clash of personal contest. *Nothing* left but stern, defenseless, hopeless 'stand-up-and-take-your-physic'—fortuitous death by an unseen missile from an unknown hand."

The loving treatment of citizen-soldiers, what they tried to do and how they thought and felt, makes *The Captain of Company K* a minor masterpiece of soldier literature. The enlisted men of Fargeon's regiment had no patience with incompetency. One of them tells Fargeon, "'Wha'd' yew s'pose . . . we came out fer?—Fer thirteen dollars a month?—Not by a jug-full!—not by a dam' sight! . . . We come t'obey orders—proper orders—live or die—an' git back home—if we're lucky enough—jest as quick as Goddlemity'll let us.'" These were the men who endured Shiloh and other fierce engagements. "How do men fall in battle?" Kirkland asks his reader. "Forward, as fall other slaughtered animals. . . . As they fall, so they lie, so they die and so they stiffen; and all the contortions seen by burial details . . . are the natural result of the removal of bodies which have fallen with faces and limbs to the earth, and grown rigid without the rearrangement of 'decent burial.'" At another point, Kirkland provides a stark analogy. "A private soldier is like a blind horse in a quarry; a precipice on every side and a lighted blast under his feet; his only comfort the bit in his mouth and the feeling of a human hand holding the reins over his back."

Despite Kirkland's unforgiving descriptions of combat and the suffering of the soldiers, he brings the story of Company K and its commander to a positive conclusion. Fargeon's life is changed by his war experience. Learning medicine because of a wound received at Shiloh, he devotes his time to treating poor people at home. Depicted as unassuming (Fargeon refuses to apply for a pension even though he deserves one), he looks back on the conflict philosophically. "Well," Kirkland writes of Fargeon, "after all is said and done, the major has more to be glad of than to be sorry for." In the tradition of the pragmatic veteran, Kirkland viewed the war experience truthfully, but with a strong and successful desire to make something positive of it. Despite coming to know war for what it was, Fargeon comes out of his wounding without bitterness. The war was a catalyst for channeling his religious impulses into self-improvement and a practical life spent helping those in need. The search for new faiths by which to gauge the worth of the war presupposed a happy ending. Both Holmes and Kirkland strove for that ending. The fact that both commentators were not naive about the nature of combat gave overwhelming credibility to their conclusions.[31]

SILENT WITNESSES

The ideological soldier, the lost soldier, and the pragmatic soldier all gave full evidence of the horrors of battle. The true nature of combat was a central feature in the writings of the latter two in particular. There existed a fourth category of veteran authors, a large group of men who ignored or minimalized the horrors of war in their memoirs. These men were not naive about the subject; they had served as faithfully and suffered as much as any member of the other three categories of veterans. Yet they chose not to dwell on the nature of battle. Instead, they concentrated on memories of comradeship, camp life, amusing incidents, foraging, marching, and a variety of other nonlethal experiences that were a large part of being a soldier in the 1860s. These men also had a tendency to avoid discussions of the cause and of the reasons for the fighting. They were not concerned with the tragedy of war, yet they knew fully what it was. They also were not concerned with justifying or analyzing the causes or results of the conflict, although they had risked everything to make it a success.

Why were they so selective in remembering the war? A recent historian argued that these veterans capitulated to the needs of Northern society for a comforting memory of the experience. They had developed a sense of separateness from the home front during the war, he argued, because of the unique and terrible experiences they had endured on the battlefield. After the conflict, it was essential for the harmony of society that they be reintegrated, that their public conception of the war experience be made to coincide with the public's unrealistic and jingoistic conception. This was a sellout, in the view of some modern students, a rejection of the veteran's duty to inform society of the true nature of war so that the public would not be so ready to resort to it in the future.[32]

There is value in this interpretation of the veteran's unwillingness to speak of the dark underside of war in his memoirs, but it is by no means the only or the most important explanation. A variety of factors influenced these men. They were not denying their genuine knowledge of reality but choosing for unstated reasons not to discuss it.

Literary standards and the dictates of polite society convinced many men to soften or sidestep certain issues. David Hunter Strother, a Unionist from Virginia who served on the staffs of several generals, revised his wartime diary when writing his reminiscences for publication in *Harper's Monthly* in 1866 and 1867. A comparison of the two versions reveals that the substance is hardly changed, but the style is altered. As the modern editor of Strother's work put it, the standards of style during the mid-nineteenth century "required a writer to discriminate nicely in his choice of diction and to soften unseemly details." Other veterans felt the same tug. The soldier-historian of the 2d Michigan Cavalry assured his readers that the "horrors of the battlefield have been touched upon as lightly as possible. The same temper of mind which unconsciously puts aside tales of horror in the daily papers, murders, disasters, etc., would not delight in perpetuating such disagreeable subjects." Victorian sensibilities seemed important in the minds of some, but by no means all, of the veterans who refused to dwell on sordidness. Softening the suffering, glossing the tragic, was the price paid by polite society for its values. Although such readers might find mention of horror in the memoirs they perused, there would be few opportunities for them to dwell on it. An Iowa veteran, writing of the battle of Pleasant Hill during the Red River campaign, described wounded Federal prisoners, himself among them, as being assailed by vermin. "The maggots trouble us a good deal, but I will leave what I saw and felt about that untold and tell something more pleasing." The "more pleasing" tale was that of a kind Southern lady who volunteered to help care for the injured prisoners. Compassion overcame horror in this man's choice of subjects.[33]

The nature of memory also worked to influence veterans' writings after the war. As one speaker told the Illinois chapter of the Military Order of the Loyal Legion, the passage of time tended to soften his memory of hard times but left his memory of good times intact. Thus, he and other men tended to recall the beauty of nature and the pleasures of good weather rather than the hardships of bad weather. They also tended to minimize the dangers of the battlefield. For another veteran, John W. Greene of Indiana, recalling one incident inevitably triggered a dozen memories of other incidents that had previously been hidden. Greene believed that an old soldier became a "most unconscionable vagarist" whenever he tried to remember anything. He could not recall one thing without tripping over many others. "To the reader many of these incidents may seem 'trifling,' they may not be 'important,' but they are characteristic. They were witnessed by the narrator; hence he writes, or tells them, with an interest infinitely greater than he feels in repeating what he has read, or has heard passing from mouth to mouth. For him the personages live, the localities exist; the real surroundings frame the picture, however valueless it may appear."[34]

Battle was not necessarily the overriding component of a veteran's memory of the war. He spent by far the greatest portion of his time in the army in camp or on the march, and the small incidents of soldier life were his war experience as much as combat was. If he chose to concentrate on them, or if the workings of his mind compelled him to write of camp life rather than of death, it was not necessarily because of a perceived imperative from society but simply a personal need to write about what was important to him. Many veterans had initially joined the army to experience the excitement and novelty of military life, to travel to unknown parts, and to test the margins of their character. They had been sustained by the strength of comradeship among their fellow soldiers. Thus it should not be surprising that they concentrated on these memories when writing of the war decades later. No veteran had a "responsibility" to describe battle as horrific, only an opportunity to do so.

Additionally, the war may not have been so awful for the hardened veteran. During the conflict, many soldiers grew used to the suffering and callously endured it. After the war, the dark side of battle, which Bierce and others dwelled on, was ignored or minimized by these men. One such veteran mentioned seeing a pile of amputated limbs at a field hospital during the Second Bull Run campaign. "It was an awful sight and one I have never forgotten. It had the appearance of a human slaughter house, and now I have another little horse story that I ought to tell of as it occurred the very day I am writing about." For this man, horror was but an incident of war, not the overriding component of it. Soldiers who were not traumatized by battle naturally would not write of it in those terms after the war was over.[35]

Finally, perhaps the most important reason that soldiers chose not to write about the terrors of the battlefield was their need to achieve a positive view of the war. Just as these men had worked hard to find ways to endure and emotionally triumph over battle, they worked hard after the conflict to achieve the same ends. This was a matter of personal well-being, self-satisfaction, and civic pride. "To *be* and to *feel* patriotic we must consistently approve our past acts, reconcile our present motives and philosophically comprehend possible results as an entailment of our doctrines and influences," wrote a veteran of the 149th Illinois. Thus they tried, as another man put it, "to forget as much as possible the hardships endured during the contest." Certain memories had to be subsumed in order to achieve a unified vision of the war that made something useful out of the suffering. Veterans felt no need to fully reconstruct the war experience if that meant raising doubts about the worth of their service. Thus, men like Borden Hicks of Michigan, even when they spoke before veterans' groups, openly admitted that they had no intention of speaking of comrades killed on the battlefield "on account of the painful recollections, that it would recall to my memory."[36]

Veterans like Hicks were not trying to deny the reality of warfare. They were engaged in a necessary process that every veteran had to undergo if he were to feel whole. War was such a unique experience that soldiers went through three psychological stages of separation and reintegration during and after their service. The first stage was separation of the civilian from peacetime society, the second was his achievement of an identity as a member of a group (the regiment), and the third was a postwar stage of reintegration into civilian society. The experience of war was, as sociologists viewed it, an experience of marginality, an outgroup experience. Few citizen-soldiers could afford to remain in that marginal group for the rest of their lives. Reintegration was absolutely essential for the Northern volunteer if he hoped to lead a normal civilian life.[37]

An important element of that reintegration was the acceptance and approval of civilian society. Northern veterans received that in abundance. Another element was their ability to perceive the war experience as a controllable part of their lives. Reminding themselves of the positive parts of that experience, making their memory of it personal and reassuring, aided many veterans in keeping their lives together after the war. They were the middle group, unable to write strongly of the ideological justification for the war, afraid to dwell on the dark side of the experience, unwilling to explore new faiths. Yet these men triumphed over the war just as much as the ideological soldier, and they bore their own kind of witness to war's awesome potential to affect the lives of those who took part in it. Theirs was a silent witness to the power of man to endure hard things and overcome them. In creating a view of the war experience as controllable, they not only helped themselves but also reinforced the nation's view that the conflict had been justified. Although this group of veteran-authors did not speak overtly about the cause, their writings indirectly bolstered its memory. Theirs was an act of personal and civic responsibility.

BACK TO THE BATTLEFIELDS

As the postwar years rolled on, veterans began to feel the urge to supplement their memoirs with visits to the battlefields of their youth. They traveled as individuals, sometimes taking their wives with them; in small groups of friends; or as part of regimental reunions. Standing on the ground; breathing Southern air; locating old landmarks, earthworks, and campsites; talking with local inhabitants; collecting souvenirs; and placing monuments all made the war physically real to them again. Many wrote about their return to the South, and their books and articles became part memoir and part travelogue.

It took some time, however, for the South to welcome this flood of Northern veterans. For many years following the war, Southerners were too numb and impoverished to care. The journalist John Townsend Trowbridge toured the war zone in the late summer of 1865 and found a region prostrated by the conflict. On battlefields such as the Wilderness and Chancellorsville, he discovered layers of discarded and rotting equipment on the ground, barely eroded earthworks lining the woods and pastures, and local inhabitants trying their best to salvage something from the catastrophe of defeat. Women, men, and children dug into the earthworks to find minié balls or retrieved old clothing from the field to wash and sell as rags. They dug up buried horses to sell bones as fertilizer, sometimes including human bones in the pile as well. Some farmers were forced to plow fields pockmarked by the graves of hundreds of soldiers. They tried to plow around them when possible, but they often dug up bones and rotted clothing without meaning to. At Chickamauga, black soldiers were methodically locating and exhuming the bodies of men who had been hastily buried where they lay and removing them to the local national cemetery. In Trowbridge's vivid description of his travels, the South seemed to have become a vast, stinking charnel house. Certainly, the Southerners were in no mood to dwell on the war. On his way to Spotsylvania, Trowbridge met a man who guessed that he was a Northerner. Trowbridge asked him how he knew. The man replied, "'Because no South'n man ever goes to the battlefields: we've seen enough of 'em.'"[38]

Given time to recover, the South grew ready to welcome its conquerors as guests. The most important inducement was the money to be made from the Northern tourist trade. Southern cities recognized the value of their nearby battlefields, entrenchments, and other landmarks as a lure for the ex-soldiers who were growing old and nostalgic. City governments promoted their Civil War heritage with travel brochures, local landowners erected small "museums" and the nineteenth-century version of visitors' centers, and out-of-work men hired themselves out as battlefield guides. To a limited degree, the tourist industry helped boost the economy of a region desperate for economic recovery.[39]

What drove Northern veterans to travel southward in an ever-increasing wave was the need to recapture their war experience. By the 1880s, when the wave was beginning to reach its peak, they had already begun to wonder if the war had been a dream. Making it real again by writing about it was one way to relieve the memory, but seeing the physical remains of the battlefields where they had become veterans was a completely different way to capture the experience.

Several veterans of the 14th Connecticut planned an excursion to Antietam and Gettysburg in September 1891, accompanied by family members. Their first night at Antietam, the regiment's first battle, brought back the war experience. They built a campfire using fence rails and logs near the Roulette farm. "To the old vets it was a vivid and pathetic reminder of the camp-fires of long ago. . . . To the ladies and civilian visitors the scene was weird, novel and exciting—entrancing. It was their first sight of what seemed a reproduction from real soldier life." Moved by the moment, old soldiers around the fire stood up, one by one, to speak their mind about the war, its meaning, and the results gained by their suffering. The next day, they eagerly explored every part of the battlefield, taking photos of one another standing in front of monuments and other landmarks. The Connecticut veterans had a similarly moving experience at Gettysburg.[40]

At the same time, western veterans were busy visiting their own battlefields. Daniel Wait Howe of the 79th Indiana toured Chickamauga with a comrade in the fall of 1899. They were impressed by the number of monuments, markers, and artillery pieces already placed by the government and thought that it was easy to "imagine the dead rising out of the ground and taking their places in mortal conflict." While standing at a monument to his old regiment near the Brotherton House, where the Indianans had captured a Confederate battery, both Howe and his companion began to cry. "Neither of us spoke, but each understood that memory had recalled the scenes of long ago and had touched some hidden spring in the human heart that causes it to overflow."[41]

Another major theme of veterans' visits to the battlefields was reconciliation. They strongly emphasized these trips as physical symbols of the reuniting of North and South, of the healing power of time. Sometimes, veterans of both armies met on the battlefields where they had tried to kill each other decades before, at Shiloh, Pea Ridge, or Gettysburg. One such reunion was described by a Michigan veteran as "the commencement of the end. It is the offering of those who fought, of a fraternal brotherhood to the future. It is the burial of the hates and animosities of the past. It is the pledge of national unity for the future." Reunions of former belligerents began as early as 1881 and extended at least until 1938, with Gettysburg the preferred site. Whenever or wherever they occurred, the events were always hailed as part of a larger process of forgetting the bitterness of the war and making friends of former enemies.[42]

Whether they traveled singly or in groups, with or without some overt mission to demonstrate reconciliation, the veterans who returned to their fields of battle did so as part of a personal exploration of their lives. They were rediscovering the kinds of men they had been long ago. Without the war experience, they might never have bothered to do so, for the conflict stood as a mighty hallmark of their personal development. The war experience had to be dealt with in some way, and many veterans found it easier to do this while standing on the very ground where it took place.

James T. Holmes, former commander of the 52d Ohio, dealt with the war experience by taking a trip in May 1897. With his wife, he traveled first to Cincinnati and then along the same route taken by his regiment in what had once been slave territory. As the train took the couple through Lexington and the Kentucky bluegrass, Holmes read parts of his wartime journal to his wife so that she could share his memories. They entered the area of his most vivid experiences when they reached Chattanooga. Holmes found Chickamauga well preserved by the War Department, which was responsible for the creation of the early national military parks, but he was irritated that a marker there identified him as J. F. Holmes rather than J. T. Holmes. Like any other tourist, he eagerly bought 125 postcard photographs of the several battlefields around Chattanooga and was delighted to meet another Northern veteran, a Mr. Converse of the 40th Ohio, who had moved to Chattanooga and was now working as a tour guide for the thousands of curious visitors who were beginning to find their way to the region.[42]

The impact of the trip on Holmes's wife was unknown, but for Holmes himself, the visit struck home. While riding over the field at Chickamauga, he vividly remembered how rifle and artillery fire had scarred and mutilated thousands of trees. Holmes recalled the "white, fresh wounds" on the vegetation as if it were "a horrid dream, a bloody drama, a patch of hell on earth." Those same trees still had the remains of bullet and shell marks. He found the discovery to be "a strange commingling of the old and new, of memories and present facts."[44]

At Kennesaw Mountain, Holmes was surprised to find the extensive earthworks well preserved. They had little vegetation growing on them, and he could stand a short distance away and easily see the line as it snaked its way over the rugged terrain. He enjoyed visiting the Channell family which owned much of the battlefield. The Channell sons collected balls, pieces of shells, and equipment to sell to tourists. They even gave away pieces of bone that they claimed were the remains of a Union soldier found buried in their yard. Holmes took a bone, although he considered it a "gruesome souvenir," but he was more interested in a small oak tree. It was no more than twenty feet tall, six inches in diameter, and it had been badly chewed up by rifle fire during the war. Barely surviving the fighting in 1864, it had nearly been cut down by a hired hand before the owner could stop him. After all that and thirty years' time, the tree could sprout only a few leaves each year. It could not grow or prosper, and many of its bullet holes were still plainly visible. But, Holmes reminded himself, it still lived. "It reminded me of many a poor fellow who went home with wounds and scars to drag out a miserable existence, never well, never strong, ever living and yet ever dying, until the end came, or will come, as come it must to the little oak of Kennesaw."[45]

The tree metaphor was meaningful to Holmes. He was not an overtly ideological soldier, but he did not consider his war experience to have been a wasted sacrifice. Holmes was sensitive to the way the war had affected many veterans. He firmly believed that all experiences had some impact on developing a man's personality. If one walked over a mountain, the scenery became part of one's life at that moment and forever. Quoting from a recent author whose thoughts on this score impressed him, Holmes wrote, "'That mountain did not absorb you; you absorbed the mountain.'" Unlike the ideological soldiers, Holmes recognized that the war had overwhelmed many men. One such veteran wrote to him after moving west that he had never revisited a Civil War battlefield, "'excepting Sigel's retreat at Carthage, Mo.,'" and he did not care to see one. "'The war was the beginning of the end of this republic.'" Holmes found this man and others like him to be sad exceptions. "The things which have touched their lives . . . seem to have become no part of themselves. No beautiful or moving pictures, 'sunshine and all,' have been ineffaceably painted on the canvas of their souls. The mountains must have absorbed them, instead of their absorbing the mountains. While they should have taken up and retained the essence of things, great and small, the essence of the higher, grander life, possible to them, had been sapped by external and internal forces."[46]

Holmes did not count himself or most of his fellow veterans among those who had allowed the mountain to absorb their lives. He and most other Union veterans mastered their war experience and became better people, or at least survived it with their personal lives intact and their faith secure. Near the end of his book describing his visit to the war grounds that had been such a big part of his life, Holmes mused on the passing of time and of personal existence. The prewar days were, he believed, "the morning of life." The war years had been "the climax, the noon-tide, of fame." Now, in the postwar era, Union veterans could only look back to recapture a sense of the fear, courage, excitement, and danger of a unique experience. "For each one there remains, not far off, the coming night."[47]

Conclusion

Here are thousands and thousands of men, who came from distant parts of the country, all engaged in one great common cause, and having the same great object in view—that of saving the country.

David E. Beem
14th Indiana

A soldier's life is one of privations and sacrifices; this I knew before I entered on it, but I was firm in the belief that plain duty required me to do it, and I am still of the same opinion after having witnessed all the realities of war. I am still firm in the belief that the authority of the government will be vindicated before long and the war honorably ended—and successfully.

P. E. Woods
Northern volunteer

You Know, my dear Nannie, that life is burdensome to me unless I can take my share in the duties, responsibilities and honors of the country.

William Ward Orme
94th Illinois

We think no more of going out to fight now than if we were going down to shoot ducks in the old marsh.

William Wallace
3d Wisconsin

I find it more disagreeable to be where I can see the marks of battle and see the suffering than it is to be upon the front line.

Hamlin Alexander Coe
19th Michigan

The worth of liberty is shown in the gallant fighting of our men; the price is seen in the ghastly corpses we have left behind.

Walter Carter
22d Massachusetts

The Northern soldier had come a long way from the innocent enthusiasm of 1861 to the grizzled embrace of war and its costs in 1865. The conflict had lasted far longer than anyone could have dreamed. It initiated a generation in the hard realities of life on the battle line and weakened the health of thousands of young men who would have to deal with lost limbs and battle wounds that refused to heal properly. It also threatened the vision of many veterans, leading them toward the possibility of losing their faith in the rightness of the cause.

Yet it was important to recognize that loss of innocence and the gaining of experience did not necessarily bring disillusionment. It was quite possible for the Northern soldier to realize the absurdity of glorifying war without rejecting the fundamental motives that had impelled him into the army in 1861. He gained a practical lesson in the reality of combat but accepted the necessity of fighting as the only way to achieve national goals. Most Northern soldiers successfully blunted the tendency to become bitter and lose faith in the war, survived the suffering that inevitably attended conflict, and managed to convince themselves that the results of the war had been worthy of their sacrifices.

The factors that enabled most soldiers to endure the war without losing their faith were varied. The love of adventure and the faith in ideological rhetoric, two major forces that had inspired them to join the army in 1861, continued to help them sustain the challenge of combat. Many other factors came into play as well. Some were more important than others, but every soldier relied on some factor, either consciously or unconsciously, to carry him through the war.

The nature of combat certainly threatened the morale of all those who endured battle. It was an unusual experience far removed from the civilian life of the Northern soldier. He had to leave behind his naive, imaginative conceptions of battle and begin crossing the gulf of experience that separated the veteran from the civilian. He had to learn that battle was an experience of the senses. The sights, sounds, and even the tactile sensations caused by near misses were his battle experience. He went a step beyond this to know the full lethality of combat as he saw his comrades hit by balls and shells and became a target himself. Actually getting hit by projectiles and experiencing life in the Union army hospitals took many soldiers even farther across the gulf of experience. Still others gave their lives as payment for preserving the Union. As the war continued its slow course, it became evident that this conflict was characterized by dubious tactical victories, prolonged defense, and the grinding trauma of total war as an entire nation collapsed of exhaustion. It was a war that fully tested the battlefield morale of its participants.

Inevitably, some proportion of the Northern army failed the emotional challenge of battle, but the exact percentage is impossible to determine. About 9 percent of Federal soldiers deserted during the war, but their motivations were difficult to pin down. Deserters simply did not write personal accounts explaining why they had left the service. Most of them deserted between battles rather than during engagements. A range of factors that were not necessarily related to combat probably led them to take that route. The evidence clearly shows that most soldiers stayed in the army and provided some sort of service to the cause.

Yet within that generalization are many interesting variations, for a large number of Union soldiers ran away from several hard-fought battles during the course of the war. Most of them did not mean to desert but simply to retire from an overpowering initial exposure to combat or to free themselves from an impossible tactical mission. Most of those men who ran away re-formed to fight another day; they did not run to take themselves permanently out of the war. There were well-documented cases of soldiers refusing to obey orders to go into action or shooting themselves to get out of combat, but these were rare. Much more common were examples of units diving for the cover of fences or ditches while advancing to attack a formidable Confederate position. In this way, common soldiers collectively took from their officers the decision to stop an attack that had only a marginal chance of success, an all-too-common tactical experience in the Civil War. Officers could not bring themselves to define this action as mutiny, giving soldiers one way to limit their exposure to danger on the battlefield without punishment or the humiliation of being branded cowards. When soldiers deviated from the line of bravery and dedication to the cause, most of them did so in this safe form. It was the common soldier's way of modifying his superior's judgment, authority, and control over the army, and it undoubtedly saved many lives without prolonging the war.

Overall, the impressive fact of the Civil War was not the scattered refusals to fight or the limited, temporary ways in which Northern soldiers shielded themselves from danger but the overpowering willingness of most Federals to throw themselves into the conflict. Spurred by their belief in the cause or whatever else motivated them to fight, they demonstrated their capacity for self-sacrifice in many engagements from Fredericksburg to Cold Harbor to Kennesaw Mountain. Few of them reacted to combat in such a way as to take an extreme course of action, such as deserting, but most deviated from the straight line to a degree that was acceptable and that allowed them to bounce back in another engagement to perform further service to the cause.

What kept these men on the firing line? One set of factors came from the society and culture around them. Morals, values, and social norms that had been taught them in the home, in the public-school system of their local communities, or in the political life of their nation provided many Northern soldiers with a firm grounding for their morale. The ideals of courage, manliness, and self-control—all of which constituted imperative guides for action—convinced many soldiers that facing battle was a supreme test of their character. Ideology had inspired many others to support the war effort in the first place, and it continued to keep their morale high even as the bullets and shells flew overhead. Inherited from the Revolution, the ideological imperative was a common property of all patriotic Northerners. Religion also played a significant role in steadying many soldiers' nerves while under fire. They were coaxed into the army by ministers, read Bibles in the field, and clung to religious beliefs when faced with imminent death. All these factors transcended the individual and connected him with larger beliefs. They were society's contribution to the mixture of emotional supports for combat morale.

Another category of factors had nothing to do with larger ideals but was centered on the devotion inspired by the bonds between individuals. The members of the military family, or, as Shakespeare called it, the "band of brothers," were tightly bound by their experiences into a mutually supportive group. Individual soldiers sustained one another's morale in a variety of ways, such as shouting to keep their spirits high under fire or keeping tight tactical formations so that a man in the battle line could get psychological comfort from the nearness of his comrades. This last phenomenon was widely noted by soldiers as the dynamic effect produced by the "touch of elbow." The intimate bonds created by the military family inspired fierce devotion. When friends were killed, infuriated survivors often fought ferociously for revenge. Good officers also could inspire the rank and file by their behavior under fire or even by the example of their deaths. Because the military family relied so heavily on itself for psychological and emotional comfort, the security of comradeship might have been the most pervasive and important support for battlefield morale.

Just as the military family supported the soldier's work, his civilian family also played an important role in his morale. Thoughts of family steadied many soldiers under fire, and the need to safeguard the home front and its institutions of freedom from the threat of an independent and aggressive slave nation in the South inspired other men to fight on. Whether interacting with members of their military families or envisioning the fate of their civilian families, soldiers found that the psychology of the group was invaluable in their ability to survive the war.

Soldiers also learned that they did not have to be passive victims of war. They had the opportunity to meet it head-on and gain some degree of control over their emotional response to it by using models and experiences from their civilian lives to understand the experience of battle. They used romantic literary descriptions of war found in novels and the news media to soften the hard reality of combat and make it more emotionally acceptable. Nature was also a common model. Soldiers often compared and contrasted scenes of war with pastoral imagery to achieve similar goals. The most common model of all, however, was work. Most Northern soldiers came from working-class occupations and lifestyles. They compared battle to working a sawmill, hoeing crops, or harvesting wheat. Loading and firing a musket on the battle line became a job as soldiers concentrated on the techniques of the soldier's task instead of the dangers of the battlefield. Officers, who were responsible for many men and thus had more work to do under fire, experienced this relief more intensely than did the rank and file. Habits of thought learned during their prewar working lives also sustained many soldiers. Their conservatism, pragmatism, and comparative lack of intellectualism made better soldiers of them. They had readily accepted patriotism as a motivation to endure battle, pragmatically accepted death, and refused to bother with things over which they had little control. Many successful soldiers simply refused to think much about combat. Using models of all kinds to get a handle on battle was a conscious effort by soldiers to understand and emotionally control this new, deadly experience.

The evidence is overwhelming that most soldiers adjusted to the experience of battle. Their youthful nature gave them a great advantage, for it made them more flexible and more easily influenced by their officers. Their accounts of battle were filled with evidence of normal behavior under fire. Sometimes they laughed at wounds received by other men, played pranks on one another even as Rebel balls sailed overhead, or coldly calculated their own chances of survival after receiving a wound. By the middle and latter part of the war, Northern soldiers learned how to coolly retreat under fire without panic or shame, quickly re-form, and continue fighting. They had become familiar with war; the experience was no longer new or particularly frightening. Even the most horrible aspects of it, the sight of death and dismemberment, became common incidents in their new lives. There was a danger, however, that soldiers would become so familiar with war that their sensibilities would become callous to humanitarian impulses. Would the war produce a class of degraded, immoral ruffians that could threaten society? Many soldiers were aware of this tendency and dealt with their feelings in letters and diaries. Most of them avoided losing their morality to the demands of the conflict.

After the war, Northern veterans struggled with their memories and produced the most voluminous collection of memoirs to come from any American war. In unpublished as well as published format, in books, articles, and newspaper pieces, they evaluated their war experiences from the perspective of time. This mass of writing was valuable for illuminating how the Northern veteran felt about his wartime service in the years following the conflict. The memoirists fell into four categories: one, those who reaffirmed their faith in the cause and the ideology that underlay it; two, a small group who constituted the "lost generation" of the Civil War, believing that the war had resulted in no worthy result and that their sacrifices had been wasted; three, veterans who expressed no belief in ideology but found new faiths to believe in, such as the war's role in their personal development; and four, the many veterans who avoided reasserting ideology, denouncing the war as a lost cause, or focusing on an inner-directed view of its value and chose instead to concentrate on retelling amusing campfire stories, writing of the value of comradeship, or reliving the excitement of campaigning in dangerous territory.

The men who wrote in all four categories had been good soldiers—even the members of the lost generation had fought well—but they interpreted the war differently in light of how they felt about their experiences long after the war had ended. Most of them did so in a positive way, even those who chose to write only of the joy of comradeship, camp life, and campaigning. Still other veterans wrote frankly about the true nature of combat without making judgments about it. Many veterans reinforced their views of the war by visiting the battlefields of their youth. The evidence is overwhelming: Most Union veterans were able, in some fashion, to remember the war positively in later years. They had not only physically survived the war but also emotionally triumphed over its legacy.

Our ability to interpret the role of the battle experience in the lives of Northern soldiers is often clouded by twentieth-century history. Beginning with World War I and continuing with dubious conflicts such as Korea and Vietnam, many Americans crafted a view of war that contrasted sharply with the view commonly held in the nineteenth century. This modernist view of armed conflict is based on a rejection of the traditional interpretation of war as being a legitimate means of achieving national goals, as playing a valuable role in personal development, and as being an exciting way for bored young men to experience adventure. The modernist view is based on an assumption that all wars are equally disastrous to victor and defeated alike. In the modernist view, war is started by manipulative politicians and arms manufacturers, stupidly conducted by insensitive generals, prolonged by jingoistic propaganda, and callously wasteful of those men who are fooled into fighting. Soldiers become tragic victims rather than honored heroes. War becomes a metaphor for waste; it solves no issues and creates only more cause for bitterness. This overwhelming sense of disillusionment about the role of war in society, culture, and politics is a dominant theme in much fictional literature and academic histories produced during the twentieth century.[1]

The modernist view has tended to be much more prominent in recent times than the traditional view, even though each has its adherents. The shock of modern warfare, with its advanced technology and its tendency to make targets of civilian populations, demanded a new attitude toward warfare that inevitably condemned it. Although this modernist view is an appropriate way to interpret World War I and other misguided military adventures, it is dangerous to assume that it applies to all conflicts. Each war must be taken on its own merits or misdeeds. Each begins differently, with differing public attitudes and divergent goals.

The modernist view of war does not necessarily apply to nineteenth-century conflicts such as the Civil War. That war was not a foreign conflict, like the world wars, but a domestic tragedy that seared the hearts of its participants and nearly wrecked the United States from the inside out. It inspired deep passions and moral fervor. Americans of the Civil War era generally placed more emphasis on ideology, patriotism, religion, and civic virtue than did their twentieth-century counterparts. Their essentially premodern culture primed them to think in more idealistic terms. Even the army that fought the Civil War was essentially a premodern military force. The North relied on a volunteer army raised by local communities rather than on a well-conceived conscription system to bring men to arms. Similarly, the federal government was much less effective in manipulating public opinion in this premodern age of communications than it was in the twentieth century. Public opinion naturally grew from a grassroots perspective that genuinely represented the thoughts of common Northerners. On the battlefield, the Northern soldier did not have to endure the horrors that his counterpart in World War I was doomed to suffer. There was less continuous contact and less trench stalemate in his campaigns, giving him more opportunity to physically and emotionally recuperate between battles.

It is certainly true that the Civil War had modern characteristics. The introduction of new military technology, the widespread use of modern transportation and communication facilities, and the experimentation with new tactics and strategies were impressive. This gave the Civil War soldier a strong taste of the battlefield horrors to come in the twentieth century, but it did not make a modern war of the conflict. Soldiers still fought with muzzle-loading muskets, marched most of the time rather than rode mechanical conveyances, and fought many pitched battles in the open, much as Napoleon's soldiers had done. The Northern soldier fought a traditional war in all respects, but particularly in his mind. The mental and emotional field of battle was the most old-fashioned of all. He looked to the past for inspiration and for guides to his own action. Thus, the example of the Founding Fathers and the ideology they created came into play more prominently than modern attitudes that would be typical of a future age.

In the end, the Northern soldier recognized that he had been through a great and nearly overwhelming experience, and he had to make sense of it if he wanted to live the rest of his life without bitterness, regret, or guilt. Most veterans found a way to do so and, in the process, helped convince their nation that the war had resulted in long-term benefits for the country. They had fought on many fields of battle from 1861 through 1865, but shaping the legacy of the Civil War during the remaining years of their lives was their greatest triumph.

Notes

CHAPTER ONE. INNOCENTS AT WAR

Epigraphs: Burrill to parents, July 11, 1862, John Burrill Papers, *Civil War Times Illustrated* Collection, U.S. Army Military History Institute; John F. Marszalek, *Sherman: A Soldier's Passion for Order* (New York, 1993), 186–87; Thomas H. Evans, "At Malvern Hill," *Civil War Times Illustrated* 6 (December 1967): 40.

1. Ruth Miller Elson, *Guardians of Tradition: American Schoolbooks of the Nineteenth Century* (Lincoln, 1964), 324–27.

2. Ibid., 329, 334.

3. Warren Lee Goss, *Recollections of a Private* (New York, 1890), 40–41.

4. Mark DeWolfe Howe, Jr., ed., *The Occasional Speeches of Justice Oliver Wendell Holmes* (Cambridge, 1962), 78–79.

5. Benjamin Smith, "Recollections of the Late War," 3, Benjamin Smith Papers, Illinois State Historical Library.

6. S. P. Jennison, "The Illusions of a Soldier," in *Glimpses of the Nation's Struggle* (St. Paul, 1887), 374–75; William W. Belknap, "The Obedience and Courage of the Private Soldier," in *War Sketches and Incidents* (Des Moines, 1893), 158.

7. William Henry Jackson, *Time Exposure: The Autobiography of William Henry Jackson* (New York, 1940), 49; George P. Metcalf Reminiscences, 63, Harrisburg Civil War Round Table–Gregory Coco Collection, U.S. Army Military History Institute.

8. Daniel Bond Reminiscences, 65, Minnesota Historical Society.

9. K. Jack Bauer, ed., *Soldiering: The Civil War Diary of Rice C. Bull, 123rd New York Volunteer Infantry* (San Rafael, 1977), 44.

10. James Cooper Miller, "Serving Under McClellan on the Peninsula in '62," *Civil War Times Illustrated* 8 (June 1969): 26; Frank L. Byrne, ed., *The View from Headquarters: Civil War Letters of Harvey Reid* (Madison, 1965), 31–32; Day to Irving Greenwood, December 28, 1862, Samuel C. Day Papers, Minnesota Historical Society.

11. Francis E. Pierce, " 'I Have with the Regiment Been Through a Terrible Battle,' " *Civil War Times Illustrated* 1 (December 1962): 9; Patrick H. White, "Civil War Diary of Patrick H. White," *Journal of the Illinois State Historical Society* 15 (October 1922–January 1923): 646.

12. Bauer, ed., *Soldiering,* 116–17.

13. Daniel McCook, "The Second Division at Shiloh," *Harper's New Monthly Magazine* 28 (May 1864): 830.

14. George R. Agassiz, ed., *Meade's Headquarters, 1863–1865: Letters of Colonel Theodore Lyman from the Wilderness to Appomattox* (Boston, 1922), 101.

15. Bauer, ed., *Soldiering*, 149; Anne A. Hage, "The Battle of Gettysburg as Seen by Minnesota Soldiers," *Minnesota History* 38 (June 1963): 256; S. H. M. Byers, "How Men Feel in Battle: Recollections of a Private at Champion Hills," *Annals of Iowa* 2 (July 1896): 444.

16. William Wheeler, *Letters of William Wheeler of the Class of 1855* (Cambridge, 1875), 418.

17. Thomas H. Evans, "'All Was Complete Chaos,'" *Civil War Times Illustrated* 6 (January 1968): Otto Eisenschiml, ed., *Vermont General: The Unusual War Experiences of Edward Hastings Ripley, 1862–1865* (New York, 1960), 250.

18. Frederick L. Hitchcock, *War from the Inside* (Philadelphia, 1904), 223–24.

19. Charles D. Page, *History of the Fourteenth Regiment, Connecticut Vol. Infantry* (Meriden, 1906), 241–42; Evans, "All Was Complete Chaos," 37.

20. Vinson Holman Diary, March 7, 1862, State Historical Society of Iowa, Iowa City; Wilcox to wife, October 9, 1862, John S. Wilcox Papers, Illinois State Historical Library.

21. Robert Goldthwaite Carter, *Four Brothers in Blue* (Austin, 1978), 308.

22. Gordon Diary, March 10, 1862, George Gordon Papers, U.S. Army Military History Institute; Thompson to wife, December 10, 1862, William G. Thompson Papers, State Historical Society of Iowa, Des Moines.

23. James H. Croushore, ed., *A Volunteer's Adventures: A Union Captain's Record of the Civil War* (New Haven, 1946), 201.

24. Albert Robinson Greene, "Campaigning in the Army of the Frontier," *Transactions of the Kansas Historical Society* 14 (1918): 299; David Herbert Donald, ed., *Gone for a Soldier: The Civil War Memoirs of Private Alfred Bellard* (Boston, 1975), 140; Charles Cowell, "An Infantryman at Corinth: The Diary of Charles Cowell," *Civil War Times Illustrated* 13 (November 1974): 12.

25. Barbee-Sue Rodman, "War and Aesthetic Sensibility: An Essay in Cultural History," *Soundings* 5 (Fall 1968): 308–26.

26. Vivian Kirkpatrick McLarty, "The Civil War Letters of Colonel Bazel F. Lazear," *Missouri Historical Review* 45 (October 1950): 56–59.

27. Croushore, ed., *A Volunteer's Adventures*, 88; Carter, *Four Brothers in Blue*, 312.

28. Emil Rosenblatt and Ruth Rosenblatt, eds., *Hard Marching Every Day: The Civil War Letters of Private Wilbur Fisk, 1861–1865* (Lawrence, 1992), 349.

29. Beem to wife, September 19, 1862, David E. Beem Papers, Indiana Historical Society; Leander Stillwell, "In the Ranks at Shiloh," in *War Talks in Kansas* (Kansas City, 1906), 111; Bauer, ed., *Soldiering*, 151; Hage, "Battle of Gettysburg," 256.

30. Henry Campbell, "Union Bugler Found Chickamauga a 'Terrible Battle,'" *Civil War Times Illustrated* 3 (May 1964): 35; John O. Holzhueter, ed., "William Wallace's Civil War Letters: The Virginia Campaign," *Wisconsin Magazine of History* 57 (Autumn 1973): 54; Joseph J. Scroggs Diary, October 27, 1864, *Civil War Times Illustrated* Collection, U.S. Army Military History Institute.

31. Mark DeWolfe Howe, Jr., ed., *Touched with Fire: Civil War Letters and Diary of Oliver Wendell Holmes, Jr., 1861–1864* (Cambridge, 1946), 50; Croushore, ed., *A Volunteer's Adventures*, 153; Charles C. Paige Memoir, 57, Wendell W. Lang, Jr., Collection, U.S. Army Military History Institute; Rosenblatt and Rosenblatt, eds., *Hard Marching Every Day*, 226.

32. Albert Castel, ed., "The War Album of Henry Dwight, Part II," *Civil War Times Illustrated* 19 (April 1980): 22.

33. Bauer, ed., *Soldiering*, 41.

34. Carter, *Four Brothers in Blue*, 306; Howe, ed., *Touched with Fire*, 49; Rosenblatt and Rosenblatt, eds., *Hard Marching Every Day*, 84.

35. Pettit to sisters, May 21, 1864, Frederick Pettit Papers, *Civil War Times Illustrated Collection*, U.S. Army Military History Institute; Thomas H. Evans, "'There Is No Use Trying to Dodge Shot,'" *Civil War Times Illustrated* 6 (August 1967): 45; Lambie to friend, January 18, 1863, Gavin A. Lambie Papers, U.S. Army Military History Institute; Welch to sister, December 27, 1862, Abraham Welch Papers, Southern Historical Collection, University of North Carolina; Edward G. Longacre, ed., "Laughing at the Screaming Bullets," *Lincoln Herald* 84 (Fall 1982): 176.

36. C. E. Lippincott letter, *Chicago Tribune*, July 28, 1862; Nathan S. Harwood, *The Pea Ridge Campaign: A Paper Read Before the Nebraska Commandery of the Military Order of the Loyal Legion of the United States* (Omaha, 1887), 16; Robert P. Mathews, "Souvenir of the Holland Company Home Guards and Phelps' Regiment, Missouri Volunteer Infantry," 25, Western Historical Manuscript Collection, University of Missouri, Columbia; Jean P. Ray, ed., *The Diary of a Dead Man: Letters and Diary of Private Ira S. Pettit* (Waverly, 1976), 129.

37. Kent to parents, July 28, 1862, William C. Kent Papers, *Civil War Times Illustrated* Collection, U.S. Army Military History Institute.

38. John Hill Ferguson Diary, March 12, 1862, Henry Pfeiffer Library, MacMurray College; Evans, "'There Is No Use Trying to Dodge Shot,'" 45; Hitchcock, *War from the Inside*, 61.

39. William Cullen Bryant II, ed., "A Yankee Soldier Looks at the Negro," *Civil War History* 7 (June 1961): 146; Byrne, ed., *View from Headquarters*, 28–29.

40. Daniel Holt, "In Captivity," *Civil War Times Illustrated* 18 (August 1979): 38.

41. Payne to parents, April 13, 1862, Edwin W. Payne Papers, Illinois State Historical Library; James P. Suiter Diary, September 20, 1863, Illinois State Historical Library; Evans, "At Malvern Hill," 41.

42. Prentice to friend, July 16, 1862, Reuben T. Prentice Papers, Illinois State Historical Library; Mr. Trueman to Mrs. Lane, November 11, 1861, Simpson Letters, Illinois State Historical Library.

43. Bauer, ed., *Soldiering*, 86; Howe, ed., *Occasional Speeches*, 82.

CHAPTER TWO. PAYING FOR VICTORY

Epigraphs: K. Jack Bauer, ed., *Soldiering: The Civil War Diary of Rice C. Bull, 123rd New York Volunteer Infantry* (San Rafael, 1977); Thomas H. Evans, "'The Cries of the Wounded Were Piercing and Horrible,' " *Civil War Times Illustrated* 7 (July 1968): 35; John Hill Ferguson Diary, June 27, 1864, Henry Pfeiffer Library, Mac-Murray College; George P. Metcalf Reminiscences, 98, Harrisburg Civil War Round Table–Gregory Coco Collection, U.S. Army Military History Institute.

1. Bauer, ed., *Soldiering*, 55–56.

2. Leo M. Kaiser, ed., "Civil War Letters of Charles W. Carr of the 21st Wisconsin Volunteers," *Wisconsin Magazine of History* 43 (Summer 1960): 268; Flegeal to siblings, October 13, 1862, Flegeal Family Papers, Harrisburg Civil War Round Table Collection, U.S. Army Military History Institute; Embley to brother and sister, April 28, 1862, Edgar Embley Papers, Harrisburg Civil War Round Table Collection, U.S. Army Military History Institute; Wilcox to wife, October 9, 1862, John S. Wilcox Papers, Illinois State Historical Library.

3. Holman S. Melcher, " 'We Were Cut Off,' " *Civil War Times Illustrated* 8 (December 1969): 12–13.

4. George P. Metcalf Reminiscences, 62, Harrisburg Civil War Round Table–Gregory Coco Collection, U.S. Army Military History Institute; Boyd Litzinger and Edward K. Eckert, eds., "On the Peninsular Campaign: Civil War Letters from William E. Dunn," *Civil War Times Illustrated* 14 (July 1975): 17; Emil Rosenblatt and Ruth Rosenblatt, eds., *Hard Marching Every Day: The Civil War Letters of Private Wilbur Fisk, 1861–1865* (Lawrence, 1992), 216.

5. Lucius W. Barber, *Army Memoirs* (Chicago, 1894), 53; Henry Houghton, "The Ordeal of Civil War: A Recollection," *Vermont History* 41 (Winter 1973): 35.

6. Oliver Willcox Norton, *Army Letters, 1861–1865* (Chicago, 1903), 91, 94.

7. Theodore A. Dodge, "Left Wounded on the Field," *Putnam's Magazine* 4 (September 1869): 321; Wilcox to wife, October 9, 1862, John S. Wilcox Papers, Illinois State Historical Library; Robert Goldthwaite Carter, *Four Brothers in Blue* (Austin, 1978), 195; Frank Wilkeson, *Recollections of a Private Soldier in the Army of the Potomac* (New York, 1887), 206.

8. Wilkinson to D. Price, November 5, 1863, Robert Price Papers, Indiana Historical Society.

9. Van Dyke to wife, September 21, 1862, Augustus Van Dyke Papers, Indiana Historical Society; George Claflin Parker to mother, October 15, 1862, George Claflin Parker Papers, *Civil War Times Illustrated* Collection, U.S. Army Military History Institute; Frederick L. Hitchcock, *War from the Inside* (Philadelphia, 1904), 60; Work to Nan, undated, Elias D. Work Papers, Indiana Historical Society.

10. Henry Gerrish Memoir, 28, *Civil War Times Illustrated* Collection, U.S. Army Military History Institute.

11. Thomas H. Evans, " 'There Is No Use Trying to Dodge Shot,' " *Civil War Times Illustrated* 6 (August 1967): 45; William Cullen Bryant II, ed., "A Yankee Soldier Looks at the Negro," *Civil War History* 7 (June 1961): 146; Gregg to wife, July 26, 1864, Sarah Gregg Papers, Illinois State Historical Library; Francis E. Pierce, " 'I Have with the Regiment Been Through a Terrible Battle,' " *Civil War Times Illustrated* 1 (December 1962): 29.

12. James H. Croushore, ed., *A Volunteer's Adventures: A Union Captain's Record of the Civil War* (New Haven, 1946), 64; John W. Appleton, "That Night at Fort

Wagner, by One Who Was There," *Putnam's Magazine* 4 (July 1869): 13; Carter, *Four Brothers in Blue*, 309; William Wheeler, *Letters of William Wheeler of the Class of 1855* (Cambridge, 1875), 409.

13. Otto Eisenschiml, ed., *Vermont General: The Unusual War Experiences of Edward Hastings Ripley, 1862–1865* (New York, 1960), 254.

14. Carter, *Four Brothers in Blue*, 196.

15. Albert S. Twitchell, *History of the Seventh Maine Light Battery* (Boston, 1892), 100; Earl J. Hess, ed., *A German in the Yankee Fatherland: The Civil War Letters of Henry A. Kircher* (Kent, 1983), 129; James O. Churchill, "Wounded at Fort Donelson," in *War Papers and Personal Reminiscences, 1861–1865*, vol. 1 (St. Louis, 1892), 164.

16. A. B. Isham, "The Story of a Gunshot Wound," in *Sketches of War History, 1861–1865*, vol. 4 (Cincinnati, 1896), 430; Ebenezer Hannaford, "In the Ranks at Stone River," *Harper's New Monthly Magazine* 27 (November 1863): 814.

17. James B. Casey, ed., "The Ordeal of Adoniram Judson Warner: His Minutes of South Mountain and Antietam," *Civil War History* 28 (September 1982): 228; Joyce Farlow and Louise Barry, eds., "Vincent B. Osborne's Civil War Experiences," *Kansas Historical Quarterly* 20 (May 1952): 120.

18. James Tanner, *Experience of a Wounded Soldier at the Second Battle of Bull Run* (N.p., 1927), 123.

19. Alonzo Abernethy, "Incidents of an Iowa Soldier's Life, or Four Years in Dixie," *Annals of Iowa*, 3d ser. 12 (1920): 406; Bruce Catton, ed., "Asa Smith Leaves the War," *American Heritage* 22 (February 1971): 58; James P. Sullivan, "The Charge of the Iron Brigade at Gettysburg," *Civil War Times Illustrated* Collection, U.S. Army Military History Institute; John A. Porter Recollection, 111, *Civil War Times Illustrated* Collection; Paul M. Angle, ed., *Three Years in the Army of the Cumberland: The Letters and Diary of James A. Connolly* (Bloomington, 1959), 49.

20. Mark DeWolfe Howe, Jr., ed., *Touched with Fire: Civil War Letters and Diary of Oliver Wendell Holmes, Jr., 1861–1864* (Cambridge, 1946), 24–32.

21. Mary Acton Hammond, ed., " 'Dear Mollie': Letters of Captain Edward A. Acton to His Wife, 1862," *Pennsylvania Magazine of History and Biography* 89 (January 1965): 28.

22. James A. Padgett, ed., "With Sherman Through Georgia and the Carolinas: Letters of a Federal Soldier," *Georgia Historical Quarterly* 32 (December 1948): 302.

23. Casey, ed., "Ordeal of Adoniram Judson Warner," 234–35.

24. Hannaford, "In the Ranks at Stone River," 814; Ebenezer Hannaford, "In Hospital After Stone River," *Harper's New Monthly Magazine* 28 (January 1864): 263–65.

25. Mildred Throne, ed., "An Iowa Doctor in Blue: The Letters of Seneca B. Thrall, 1862–1864," *Iowa Journal of History* 58 (April 1960); 151; Claiborne J. Walton, " 'One Continued Scene of Carnage,' " *Civil War Times Illustrated* 15 (August 1976): 34–36.

26. Frederick Winsor, "The Surgeon at the Field Hospital," *Atlantic Monthly* 46 (August 1880): 186.

27. Wheeler, *Letters*, 400.

28. Carter, *Four Brothers in Blue*, 324–25.

29. David Coe, ed., *Mine Eyes Have Seen the Glory: Combat Diaries of Union Sergeant Hamlin Alexander Coe* (Rutherford, 1975), 179; Croushore, ed., *A Volunteer's Adventures*, 215.

30. Abernethy, "Incidents of an Iowa Soldier's Life," 410.

31. Carter, *Four Brothers in Blue*, 200–201; George P. Metcalf Reminiscences, 100, Harrisburg Civil War Round Table–Gregory Coco Collection, U.S. Army Military History Institute.

32. Merchant to Henry Yates, February 26, 1862, Ira Merchant Papers, Illinois State Historical Library.

33. Cecil D. Eby, ed., *A Virginia Yankee in the Civil War: The Diaries of David Hunter Strother* (Chapel Hill, 1961), 108; William A. Moore Memoir, 27, Civil War Miscellaneous Collection, U.S. Army Military History Institute; Carter, *Four Brothers in Blue*, 131, 452; Thomas White Stephens Diary, June 23, 1864, State Historical Society of Missouri; Harrison T. Chandler Diary, July 15, 1864, Illinois State Historical Library; Chauncey H. Cooke, "A Badger Boy in Blue: The Letters of Chauncey H. Cooke," *Wisconsin Magazine of History* 5 (September 1921): 92.

34. Wilcox to wife, October 9, 1862, John S. Wilcox Papers, Illinois State Historical Library; Burrill to parents, July 13, 1862, John Burrill Papers, *Civil War Times Illustrated* Collection, U.S. Army Military History Institute.

35. Perkins to friend, September 21, 1862, Hugh C. Perkins Papers, Harrisburg Civil War Round Table Collection, U.S. Army Military History Institute; George P. Metcalf Reminiscences, 104, Harrisburg Civil War Round Table–Gregory Coco Collection, U.S. Army Military History Institute; John H. Brinton, *Personal Memoirs* (New York, 1914), 207–9; George Carrington Diary, May 16, 1863, Chicago Historical Society.

36. John A. Porter Recollection, 90, *Civil War Times Illustrated* Collection, U.S. Army Military History Institute.

37. Carter, *Four Brothers in Blue*, 325; David Herbert Donald, ed., *Gone for a Soldier: The Civil War Memoirs of Private Alfred Bellard* (Boston, 1975), 85.

38. S. H. M. Byers, "How Men Feel in Battle: Recollections of a Private at Champion Hills," *Annals of Iowa* 2 (July 1896): 448–49.

39. Albert Castel, ed., "The War Album of Henry Dwight, Part III," *Civil War Times Illustrated* 19 (May 1980): 36.

40. Ira Seymour Dodd, *The Song of the Rappahannock: Sketches of the Civil War* (New York, 1898), 109–10.

41. Frank E. Vandiver, *Blood Brothers: A Short History of the Civil War* (College Station, 1992), 178.

42. Stanley P. Wasson, ed., "Civil War Letters of Darwin Cody," *Ohio Historical Quarterly* 68 (October 1959): 383–84.

CHAPTER THREE. THE NATURE OF BATTLE

Epigraphs: Thomas H. Evans, "All Was Complete Chaos,'" *Civil War Times Illustrated* 6 (January 1968): 37; Pettit to sister, October 9, 1862, Frederick Pettit Papers,

Civil War Times Illustrated Collection, U.S. Army Military History Institute; Claiborne J. Walton, " 'One Continued Scene of Carnage,' " *Civil War Times Illustrated* 15 (August 1976): 34.

1. James Franklin Fitts, "In the Ranks at Cedar Creek," *Galaxy* 1 (1866): 538; Ebenezer Hannaford, "In the Ranks at Stone River," *Harper's New Monthly Magazine* 27 (November 1863): 813; Jacob Heffelfinger Diary, June 29, 1862, *Civil War Times Illustrated* Collection, U.S. Army Military History Institute.

2. Lewis M. Hosea, "The Second Day at Shiloh," in *Sketches of War History, 1861–1865,* vol. 6 (Cincinnati, 1908), 199–200.

3. Eric J. Leed, *No Man's Land: Combat and Identity in World War I* (New York, 1979), 132–36.

4. David L. Thompson, "With Burnside at Antietam," in *Battles and Leaders of the Civil War,* vol. 2 (New York, 1956), 660.

5. Maps and descriptions of the cluttered vegetation on Civil War battlefields can be found in many studies, such as William L. Shea and Earl J. Hess, *Pea Ridge: Civil War Campaign in the West* (Chapel Hill, 1992); John J. Hennessy, *Return to Bull Run: The Campaign and Battle of Second Manassas* (New York, 1993); and Robert Garth Scott, *Into the Wilderness with the Army of the Potomac* (Bloomington, 1992). The maps published in the *Atlas to Accompany the Official Records of the Union and Confederate Armies* (Washington, 1891–1895) are extremely helpful as well. George R. Agassiz, ed., *Meade's Headquarters, 1863–1865: Letters of Colonel Theodore Lyman from the Wilderness to Appomattox* (Boston, 1922), 173–74.

6. Raffen to Grace, March 22, 1864, Alexander W. Raffen Papers, Illinois State Historical Library; Thomas to sister, April 19, 1862, James S. Thomas Papers, Indiana Historical Society.

7. James H. Croushore, ed., *A Volunteer's Adventures: A Union Captain's Record of the Civil War* (New Haven, 1946), 109.

8. William D. Matter, *If It Takes All Summer: The Battle of Spotsylvania* (Chapel Hill, 1988), 259, 373.

9. In addition to artillery and small-arms fire, the clear-cutting of fields of fire in front of defensive positions devastated the natural environment. Captain Marcus M. Spiegel of the 67th Ohio was awed by the wholesale nipping of the woods at Harrison's Landing after the Seven Days campaign. "You can possibly have no Idea of the slashing of trees there has been done since we came here; 8 or 10 miles of a wild and picturesque forest has been leveled to the ground and the trees felled every way mixed, so as to keep the enemy from using any Artillery and Cavelery against us." Frank L. Byrne and Jean Powers Soman, eds., *Your True Marcus: The Civil War Letters of a Jewish Colonel* (Kent, 1985), 126.

10. Agassiz, ed., *Meade's Headquarters,* 202.

11. William Ketcham to Pa, October 30, 1864, John Lewis Ketcham Papers, Indiana Historical Society; Thomas White Stephens Diary, June 7, 1864, State Historical Society of Missouri; Earl J. Hess, ed., *A German in the Yankee Fatherland: The Civil War Letters of Henry A. Kircher* (Kent, 1983), 100.

12. Holman S. Melcher, " 'We Were Cut Off,' " *Civil War Times Illustrated* 8 (December 1969): 14.

13. Nicholas B. Wainwright, ed., *A Philadelphia Perspective: The Diary of Sidney George Fisher Covering the Years 1834–1871* (Philadelphia, 1967), 436.

14. Henry Otis Dwight, "How We Fight at Atlanta," *Harper's New Monthly Magazine* 29 (October 1864): 665; John Buechler, " 'Give 'em the Bayonet'—A Note on Civil War Mythology," *Civil War History* 7 (June 1961): 128–32.

15. *War of the Rebellion: A Compilation of the Official Records of the Union and Confederate Armies* (Washington, D.C., 1880–1901), vol. 31, pt. 1, 112–16, 133, 135; (hereafter cited as *OR*).

16. Ibid., vol. 38, pt. 3, 522; Chauncey H. Cooke, "A Badger Boy in Blue: The Letters of Chauncey H. Cooke," *Wisconsin Magazine of History* 5 (September 1921): 79–80.

17. Herman Hattaway and Archer Jones, *How the North Won: A Military History of the Civil War* (Urbana, 1983), 47.

18. Ibid.

19. Earl J. Coates and Dean S. Thomas, *An Introduction to Civil War Small Arms* (Gettysburg, 1990), 13–29.

20. Thomas L. Livermore, "The Northern Volunteers," *Journal of the Military Service Institution of the United States* 12 (September 1891): 934.

21. Charles C. Paige Memoir, 24, 27, Wendell W. Lang, Jr., Collection, U.S. Army Military History Institute; *OR*, vol. 21, 329.

22. Annette Tapert, *The Brothers' War: Civil War Letters to Their Loved Ones from the Blue & Gray* (New York, 1989), 227. There are numerous ways to determine the range at which Civil War soldiers commonly fired their weapons. Many mentioned this information in their reports and personal correspondence. Paddy Griffith, *Battle Tactics of the Civil War* (New Haven, 1989), 145–50. Battlefields such as Chickamauga have many markers, erected by veterans of the fighting, that precisely place the location of regiments and thus vividly demonstrate the closeness of the opposing lines.

23. Grady McWhiney and Perry D. Jamieson, *Attack and Die: Civil War Military Tactics and the Southern Heritage* (Tuscaloosa, 1982), 31–32.

24. Griffith, *Battle Tactics of the Civil War*, 73–90.

25. Bell Irvin Wiley, *The Life of Billy Yank: The Common Soldier of the Union* (Baton Rouge, 1952), 17–30. For useful commentary on the deficiencies of the volunteer army, see Thomas Wentworth Higginson, "Regular and Volunteer Officers," *Atlantic Monthly* 14 (September 1864): 348–57, and Allan Nevins, ed., *A Diary of Battle: The Personal Journals of Colonel Charles S. Wainwright, 1861–1865* (New York, 1962), 273.

26. Hattaway and Jones, *How the North Won*, 11–14.

27. Ibid., 102–7.

28. Brent Nosworthy, *The Anatomy of Victory: Battle Tactics, 1689–1763* (New York, 1992), 86; Gunther E. Rothenberg, *The Art of Warfare in the Age of Napoleon* (Bloomington, 1980), 153–54.

29. Evidence of the breakdown of lateral control can be found throughout the battle reports in *OR*. Additional evidence can be found in soldiers' personal

accounts. For an analysis of this phenomenon in one battle, see Shea and Hess, *Pea Ridge,* 128–33, 313–16. See also Griffith, *Battle Tactics of the Civil War,* 140–45.

30. See, for example, the discussion of the Confederate assaults at Stones River in James Lee McDonough, *Stones River: Bloody Winter in Tennessee* (Knoxville, 1980), 148–49.

31. Kenneth A. Hafendorfer, *Perryville: Battle for Kentucky* (Louisville, 1991), 260–68.

32. Albert Castel, "Mars and the Reverend Longstreet: Or, Attacking and Dying in the Civil War," *Civil War History* 33 (June 1987): 103–14.

33. William T. Sherman, *Memoirs,* vol. 2 (New York, 1875), 885.

34. Wiley Sword, *The Confederacy's Last Hurrah: Spring Hill, Franklin, and Nashville* (Lawrence, 1992), 392–422.

35. Hennessy, *Return to Bull Run,* 259–60; Lyman Jackman, *History of the Sixth New Hampshire Regiment in the War for the Union* (Concord, 1891), 78.

36. Tapert, *The Brothers' War,* 81; Jackman, *History of the Sixth New Hampshire Regiment,* 80; Hennessy, *Return to Bull Run,* 261–63.

37. Hennessy, *Return to Bull Run,* 263–64; Tapert, *The Brothers' War,* 82; Jackman, *History of the Sixth New Hampshire Regiment,* 81–82.

38. Hennessy, *Return to Bull Run,* 264–68.

39. Ibid., 268; Jackman, *History of the Sixth New Hampshire Regiment,* 84.

40. Tapert, *The Brothers' War,* 84–85.

41. Mark DeWolfe Howe, Jr., ed., *The Occasional Speeches of Justice Oliver Wendell Holmes* (Cambridge, 1962), 76.

42. Griffith, *Battle Tactics of the Civil War,* 190.

43. Hattaway and Jones, *How the North Won,* 515–19.

44. Dwight, "How We Fight at Atlanta," 664.

45. Hattaway and Jones, *How the North Won,* 538–45.

46. Ibid., 552–67.

47. Ibid., 577–81.

48. James M. McPherson, *Battle Cry of Freedom: The Civil War Era* (New York, 1988), 742.

49. Ibid., 743–50.

50. Mark DeWolfe Howe, Jr., ed., *Touched with Fire: Civil War Letters and Diary of Oliver Wendell Holmes, Jr., 1861–1864* (Cambridge, 1946), 149–50; Matter, *If It Takes All Summer,* 257.

51. Stephen Pierson, "From Chattanooga to Atlanta in 1864," *Proceedings of the New Jersey Historical Society* 16 (1931): 339–40.

52. Edward Hagerman, *The American Civil War and the Origins of Modern Warfare* (Bloomington, 1988), index; Griffith, *Battle Tactics of the Civil War,* 123–35.

53. William H. Powell, "The Battle of the Petersburg Crater," in *Battles and Leaders of the Civil War,* vol. 4 (New York, 1956), 551, 553–54; Charles H. Houghton, "In the Crater," in ibid., 562.

54. G. Norton Galloway, "Hand-to-Hand Fighting at Spotsylvania," in *Battles and Leaders of the Civil War,* vol. 4 (New York, 1956), 172–73; Thomas W. Hyde,

Following the Greek Cross or, Memories of the Sixth Army Corps (Boston, 1894), 202; Matter, *If It Takes All Summer,* 266–67.

55. *OR,* vol. 38, pt. 2, 131.

56. J. T. Holmes, *52d O.V.I., Then and Now* (Columbus, 1898), 183; Edwin W. Payne, *History of the Thirty-fourth Regiment of Illinois Volunteer Infantry* (Clinton, 1902), 131–32.

57. Payne, *History of the Thirty-fourth Illinois,* 133–34; Holmes, *52d O.V.I.,* 183, 187; "A Rash Deed at Dead Angle," *Confederate Veteran* 12 (August 1904): 394.

58. McPherson, *Battle Cry of Freedom,* 821.

CHAPTER FOUR. DEFINING COURAGE

Epigraphs: George P. Metcalf Reminiscences, 92, Harrisburg Civil War Round Table–Gregory Coco Collection, U.S. Army Military History Institute; George F. Williams, "Lights and Shadows of Army Life," *Century* 28 (October 1884): 812–13; James H. Croushore, ed., *A Volunteer's Adventures: A Union Captain's Record of the Civil War* (New Haven, 1946), 124; Lewis M. Hosea, "The Second Day at Shiloh," in *Sketches of War History, 1861–1865,* vol. 6 (Cincinnati, 1908), 201.

1. William A. Ketcham Reminiscences, 24, Indiana Historical Society; Horace Porter, "The Philosophy of Courage," *Century* 36 (June 1888): 250.

2. William T. Sherman, *Memoirs,* vol. 2 (New York, 1875), 395; Porter, "Philosophy of Courage," 248, 254.

3. William A. Moore Memoir, 26, 28, Civil War Miscellaneous Collection, U.S. Army Military History Institute.

4. Frank Holsinger, "How Does One Feel Under Fire?" in *War Talks in Kansas* (Kansas City, 1906), 291.

5. William C. Davis, *Battle at Bull Run* (Baton Rouge, 1977), 232–38.

6. Oliver Haskell Reminiscence, Indiana Historical Society; Allen to W. H. Fairbanks, September 8, 1862, Edward B. Allen Papers, Indiana Historical Society.

7. Allen to W. H. Fairbanks, September 8, 1862, Edward B. Allen Papers, Indiana Historical Society; *War of the Rebellion: A Compilation of the Official Records of the Union and Confederate Armies* (Washington, D.C., 1880–1901), vol. 16, pt. 1, 909, 915.

8. Alonzo Marshall to Elvira, December 19, 1862, Thomas Marshall Collection, Indiana Historical Society.

9. James Franklin Fitts, "In the Ranks at Cedar Creek," *Galaxy* 1 (1866): 536.

10. Robert Goldthwaite Carter, *Four Brothers in Blue* (Austin, 1978), 114.

11. George P. Metcalf Reminiscences, 99, Harrisburg Civil War Round Table–Gregory Coco Collection, U.S. Army Military History Institute.

12. Croushore, ed., *A Volunteer's Adventures,* 63.

13. Theodore A. Dodge, "Left Wounded on the Field," *Putnam's Magazine* 4 (September 1869): 320–21; James I. Robertson, Jr., ed., "A Federal Surgeon at Sharpsburg," *Civil War History* 6 (June 1960): 147; John M. Schofield, *Forty-six Years in the Army* (New York, 1897), 45.

14. Dodge, "Left Wounded on the Field," 321; Croushore, ed., *A Volunteer's Adventures*, 110.

15. Mortimer D. Leggett, "The Military and the Mob," in *Sketches of War History, 1861–1865*, vol. 1 (Cincinnati, 1888), 195; Cecil D. Eby, ed., *A Virginia Yankee in the Civil War: The Diaries of David Hunter Strother* (Chapel Hill, 1961), 42.

16. William A. Ketcham Reminiscences, 17, Indiana Historical Society; Allan Nevins, ed., *A Diary of Battle: The Personal Journals of Colonel Charles S. Wainwright, 1861–1865* (New York, 1962), 252.

17. David L. Thompson, "With Burnside at Antietam," in *Battles and Leaders of the Civil War*, vol. 2 (New York, 1956), 662.

18. Porter, "Philosophy of Courage," 247.

19. Joseph J. Scroggs Diary, September 29, 1864, *Civil War Times Illustrated* Collection, U.S. Army Military History Institute.

20. Ambrose Bierce, *The Collected Works of Ambrose Bierce*, 11 vols. (New York, 1909), 1:287–95.

21. Joseph Allan Frank and George A. Reaves, *"Seeing the Elephant": Raw Recruits at the Battle of Shiloh* (Westport, 1989), 135, 139.

22. Emil Rosenblatt and Ruth Rosenblatt, eds., *Hard Marching Every Day: The Civil War Letters of Private Wilbur Fisk, 1861–1865* (Lawrence, 1992), 216–17.

23. Frank and Reaves, *Seeing the Elephant*, 97.

24. Rankin, "What I Thought at Antietam," in Benjamin Wilson Smith Papers, pt. 2, 1, 8–13, Indiana Historical Society.

25. Frank and Reaves, *Seeing the Elephant*, 113; Pettit to parents, brothers, and sisters, June 27, 1864, Frederick Pettit Papers, *Civil War Times Illustrated* Collection, U.S. Army Military History Institute.

26. Albert Castel, *Decision in the West: The Atlanta Campaign of 1864* (Lawrence, 1992), 225, 481.

27. George Bowen Diary, June 18, 1864, Petersburg National Battlefield.

28. James W. Geary, *We Need Men: The Union Draft in the Civil War* (DeKalb, 1991), 15; James M. McPherson, *Ordeal by Fire: The Civil War and Reconstruction* (New York, 1982), 468; Earl J. Hess, "The 12th Missouri Infantry: A Socio-Military Profile of a Union Regiment," *Missouri Historical Review* 76 (October 1981): 71–72; Judith Lee Hallock, "The Role of the Community in Civil War Desertion," *Civil War History* 29 (June 1983): 125, 134.

29. James M. McPherson, *Battle Cry of Freedom: The Civil War Era* (New York, 1988), 720; Hess, "The 12th Missouri Infantry," 75–76; Earl J. Hess, ed., *A German in the Yankee Fatherland: The Civil War Letters of Henry A. Kircher* (Kent, 1983), 157.

30. W. J. Rorabaugh, "Who Fought for the North in the Civil War? Concord, Massachusetts, Enlistments," *Journal of American History* 73 (December 1986): 699; Emily J. Harris, "Sons and Soldiers: Deerfield, Massachusetts, and the Civil War," *Civil War History* 30 (June 1984): 159–69; Hallock, "Role of the Community," 123; Richard E. Matthews, *The 149th Pennsylvania Volunteer Infantry Unit in the Civil War* (Jefferson, 1994), 127–30.

31. Thomas F. Barr, "Costs and Compensations of the War," in *Military Essays and Recollections*, vol. 1 (Chicago, 1891), 523; Joseph Harrington Trego Diary, June

10, 1861, Kansas State Historical Society; William P. Hogarty, "A Medal of Honor," in *War Talks in Kansas* (Kansas City, 1906), 357; Thomas H. Evans, " 'The Cries of the Wounded Were Piercing and Horrible,' " *Civil War Times Illustrated* 7 (July 1968): 33.

32. Wilcox to wife, October 9, 1862, John S. Wilcox Papers, Illinois State Historical Library.

33. William Wheeler, *Letters of William Wheeler of the Class of 1855* (Cambridge, 1875), 411, 418, 436.

34. Croushore, ed., *A Volunteer's Adventures*, 112; Daniel McCook, "The Second Division at Shiloh," *Harper's New Monthly Magazine* 28 (May 1864): 831; Otto Eisenschiml, ed., *Vermont General: The Unusual War Experiences of Edward Hastings Ripley, 1862–1865* (New York, 1960), 250; William Camm, "Diary of Colonel William Camm, 1861 to 1865," *Journal of the Illinois State Historical Society* 18 (January 1926): 857.

35. Paul M. Angle, ed., *Three Years in the Army of the Cumberland: The Letters and Diary of James A. Connolly* (Bloomington, 1959), 258.

36. Croushore, ed., *A Volunteer's Adventures*, 112, 123; Nevins, ed., *Diary of Battle*, 186; Mildred Throne, ed., "An Iowa Doctor in Blue: The Letters of Seneca B. Thrall, 1862–1864," *Iowa Journal of History* 58 (April 1960): 104.

CHAPTER FIVE. HOLDING ON

Epigraphs: William A. Ketcham Reminiscences, Indiana Historical Society; J. Spangler Kieffer to Robert Weidensall, October 4, 1862, Robert Weidensall Papers, George Williams College; W. C. Littlefield to parents, December 17, 1863, W. C. Littlefield Papers, Illinois State Historical Library; Henry N. Blake, *Three Years in the Army of the Potomac* (Boston, 1865), 309; David E. Beem to Hala, July 1861, David E. Beem Papers, Indiana Historical Society.

1. Gerald F. Linderman, *Embattled Courage: The Experience of Combat in the American Civil War* (New York, 1987), 8–17; Michael Barton, *Goodmen: The Character of Civil War Soldiers* (University Park, 1981), 5, 21, 33; E. Anthony Rotundo, "Body and Soul: Changing Ideals of American Middle-Class Manhood, 1770–1920," *Journal of Social History* 16 (Summer 1983): 23–38.

2. Joshua Lawrence Chamberlain, *The Passing of the Armies* (New York, 1915), 11, 15–16.

3. George W. Crosley, "Some Reminiscences of an Iowa Soldier," *Annals of Iowa* 10 (July 1911): 121; Leander Stillwell, *The Story of a Common Soldier of Army Life in the Civil War, 1861–1865* (Kansas City, 1920), 270–71.

4. William A. Ketcham Reminiscences, Indiana Historical Society; H. L. Brush to Charles H. Brush, January 23, 1863, Brush Family Papers, Illinois State Historical Library; Lysander Wheeler to parents and sister, November 7, 1862, Lysander Wheeler Papers, Illinois State Historical Library.

5. Charles Richard Williams, ed., *Diary & Letters of Rutherford Birchard Hayes*, vol. 2 (Columbus, 1922), 50; Stephen S. Rogers to parents, May 19, 1864, Stephen S. Rogers Papers, Illinois State Historical Library.

6. John A. Lynn, *Bayonets of the Republic: Motivation and Tactics in the Army of Revolutionary France, 1791–94* (Urbana, 1984), 34, and John Baynes, *Morale: A Study of Men and Courage* (Garden City Park, 1967), 224–25, 228–30, 235, 253–54, discuss patriotism and ideology in the French revolutionary wars and World War I. For studies that downplay the role of ideology in the Civil War, see Bell Irvin Wiley, *The Life of Billy Yank: The Common Soldier of the Union* (Baton Rouge, 1952), 44, and Pete Maslowski, "A Study of Morale in Civil War Soldiers," *Military Affairs* 34 (December 1970): 123–24.

7. James Abraham to Will, August 7, 1862, James Abraham Papers, *Civil War Times Illustrated* Collection, U.S. Army Military History Institute; Alexis W. Tallman to brother and sister, March 20, 1864, Alexis W. Tallman Papers, *Civil War Times Illustrated* Collection, U.S. Army Military History Institute.

8. John Stahl Peterson, "The Issues of the War," *Continental Monthly* 5 (1864): 274.

9. Chamberlain, *The Passing of the Armies*, 18.

10. Robert Goldthwaite Carter, *Four Brothers in Blue* (Austin, 1978), 212.

11. Henry Henney to Libby, March 17, 1863; to sister, April 1, 1863; and diary, April 26, 1863, Henry Henney Papers, *Civil War Times Illustrated* Collection, U.S. Army Military History Institute.

12. Daniel Holt to wife, May 15, 1863, Daniel Holt Papers, New York State Historical Association; Jacob Heffelfinger Diary, May 7, 1863, *Civil War Times Illustrated* Collection, U.S. Army Military History Institute.

13. Joseph H. Sweney, "Nursed a Wounded Brother," *Annals of Iowa* 31 (January 1952): 192–93.

14. Earl J. Hess, *Liberty, Virtue, and Progress: Northerners and Their War for the Union* (New York, 1988), 32–55.

15. Ibid., 78–80; Reid Mitchell, *Civil War Soldiers: Their Expectations and Their Experiences* (New York, 1988), 109–17.

16. R. G. Plumb, ed., "Letters of a Fifth Wisconsin Volunteer," *Wisconsin Magazine of History* 3 (September 1919): 66.

17. William Wheeler, *Letters of William Wheeler of the Class of 1855* (Cambridge, 1875), 417.

18. Will C. Robinson to Charlie, April 28, 1861, Will C. Robinson Papers, Illinois State Historical Library; Rollin W. Quimby, "Recurrent Themes and Purposes in the Sermons of the Union Army Chaplain," *Speech Monographs* 31 (November 1964): 433.

19. Richard N. Ellis, ed., "The Civil War Letters of an Iowa Family," *Annals of Iowa* 39 (Spring 1969): 585; Jacob Behm to sister and brother, February 1, 1864, Jacob Behm Papers, *Civil War Times Illustrated* Collection, U.S. Army Military History Institute.

20. Knox Mellon, Jr., ed., "Letters of James Greenalch," *Michigan History* 44 (June 1960): 199.

21. Frederick Pettit to parents, May 20, 1864, Frederick Pettit Papers, *Civil War Times Illustrated* Collection, U.S. Army Military History Institute.

22. Lewis O. Saum, "Providence in the Popular Mind of Pre–Civil War America," *Indiana Magazine of History* 72 (December 1976): 326, 344.

23. Ferdinand Davis to brother, April 20, 1862, Raymond Cazallis Davis Papers, Michigan History Collection; Nelson Chapin to wife, April 26, 1862, Nelson Chapin Papers, *Civil War Times Illustrated* Collection, U.S. Army Military History Institute; Arthur Lee Bailhache to brother, October 22, 1861, Bailhache-Brayman Collection, Illinois State Historical Library.

24. Nathan B. Webb Diary, April 15, 1863, Illinois State Historical Library; Chauncey H. Cooke, "A Badger Boy in Blue: The Letters of Chauncey H. Cooke," *Wisconsin Magazine of History* 5 (September 1921): 73.

25. Eric J. Leed, *No Man's Land: Combat and Identity in World War I* (New York, 1979), 6–12; Francis A. Riddle, "The Soldier's Place in Civilization," in *Military Essays and Recollections*, vol. 2 (Chicago, 1894), 515–17.

26. John Russell to sister, December 8, 1862, John Russell Papers, *Civil War Times Illustrated* Collection, U.S. Army Military History Institute; Charles C. Paige Memoir, 4, Wendell W. Lang, Jr., Collection, U.S. Army Military History Institute.

27. James J. Heslin, ed., "A Yankee Soldier in a New York Regiment," *New York Historical Quarterly* 50 (April 1966): 116.

28. Williams, ed., *Diary & Letters*, 104; George P. Metcalf Reminiscences, 129, Harrisburg Civil War Round Table–Gregory Coco Collection, U.S. Army Military History Institute.

29. Henry Otis Dwight, "How We Fight at Atlanta," *Harper's New Monthly Magazine* 29 (October 1864): 666.

30. James H. Croushore, ed., *A Volunteer's Adventures: A Union Captain's Record of the Civil War* (New Haven, 1946), 144; George R. Agassiz, ed., *Meade's Headquarters, 1863–1865: Letters of Colonel Theodore Lyman from the Wilderness to Appomattox* (Boston, 1922), 109; Frank Wilkeson, *Recollections of a Private Soldier in the Army of the Potomac* (New York, 1887), 121.

31. Benjamin W. Thompson Memoir, 40, *Civil War Times Illustrated* Collection, U.S. Army Military History Institute; William A. Ketcham Reminiscences, 81, Indiana Historical Society; R. E. McBride, *In the Ranks from the Wilderness to Appomattox Court House* (Cincinnati, 1881), 97–98.

32. Edward Tabor Linenthal, *Changing Images of the Warrior Hero in America: A History of Popular Symbolism* (New York, 1982), xvi–xvii, 4–5.

33. Ibid., ix–xvii, 69–90; Richard Slotkin, *Regeneration Through Violence: The Mythology of the American Frontier, 1600-1860* (Middletown, 1973), 5.

34. Howard Stevens to uncle, July 21, 1863, Howard Stevens Papers, Harrisburg Civil War Round Table–Gregory A. Coco Collection, U.S. Army Military History Institute.

CHAPTER SIX. THE PSYCHOLOGY OF THE BATTLE LINE

Epigraphs: E. L. Marsh, "Military Discipline," in *War Sketches and Incidents*, vol. 2 (Des Moines, 1898), 107; Rufus R. Dawes, "With the Sixth Wisconsin at Gettysburg," in *Sketches of War History, 1861–1865*, vol. 3 (Cincinnati, 1890), 368; Edward G. Longacre, ed., " 'Laughing at the Screaming Bullets,' " *Lincoln Her-*

ald 84 (Fall 1982): 177–78; John W. DeForest, "Our Military Past and Present," *Atlantic Monthly* 44 (November 1879): 569; Jones to sister, April 19, 1863, A. Stokes Jones Papers, Harrisburg Civil War Round Table Collection, U.S. Army Military History Institute.

1. Bell Irvin Wiley, *The Life of Billy Yank: The Common Soldier of the Union* (Baton Rouge, 1952), 73–75; James H. Croushore, ed., *A Volunteer's Adventures: A Union Captain's Record of the Civil War* (New Haven, 1946), 65, 70.

2. Ira Seymour Dodd,"The Making of a Regiment," *McClure's Magazine* 9 (1897): 1044.

3. Frederick L. Hitchcock, *War from the Inside* (Philadelphia, 1904), 219; James C. Mohr, ed., *The Cormany Diaries: A Northern Family in the Civil War* (Pittsburgh, 1982), 438.

4. James Lee McDonough, *Stones River: Bloody Winter in Tennessee* (Knoxville, 1980), 78.

5. Horace Porter, "The Philosophy of Courage," *Century* 36 (June 1888): 248; Ira Seymour Dodd, *The Song of the Rappahannock: Sketches of the Civil War* (New York, 1898), 151; Stowe to friends, July 11, 1862, J. P. Stowe Papers, *Civil War Times Illustrated* Collection, U.S. Army Military History Institute.

6. Charles Mackenzie, "The Great American Civil War," in *War Sketches and Incidents,* vol. 1 (Des Moines, 1893), 359–60.

7. William Thompson Lusk, *War Letters of William Thompson Lusk* (New York, 1911), 247–48.

8. Thomas L. Livermore, "The Northern Volunteers," *Journal of the Military Service Institution of the United States* 12 (September 1891): 918.

9. Croushore, ed., *A Volunteer's Adventures,* 60.

10. Ira Seymour Dodd, "The Song of the Rappahannock," *McClure's Magazine* 8 (1896–1897): 316.

11. Frank Wilkeson, *Recollections of a Private Soldier in the Army of the Potomac* (New York, 1887), 202.

12. Croushore, ed., *A Volunteer's Adventures,* 182; Ambrose Bierce, *The Collected Works of Ambrose Bierce,* 11 vols. (New York, 1909), 1:286–88.

13. Frank Holsinger, "How Does One Feel Under Fire?" in *War Talks in Kansas* (Kansas City, 1906), 300; Fred Albert Shannon, ed., *The Civil War Letters of Sergeant Onley Andrus* (Urbana, 1947), 53; John A. Logan, *The Volunteer Soldier of America* (Chicago, 1887), 472.

14. J. Glenn Gray, *The Warriors: Reflections on Men in Battle* (New York, 1970), 41–44, 56; S. L. A. Marshall, *Men Against Fire: The Problem of Battle Command in Future War* (New York, 1947), 41–42; Lord Moran, *The Anatomy of Courage* (Garden City, 1966), 183.

15. Alva C. Griest Journal, 23, Harrisburg Civil War Round Table Collection, U.S. Army Military History Institute.

16. Alexander B. Pattison Diary, May 12, 29, 1864, Indiana Historical Society.

17. Thomas H. Benton to sister, July 18, 1862, Thomas H. Benton Papers, Indiana Historical Society; Paul M. Angle, ed., *Three Years in the Army of the Cumberland: The Letters and Diary of James A. Connolly* (Bloomington, 1959), 105; Albinus

R. Fell to Lydia, May 12, 1863, Albinus R. Fell Papers, Civil War Miscellaneous Collection, U.S. Army Military History Institute.

18. John S. Wilcox to wife, October 9, 1862, John S. Wilcox Papers, Illinois State Historical Library; Chauncey H. Cooke, "A Badger Boy in Blue: The Letters of Chauncey H. Cooke," *Wisconsin Magazine of History* 5 (September 1921): 91; Oliver Willcox Norton, *Army Letters, 1861–1865* (Chicago, 1903), 107–9.

19. Stephen S. Rogers to parents, September 28, 1862, Stephen S. Rogers Papers, Illinois State Historical Library; Daniel Holt to wife, May 15, 1863, Daniel Holt Papers, New York State Historical Association; William P. Barker to daughter, February 23, 1865, William P. Barker Papers, New York State Historical Association.

20. George H. Barker to James Miner, September 16, 1861, Miner Family Papers, Illinois State Historical Library; Pete Maslowski, "A Study of Morale in Civil War Soldiers," *Military Affairs* 34 (December 1970): 124–25.

21. James B. Casey, ed., "The Ordeal of Adoniram Judson Warner: His Minutes of South Mountain and Antietam," *Civil War History* 28 (September 1982): 226; F. Clever Bald, "Detroit's Little French Corporal," *Michigan History Magazine* 46 (June 1962): 140.

22. James Franklin Fitts, "In the Ranks at Cedar Creek," *Galaxy* 1 (1866): 540.

23. Philip H. Sheridan, *Personal Memoirs,* vol. 2 (New York, 1888), 71–93; Fitts, "In the Ranks at Cedar Creek," 540–41.

24. Caroline D. Sherman, "A New England Boy in the Civil War," *New England Quarterly* 5 (April 1932): 332–33.

25. Earl J. Hess, *Liberty, Virtue, and Progress: Northerners and Their War for the Union* (New York, 1988), 66.

26. Reid Mitchell, *The Vacant Chair: The Northern Soldier Leaves Home* (New York, 1993), 19–37, 71–87.

27. John S. Wilcox to wife, October 9, 1862, John S. Wilcox Papers, Illinois State Historical Library; Nelson Chapin to wife, April 26, 1862, Nelson Chapin Papers, *Civil War Times Illustrated* Collection, U.S. Army Military History Institute; Mark DeWolfe Howe, Jr., ed., *Touched with Fire: Civil War Letters and Diary of Oliver Wendell Homes, Jr., 1861–1864* (Cambridge, 1946), 60.

28. Richard N. Ellis, ed., "The Civil War Letters of an Iowa Family," *Annals of Iowa* 39 (Spring 1969): 576; Robert Goldthwaite Carter, *Four Brothers in Blue* (Austin, 1978), 421.

29. Hess, *Liberty, Virtue, and Progress,* 23–25.

30. W. H. L. Wallace to Ann, April 28, 1861, Wallace-Dickey Collection, Illinois State Historical Library; Mackenzie, "The Great American Civil War," 361.

31. Claiborne J. Walton, " 'One Continued Scene of Carnage,' " *Civil War Times Illustrated* 15 (August 1976): 36.

32. Angle, ed., *Three Years in the Army of the Cumberland,* 38.

33. Lysander Wheeler to parents and sister, December 29, 1862, Lysander Wheeler Papers, Illinois State Historical Library.

34. Joseph H. Sweney, "Nursed a Wounded Brother," *Annals of Iowa* 31 (January 1952): 189.

CHAPTER SEVEN. SHAPING THE BATTLE EXPERIENCE

Epigraphs: Frank Holsinger, "How Does One Feel Under Fire?" in *War Talks in Kansas* (Kansas City, 1906), 294; S. H. M. Byers, "How Men Feel in Battle: Recollections of a Private at Champion Hills," *Annals of Iowa* 2 (July 1896): 443; Edgar Embley to brother and sister, April 28, 1862, Edgar Embley Papers, Harrisburg Civil War Round Table Collection, U.S. Army Military History Institute.

1. Daniel McCook, "The Second Division at Shiloh," *Harper's New Monthly Magazine* 28 (May 1864): 831–32.

2. William Camm, "Diary of Colonel William Camm, 1861 to 1865," *Journal of the Illinois State Historical Society* 18 (January 1926): 853.

3. Paul M. Angle, ed., *Three Years in the Army of the Cumberland: The Letters and Diary of James A. Connolly* (Bloomington, 1959), 158.

4. Frank H. Schell, " 'A Great Raging Battlefield Is Hell,' " *Civil War Times Illustrated* 8 (June 1969): 22; Angle, ed., *Three Years in the Army of the Cumberland*, 21.

5. John K. Ely Diary, October 24, 1863, Judy Beal Collection.

6. George Claflin Parker to mother, October 15, 1862, George Claflin Parker Papers, *Civil War Times Illustrated* Collection, U.S. Army Military History Institute; James H. Croushore, ed., *A Volunteer's Adventures: A Union Captain's Record of the Civil War* (New Haven, 1946), 216.

7. Eric J. Leed, *No Man's Land: Combat and Identity in World War I* (New York, 1979), 64, 66; Earl J. Hess, *Liberty, Virtue, and Progress: Northerners and Their War for the Union* (New York, 1988), 55, 120–27.

8. James I. Robertson, Jr., ed., *The Civil War Letters of General Robert McAllister* (New Brunswick, 1965), 322; Frederick M. Woodruff, ed., "The Civil War Notebook of Montgomery Schuyler Woodruff," *Missouri Historical Society Bulletin* 29 (April 1973): 173.

9. George F. Noyes, "The Battle of Antietam," *Harper's New Monthly Magazine* 27 (September 1863): 540–41.

10. Oliver Willcox Norton, *Army Letters, 1861–1865* (Chicago, 1903), 119.

11. Bell Irvin Wiley, *The Life of Billy Yank: The Common Soldier of the Union* (Baton Rouge, 1952), 304; Mark H. Dunkelman and Michael J. Winey, *The Hardtack Regiment: An Illustrated History of the 154th Regiment, New York State Infantry Volunteers* (Rutherford, 1981), 195–96; Earl J. Hess, "The 12th Missouri Infantry: A Socio-Military Profile of a Union Regiment," *Missouri Historical Review* 76 (October 1981): 62.

12. Lee Soltow and Edward Stevens, *The Rise of Literacy and the Common School in the United States: A Socioeconomic Analysis to 1870* (Chicago, 1981), 117, 155; David Kaser, *Books and Libraries in Camp and Battle: The Civil War Experience* (Westport, 1984), 3.

13. Leed, *No Man's Land*, 88–90.

14. Lord Moran, *The Anatomy of Courage* (Garden City, 1966), 4, 9–10, 188.

15. Cecil D. Eby, ed., *A Virginia Yankee in the Civil War: The Diaries of David Hunter Strother* (Chapel Hill, 1961), 281.

16. Leander Stillwell, *The Story of a Common Soldier of Army Life in the Civil War, 1861–1865* (Kansas City, 1920), 177.

17. Angle, ed., *Three Years in the Army of the Cumberland*, 52; Joseph H. Sweney, "Nursed a Wounded Brother," *Annals of Iowa* 31 (January 1952): 186.

18. John O. Holzhueter, ed., "William Wallace's Civil War Letters: The Atlanta Campaign," *Wisconsin Magazine of History* 57 (Winter 1973–1974): 94; Hugh C. Perkins to friend, September 21, 1862, Hugh C. Perkins Papers, Harrisburg Civil War Round Table Collection, U.S. Army Military History Institute; John M. Schofield, *Forty-six Years in the Army* (New York, 1897), 145.

19. Lewis M. Hosea, "The Second Day at Shiloh," in *Sketches of War History, 1861–1865*, vol. 6 (Cincinnati, 1908), 198.

20. Ebenezer Hannaford, "In the Ranks at Stone River," *Harper's New Monthly Magazine* 27 (November 1863): 813; James O. Smith, "My First Campaign and Battle: A Jersey Boy at Antietam—Seventeen Days from Home," *Blue and Gray* 1 (1893): 285.

21. Angle, ed., *Three Years in the Army of the Cumberland*, 25; Worthington Chauncey Ford, ed., *A Cycle of Adams Letters, 1861–1865*, vol. 1 (Boston, 1920), 158.

22. William Wheeler, *Letters of William Wheeler of the Class of 1855* (Cambridge, 1875), 357; Croushore, ed., *A Volunteer's Adventures*, 65–66, 75; Angle, ed., *Three Years in the Army of the Cumberland*, 21–22.

23. Lewis O. Saum, "Death in the Popular Mind of Pre–Civil War America," *American Quarterly* 26 (December 1974): 479, 481.

24. Wiley, *The Life of Billy Yank*, 124; Stephen E. Ambrose, ed., *A Wisconsin Boy in Dixie: The Selected Letters of James K. Newton* (Madison, 1961), 73–74.

25. Thomas F. Miller to Benjamin Newton, May 2, 1862, Thomas F. Miller Papers, Illinois State Historical Library.

26. Charles F. Weller to Kate, March 31, 1864, Charles F. Weller Papers, Civil War Miscellaneous Collection, U.S. Army Military History Institute; W. H. Clune to Maggie, April 16, 1862, W. H. Clune Papers, Iowa State Department of History and Archives.

27. John T. Hubbell, ed., "Stand by the Colors: The Civil War Letters of Leander Stem," *Register of the Kentucky Historical Society* 73 (July 1975): 305; Edward Meeker, "The Improving Health of the United States, 1850–1915," *Explorations in Economic History* 9 (Summer 1972): 362, 367; Thomas H. Benton to sister, July 2, 1862, Thomas H. Benton Papers, Indiana Historical Society.

28. Jacob Behm to brother and sister, April 27, 1862, Jacob Behm Papers, *Civil War Times Illustrated* Collection, U.S. Army Military History Institute; Fred Albert Shannon, ed., *The Civil War Letters of Sergeant Onley Andrus* (Urbana, 1947), 53.

29. Luther C. Furst Diary, May 16, 1861, Harrisburg Civil War Round Table Collection, U.S. Army Military History Institute; Dietrich C. Smith to Carrie, April 21, 1861, Dietrich C. Smith Papers, Illinois State Historical Library.

30. Dietrich C. Smith to Carrie, February 20, 1862, Dietrich C. Smith Papers, Illinois State Historical Library; Vivian C. Hopkins, ed., "Soldier of the 92nd Illinois: Letters of William H. Brown and His Fiancee, Emma Jane Frazey," *Bulletin*

of the New York Public Library 73 (February 1969): 123; James H. Bradd Diary, April 18, 1864, James H. Bradd Papers, U.S. Army Military History Institute.

31. Alva C. Griest Journal, October 31, 1862, Harrisburg Civil War Round Table Collection, U.S. Army Military History Institute; Nannie M. Tilley, ed., *Federals on the Frontier: The Diary of Benjamin F. McInyre, 1862–1864* (Austin, 1963), 117; Robert Goldthwaite Carter, *Four Brothers in Blue* (Austin, 1978), 129.

CHAPTER EIGHT. KNOWING WAR

Epigraphs: David Cornwell Memoir, Civil War Miscellaneous Collection, U.S. Army Military History Institute; George R. Agassiz, ed., *Meade's Headquarters, 1863–1865: Letters of Colonel Theodore Lyman from the Wilderness to Appomattox* (Boston, 1922), 245; Henry F. Lyster, "Recollections of the Bull Run Campaign After Twenty-seven Years," *A Paper Read Before Michigan Commandery of the Military Order of the Loyal Legion of the United States, February 1, 1887* (Detroit, 1888), 17.

1. Bell Irvin Wiley, *The Life of Billy Yank: The Common Soldier of the Union* (Baton Rouge, 1952), 292, 303.

2. Ira Seymour Dodd, "The Making of a Regiment," *McClure's Magazine* 9 (1897): 1041; Jacob Dolson Cox, *Military Reminiscences of the Civil War*, vol. 1 (New York, 1900), 169–70; Thomas Wentworth Higginson, *Army Life in a Black Regiment* (Boston, 1882), 10; Theodore A. Dodge, "Left Wounded on the Field," *Putnam's Magazine* 4 (September 1869): 318.

3. Jacob Heffelfinger Diary, June 27, 1862, *Civil War Times Illustrated* Collection, U.S. Army Military History Institute; Frank Holsinger, "How Does One Feel Under Fire?" in *War Talks in Kansas* (Kansas City, 1906), 291; Frank L. Byrne, ed., *The View from Headquarters: Civil War Letters of Harvey Reid* (Madison, 1965), 35; James H. Croushore, ed., *A Volunteer's Adventures: A Union Captain's Record of the Civil War* (New Haven, 1946), 61–62; Allan Nevins, ed., *A Diary of Battle: The Personal Journals of Colonel Charles S. Wainwright, 1861–1865* (New York, 1962), 56.

4. Harry E. Pratt, ed., "The Civil War Letters of Brigadier General William Ward Orme, 1862–1866," *Journal of the Illinois State Historical Society* 23 (July 1930): 256; George F. Williams, "Lights and Shadows of Army Life," *Century* 28 (October 1884): 813; Daniel Faust to mother, July 14, 1863, Daniel Faust Papers, Harrisburg Civil War Round Table Collection, U.S. Army Military History Institute; William Wheeler, *Letters of William Wheeler of the Class of 1855* (Cambridge, 1875), 419.

5. Nicholas B. Wainwright, ed., *A Philadelphia Perspective: The Diary of Sidney George Fisher Covering the Years 1834–1871* (Philadelphia, 1967), 436.

6. Abner R. Small, *The Road to Richmond* (Berkeley, 1939), 193; George P. Metcalf Reminiscences, 137, Harrisburg Civil War Round Table–Gregory Coco Collection, U.S. Army Military History Institute; James Samuel Clark, *Life in the Middle West* (Chicago, 1916), 54; John K. Ely Diary, October 23, 1863, Judy Beal Collection.

7. Mildred Throne, ed., "Reminiscences of Jacob C. Switzer of the 22nd Iowa," *Iowa Journal of History* 55 (October 1957): 343; Charles E. Davis, Jr., *Three Years in the Army: The Story of the Thirteenth Massachusetts Volunteers* (Boston, 1894), 374.

8. Thomas R. Bright, "Yankees in Arms: The Civil War as a Personal Experience," *Civil War History* 19 (September 1973): 201, 204.

9. Arnold Gates, ed., *The Rough Side of War: The Civil War Journal of Chesley A. Mosman* (Garden City, 1987), 235, 248.

10. Cecil D. Eby, ed., *A Virginia Yankee in the Civil War: The Diaries of David Hunter Strother* (Chapel Hill, 1961), 112–13.

11. Horace Porter, "The Philosophy of Courage," *Century* 36 (June 1888): 248.

12. Holsinger, "How Does One Feel Under Fire?" 301; Paul M. Angle, ed., *Three Years in the Army of the Cumberland: The Letters and Diary of James A. Connolly* (Bloomington, 1959), 224–25; R. E. McBride, *In the Ranks from the Wilderness to Appomattox Court House* (Cincinnati, 1881), 95; Edward G. Longacre, ed., " 'Laughing at the Screaming Bullets,' " *Lincoln Herald* 84 (Fall 1982): 178.

13. Earl J. Hess, ed., *A German in the Yankee Fatherland: The Civil War Letters of Henry A. Kircher* (Kent, 1983), 101; Richard N. Ellis, ed., "The Civil War Letters of an Iowa Family," *Annals of Iowa* 39 (Spring 1969): 568.

14. William W. Belknap, "The Obedience and Courage of the Private Soldier," in *War Sketches and Incidents,* vol. 1 (Des Moines, 1893), 166–67.

15. Frank Wilkeson, *Recollections of a Private Soldier in the Army of the Potomac* (New York, 1887), 207; Charles A. Partridge, ed., *History of the Ninety-sixth Regiment Illinois Volunteer Infantry* (Chicago, 1887), 215.

16. Thomas White Stephens Diary, June 9, July 4, 1864, State Historical Society of Missouri.

17. William H. James, "Blue and Gray: A Baltimore Volunteer of 1864," *Maryland Historical Magazine* 36 (March 1941): 28; William A. Ketcham Reminiscences, 8, Indiana Historical Society.

18. Croushore, ed., *A Volunteer's Adventures,* 59; Porter, "Philosophy of Courage," 250.

19. Annette Tapert, *The Brothers' War: Civil War Letters to Their Loves Ones from the Blue & Gray* (New York, 1989), 84; S. H. M. Byers, "How Men Feel in Battle: Recollections of a Private at Champion Hills," *Annals of Iowa* 2 (July 1896): 445.

20. James B. Casey, ed., "The Ordeal of Adoniram Judson Warner: His Minutes of South Mountain and Antietam," *Civil War History* 28 (September 1982): 229–30.

21. Croushore, ed., *A Volunteer's Adventures,* 210–11, 220; James Franklin Fitts, "In the Ranks at Cedar Creek," *Galaxy* 1 (1866): 541.

22. Warren Olney, "Shiloh as Seen by a Private Soldier," *A Paper Read Before California Commandery of the Military Order of the Loyal Legion of the United States, May 31, 1889* (n.p., n.d.), 21; Nevins, ed., *Diary of Battle,* 467; Thomas H. Evans, "At Malvern Hill," *Civil War Times Illustrated* 6 (December 1967): 40.

23. Worthington Chauncey Ford, ed., *A Cycle of Adams Letters, 1861–1865,* vol. 1 (Boston, 1920), 190; Wheeler, *Letters,* 435–36; Ebenezer Hannaford, "In the Ranks at Stone River," *Harper's New Monthly Magazine* 27 (November 1863): 812.

24. Agassiz, ed., *Meade's Headquarters*, 165; Nevins, ed., *Diary of Battle*, 252.

25. Small, *Road to Richmond*, 186, 190.

26. Robert Goldthwaite Carter, *Four Brothers in Blue* (Austin, 1978), 116; Frederick L. Hitchcock, *War from the Inside* (Philadelphia, 1904), 71–72; Croushore, ed., *A Volunteer's Adventures*, 108; William Camm, "Diary of Colonel William Camm, 1861 to 1865," *Journal of the Illinois State Historical Society* 18 (January 1926): 832.

27. Amos W. Hostetler to Mr. and Mrs. O. P. Miles, January 29, 1863, Amos W. Hostetler Papers, Illinois State Historical Library.

28. Dodd, "The Making of a Regiment," 1033–34, 1044; Robert W. McClaughry, "The Boys of 1861—And Their Boys," in *Military Essays and Recollections*, vol. 3 (Chicago, 1899), 397–412.

CHAPTER NINE. MEMORIES

Epigraphs: Daniel Bond Reminiscences, 1, Minnesota Historical Society; George F. Williams, "Lights and Shadows of Army Life," *Century* 28 (October 1884): 803; Lemuel Adams Autobiography, 106, Illinois State Historical Library; John H. Brinton, *Personal Memoirs* (New York, 1914), 11; Mark DeWolfe Howe, Jr., ed., *The Occasional Speeches of Justice Oliver Wendell Holmes* (Cambridge, 1962), 80; Henry M. Rogers Remarks, May 5, 1909, Massachusetts MOLLUS Collection, U.S. Army Military History Institute.

1. Michael H. Fitch, *Echoes of the Civil War as I Hear Them* (New York, 1905), 343–44; J. O. Kerby, *On the War Path: A Journey over the Historic Grounds of the Late Civil War* (Chicago, 1890), 149; J. T. Holmes, *52d O.V.I., Then and Now* (Columbus, 1898), 166.

2. James H. Patton to Dorothy, April 17, 1907, James H. Patton Papers, Civil War Miscellaneous Collection, U.S. Army Military History Institute; John D. Billings, *Hardtack and Coffee, or the Unwritten Story of Army Life* (Boston, 1887), v.

3. Charles H. Roundy, "Reminiscences and Recollections of the Civil War, 1861–1864," Civil War Miscellaneous Collection, U.S. Army Military History Institute; George H. Allen, *Forty-six Months with the Fourth R.I. Volunteers* (Providence, 1887), 5; Frank Wilkeson, *Recollections of a Private Soldier in the Army of the Potomac* (New York, 1887), vi; Henry N. Blake, *Three Years in the Army of the Potomac* (Boston, 1865), iii; Charles Church Reminiscences, 2, Civil War Miscellaneous Collection, U.S. Army Military History Institute; Stephen Minot Weld, *War Diary and Letters of Stephen Minot Weld, 1861–1865* (Boston, 1979), 3; Nixon B. Stewart, *Dan McCook's Regiment, 52nd O.V.I.* (Alliance, 1900), 9; S. H. M. Byers, "How Men Feel in Battle: Recollections of a Private at Champion Hills," *Annals of Iowa* 2 (July 1896): 449.

4. David Cornwell Memoir, 1, Civil War Miscellaneous Collection, U.S. Army Military History Institute; Jasper P. George Autobiography, 45, ibid.; Josiah Marshall Favill, *The Diary of a Young Officer* (Chicago, 1909), 7; Leander Stillwell, *The Story of a Common Soldier of Army Life in the Civil War, 1861–1865* (Kansas City,

1920), 7–8; Melvin Grigsby, *The Smoked Yank* (Sioux Falls, 1888), 14; Peter Michie, "Reminiscences of Cadet and Army Service," in *Personal Recollections of the War of the Rebellion*, 2d ser. (New York, 1897), 183.

5. Borden M. Hicks, "Personal Recollections of the War of the Rebellion," in *Glimpses of the Nation's Struggle*, 6th ser. (Minneapolis, 1909), 519; Charles O. Brown, *Battle-Fields Revisited* (Kalamazoo, 1886), 4; Charles Morton, "A Boy at Shiloh," in *Personal Recollections of the War of the Rebellion*, 3d ser. (New York, 1907), 53.

6. Holmes, *52d O.V.I.*, dedication.

7. James R. Carnahan, "Personal Recollections of Chickamauga," in *Sketches of War History, 1861–1865*, vol. 1 (Cincinnati, 1888), 401–2; Ira Seymour Dodd, "The Song of the Rappahannock," *McClure's Magazine* 8 (1896–1897): 314–18.

8. James O. Smith, "My First Campaign and Battle: A Jersey Boy at Antietam—Seventeen Days from Home," *Blue and Gray* 1 (1893): 290.

9. Earl J. Hess, *Liberty, Virtue, and Progress: Northerners and Their War for the Union* (New York, 1988), 103–15.

10. R. L. Ashhurst, *Address to the Survivors' Association of the 150th Regiment, Pennsylvania Volunteers* (Philadelphia, 1896), 9; Gilbert C. Kniffin, "A Retrospect," in *War Papers, Military Order of the Loyal Legion of the United States, Commandery of the District of Columbia* (n.p., n.d.), 6; William P. Hogarty, "A Medal of Honor," in *War Talks in Kansas* (Kansas City, 1906), 356–57.

11. George R. Skinner, "Impressions and Realities of War," in *War Sketches and Incidents*, vol. 1 (Des Moines, 1893), 342; Ira Seymour Dodd, *The Song of the Rappahannock: Sketches of the Civil War* (New York, 1898), 253; Thomas F. Barr, "Costs and Compensations of the War," in *Military Essays and Recollections*, vol. 1 (Chicago, 1891), 519–28.

12. Lemuel Adams Autobiography, 105, Illinois State Historical Library; Mildred Throne, ed., "Reminiscences of Jacob C. Switzer of the 22nd Iowa," *Iowa Journal of History* 56 (January 1958): 75.

13. Levi Wagner Memoir, 5, *Civil War Times Illustrated* Collection, U.S. Army Military History Institute.

14. Charles A. Woodruff, "Our Boys in the War of the Rebellion," *A Paper Prepared and Read Before California Commandery of the Military Order of the Loyal Legion of the United States, November 12, 1890* (n.p., n.d.), 21; Charles Robinson, "My Experiences in the Civil War," *Michigan History Magazine* 24 (Winter 1940): 50.

15. Henry A. Castle, "Some Experiences of an Enlisted Man," in *Glimpses of the Nation's Struggle*, 1st ser. (St. Paul, 1887), 129–33; George E. Sutherland, "The Negro in the Late War," in *War Papers Read Before the Commandery of the State of Wisconsin, Military Order of the Loyal Legion of the United States*, vol. 1 (Milwaukee, 1891), 187; Henry A. Barnum, *Society of the Army of the Cumberland, Fifth Reunion, Detroit, 1871* (Cincinnati, 1872), 57–58.

16. Cruce Stark, "Brothers at/in War: One Phase of Post–Civil War Reconciliation," *Canadian Review of American Studies* 6 (Fall 1975): 177–78; Skinner, "Impressions and Realities of War," 344–53.

17. John W. DeForest, *Miss Ravenel's Conversion from Secession to Loyalty* (Columbus, 1969), passim.

18. Gerald F. Linderman, *Embattled Courage: The Experience of Combat in the American Civil War* (New York, 1987), 284–94.

19. Abner R. Small, *The Road to Richmond* (Berkeley, 1939), 185, 194–95, 202–3.

20. Daniel Aaron, *The Unwritten War: American Writers and the Civil War* (New York, 1973), 184, 189; Cathy N. Davidson, *The Experimental Fictions of Ambrose Bierce: Structuring the Ineffable* (Lincoln, 1984), 16; Lawrence I. Berkove, "Two Impossible Dreams: Ambrose Bierce on Utopia and America," *Huntington Library Quarterly* 44 (Autumn 1981): 283–92; Lawrence I. Berkove, "The Heart Has Its Reasons: Ambrose Bierce's Successful Failure at Philosophy," in *Critical Essays on Ambrose Bierce,* ed. Cathy N. Davidson (Boston, 1982), 137.

21. Ambrose Bierce, *The Collected Works of Ambrose Bierce,* 11 vols. (New York, 1909), 4:115–18.

22. Ibid., 1:225–33, 270–78, 297–327.

23. Ibid., 1:254, 269.

24. Ibid., 1:279–96.

25. Ibid., 2:15–26, 46–104, 197–208, 218–29.

26. Albion W. Tourgee, *An Appeal to Caesar* (New York, 1884), and *The Veteran and His Pipe* (Chicago, 1888), both passim.

27. George M. Fredrickson, *The Inner Civil War: Northern Intellectuals and the Crisis of the Union* (New York, 1965), 168, 171, 175, 211; Thomas C. Leonard, *Above the Battle: War-Making in America from Appomattox to Versailles* (New York, 1978), 20–24.

28. Howe, ed., *Occasional Speeches,* 10, 90–91.

29. Ibid., 73–83.

30. Ibid., 15.

31. Stanley J. Kunitz and Howard Haycraft, eds., *American Authors, 1600–1900* (New York, 1938), 441; Francis B. Heitman, *Historical Register and Dictionary of the United States Army,* vol. 1 (Washington, D.C., 1903), 604; Joseph Kirkland, *The Captain of Company K* (Ridgewood, 1968), passim.

32. Linderman, *Embattled Courage,* 284–94.

33. Cecil D. Eby, ed., *A Virginia Yankee in the Civil War: The Diaries of David Hunter Strother* (Chapel Hill, 1961), xvi; Marshall P. Thatcher, *A Hundred Battles in the West* (Detroit, 1884), viii; Michael Ackerman, "After the Battle of Pleasant Hill, La.," *Annals of Iowa* 11 (July–October 1913): 221.

34. Sartell Prentice, "The Opening Hours in the Wilderness in 1864," in *Military Essays and Recollections,* vol. 2 (Chicago, 1894), 99–100; John W. Greene, *Camp Ford Prison; and How I Escaped* (Toledo, 1893), 7.

35. Robert D. Hofsommer, "On the Death of Reynolds," *Civil War Times Illustrated* 21 (June 1982): 17.

36. S. D. Mercer, "Forty Years in the Field," in *Civil War Sketches and Incidents* (Omaha, 1902), 226; John W. Lewis, "Libby," in *War Papers, Military Order of the Loyal Legion of the United States, Commandery of the District of Columbia* (n.p., n.d.),

3; Hicks, "Personal Recollections of the War of the Rebellion," 544.

37. Eric J. Leed, *No Man's Land: Combat and Identity in World War I* (New York, 1979), 12–15, 32–33, 132; Linderman, *Embattled Courage*, 266–97.

38. John Townsend Trowbridge, *The South: A Tour of Its Battle-Fields and Ruined Cities* (Hartford, 1866), 46–47, 115, 121, 125, 131, 141, 266.

39. Anthonette L. McDaniel, " 'Just Watch Us Make Things Hum': Chattanooga, Adolph S. Ochs, and the Memorialization of the Civil War," *East Tennessee Historical Society's Publications* 61 (1989): 3–14.

40. H. S. Stevens, *Souvenir of Excursion to Battlefields by the Society of the Fourteenth Connecticut Regiment and Reunion at Antietam, September 1891* (Washington, 1893), 40, 46–47, 63–68, 87.

41. Daniel Wait Howe, *Civil War Times, 1861–1865* (Indianapolis, 1902), 363.

42. George W. McBride, "Shiloh, After Thirty-two Years," *Blue and Gray* 3 (1894): 310; Paul L. Roy, *The Last Reunion of the Blue and Gray* (Gettysburg, 1950), 18; Walter H. Blake, *Hand Grips: The Story of the Great Gettysburg Reunion, July, 1913* (Vineland, 1913), 31; *On to Richmond! By Post No. 23, G.A.R., Department of New Jersey, and Its Friends, October 16th, 1881* (Trenton, 1881), 3–8, 21–68.

43. Holmes, *52d O.V.I.*, 42, 44, 107, 137, 140, 144–45.

44. Ibid., 143, 193.

45. Ibid., 188–89, 190–99.

46. Ibid., 172–74.

47. Ibid., 200.

CONCLUSION

Epigraphs: David E. Beem to Hala, July 6, 1862, Davis E. Beem Papers, Indiana Historical Society; P. E. Woods to father and mother, November 23, 1862, Dumas Jones Papers, Illinois State Historical Library; Harry E. Pratt, ed., "The Civil War Letters of Brigadier General William Ward Orme, 1862–1866," *Journal of the Illinois State Historical Society* 23 (July 1930): 277–78; John O. Holzhueter, ed., "William Wallace's Civil War Letters: The Virginia Campaign," *Wisconsin Magazine of History* 57 (Autumn 1973): 45; David Coe, ed., *Mine Eyes Have Seen the Glory: Combat Diaries of Union Sergeant Hamlin Alexander Coe* (Rutherford, 1975), 157; Robert Goldthwaite Carter, *Four Brothers in Blue* (Austin, 1978), 210.

1. For examples of the modernist view of war as expressed by fiction writers, see the works of Ernest Hemingway, particularly *For Whom the Bell Tolls*, and Norman Mailer's *The Naked and the Dead*. Examples of this view in the work of academic historians include Gerald F. Linderman, *Embattled Courage: The Experience of Combat in the American Civil War* (New York, 1987), and Richard A. Gabriel, *No More Heroes: Madness and Psychiatry in War* (New York, 1987).

Bibliography

MANUSCRIPTS

Chicago Historical Society
   George Carrington Diary
George Williams College, Downer's Grove, Illinois
   Robert Weidensall Papers
Henry Pfeiffer Library, MacMurray College, Jacksonville, Illinois
   John Hill Ferguson Diary
Illinois State Historical Library
   Lemuel Adams Autobiography
   Bailhache-Brayman Collection
   Brush Family Papers
   Harrison T. Chandler Diary
   Sarah Gregg Papers
   Amos W. Hostetler Papers
   Dumas Jones Papers
   W. C. Littlefield Papers
   Ira Merchant Papers
   Thomas F. Miller Papers
   Miner Family Papers
   Edwin W. Payne Papers
   Reuben T. Prentice Papers
   Alexander W. Raffen Papers
   Will C. Robinson Papers
   Stephen S. Rogers Papers
   Simpson Letters
   Benjamin Smith Papers
   Dietrich C. Smith Papers
   James P. Suiter Diary
   Wallace-Dickey Collection
   Nathan B. Webb Diary
   Lysander Wheeler Papers
   John S. Wilcox Papers

Indiana Historical Society
   Edward B. Allen Papers
   David E. Beem Papers
   Thomas H. Benton Papers
   Oliver Haskell Reminiscence
   John Lewis Ketcham Papers
   William A. Ketcham Reminiscences
   Thomas Marshall Collection
   Alexander B. Pattison Diary
   Robert Price Papers
   Benjamin Wilson Smith Papers
   James S. Thomas Papers
   Augustus Van Dyke Papers
   Elias D. Work Papers
Judy Beal Collection, Harrogate, Tennessee
   John K. Ely Diary
Kansas State Historical Society
   Joseph Harrington Trego Diary
Michigan History Collection
   Raymond Cazallis Davis Papers
Minnesota Historical Society
   Daniel Bond Reminiscences
   Samuel C. Day Papers
New York State Historical Association
   William P. Barker Papers
   Daniel Holt Papers
Petersburg (Virginia) National Battlefield
   George Bowen Diary
Southern Historical Collection, University of North Carolina
   Abraham Welch Papers
State Historical Society of Iowa, Des Moines
   W. H. Clune Papers
   William G. Thompson Papers
State Historical Society of Iowa, Iowa City
   Vinson Holman Diary
State Historical Society of Missouri
   Thomas White Stephens Diary
U.S. Army Military History Institute, Carlisle Barracks, Carlisle, Pennsylvania
   James H. Bradd Papers
   George Gordon Papers
   Gavin A. Lambie Papers
_____. Civil War Miscellaneous Collection
   Charles Church Reminiscences
   David Cornwell Memoir

Albinus R. Fell Papers
Jasper P. George Autobiography
William A. Moore Memoir
James H. Patton Papers
Charles H. Roundy, "Reminiscences and Recollections of the Civil War,
    1861–1864"
Charles F. Weller Papers
_____. *Civil War Times Illustrated* Collection
James Abraham Papers
Jacob Behm Papers
John Burrill Papers
Nelson Chapin Papers
Henry Gerrish Memoir
Jacob Heffelfinger Diary
Henry Henney Papers
William C. Kent Papers
George Claflin Parker Papers
Frederick Pettit Papers
John A. Porter Recollection
John Russell Papers
Joseph J. Scroggs Diary
J. P. Stowe Papers
James P. Sullivan, "The Charge of the Iron Brigade at Gettysburg"
Alexis W. Tallman Papers
Benjamin W. Thompson Memoir
Levi Wagner Memoir
_____. Harrisburg Civil War Round Table Collection
Edgar Embley Papers
Daniel Faust Papers
Flegeal Family Papers
Luther C. Furst Diary
Alva C. Griest Journal
A. Stokes Jones Papers
George P. Metcalf Reminiscences
Hugh C. Perkins Papers
Howard Stevens Papers
_____. Massachusetts Military Order of the Loyal Legion of the United States
(MOLLUS) Collection
Henry M. Rogers Remarks, May 5, 1909
_____. Wendell W. Lang, Jr., Collection
Charles C. Paige Memoir
Western Historical Manuscript Collection, University of Missouri, Columbia
    Robert P. Mathews, "Souvenir of the Holland Company Home Guards and
        Phelps' Regiment, Missouri Volunteer Infantry"

PUBLISHED WORKS

Aaron, Daniel. *The Unwritten War: American Writers and the Civil War.* New York, 1973.

Abernethy, Alonzo. "Incidents of an Iowa Soldier's Life, or Four Years in Dixie." *Annals of Iowa*, 3d ser. 12 (1920): 401–28.

Ackerman, Michael. "After the Battle of Pleasant Hill, La." *Annals of Iowa* 11 (July–October 1913): 218–24.

Agassiz, George R., ed. *Meade's Headquarters, 1863–1865: Letters of Colonel Theodore Lyman from the Wilderness to Appomattox.* Boston, 1922.

Allen, George H. *Forty-six Months with the Fourth R.I. Volunteers.* Providence, 1887.

Ambrose, Stephen E., ed. *A Wisconsin Boy in Dixie: The Selected Letters of James K. Newton.* Madison, 1961.

Angle, Paul M., ed. *Three Years in the Army of the Cumberland: The Letters and Diary of James A. Connolly.* Bloomington, 1959.

Appleton, John W. "That Night at Fort Wagner, by One Who Was There." *Putnam's Magazine* 4 (July 1869): 9–16.

Ashhurst, R. L. *Address to the Survivors' Association of the 150th Regiment, Pennsylvania Volunteers.* Philadelphia, 1896.

Atlas to Accompany the Official Records of the Union and Confederate Armies. Washington, D.C., 1891–1895.

Bald, F. Clever. "Detroit's Little French Corporal." *Michigan History Magazine* 46 (June 1962): 126–46.

Barber, Lucius W. *Army Memoirs.* Chicago, 1894.

Barnum, Henry A. *Society of the Army of the Cumberland, Fifth Re-Union, Detroit, 1871.* Cincinnati, 1872.

Barr, Thomas F. "Costs and Compensations of the War." *Military Essays and Recollections: Papers Read Before the Commandery of the State of Illinois, Military Order of the Loyal Legion of the United States.* Vol. 1. Chicago, 1891.

Barton, Michael. *Goodmen: The Character of Civil War Soldiers.* University Park, 1981.

Bauer, K. Jack, ed. *Soldiering: The Civil War Diary of Rice C. Bull, 123rd New York Volunteer Infantry.* San Rafael, 1977.

Baynes, John. *Morale: A Study of Men and Courage.* Garden City Park, 1967.

Belknap, William W. "The Obedience and Courage of the Private Soldier." *War Sketches and Incidents* (Iowa Commandery, Military Order of the Loyal Legion of the United States). Vol. 1. Des Moines, 1893.

Berkove, Lawrence I. "The Heart Has Its Reasons: Ambrose Bierce's Successful Failure at Philosophy." *Critical Essays on Ambrose Bierce.* Ed. Cathy N. Davidson. Boston, 1982.

———. "Two Impossible Dreams: Ambrose Bierce on Utopia and America." *Huntington Library Quarterly* 44 (Autumn 1981): 283–92.

Bierce, Ambrose. *The Collected Works of Ambrose Bierce.* 11 vols. New York, 1909.

Billings, John D. *Hardtack and Coffee, or the Unwritten Story of Army Life.* Boston, 1887.

Blake, Henry N. *Three Years in the Army of the Potomac.* Boston, 1865.

Blake, Walter H. *Hand Grips: The Story of the Great Gettysburg Reunion, July, 1913.* Vineland, 1913.

Bright, Thomas R. "Yankees in Arms: The Civil War as a Personal Experience." *Civil War History* 19 (September 1973): 197–218.

Brinton, John H. *Personal Memoirs.* New York, 1914.

Brown, Charles O. *Battle-Fields Revisited.* Kalamazoo, 1886.

Bryant, William Cullen, II, ed. "A Yankee Soldier Looks at the Negro." *Civil War History* 7 (June 1961): 133–48.

Buechler, John. "'Give 'em the Bayonet'—A Note on Civil War Mythology." *Civil War History* 7 (June 1961): 128–32.

Byers, S. H. M. "How Men Feel in Battle: Recollections of a Private at Champion Hills." *Annals of Iowa* 2 (July 1896): 438–49.

Byrne, Frank L., ed. *The View from Headquarters: Civil War Letters of Harvey Reid.* Madison, 1965.

Byrne, Frank L., and Jean Powers Soman, eds. *Your True Marcus: The Civil War Letters of a Jewish Colonel.* Kent, 1985.

Cain, Marvin R. "A 'Face of Battle' Needed: An Assessment of Motives and Men in Civil War Historiography." *Civil War History* 28 (March 1982): 5–27.

Camm, William. "Diary of Colonel William Camm, 1861 to 1865." *Journal of the Illinois State Historical Society* 18 (January 1926): 793–969.

Campbell, Henry. "Union Bugler Found Chickamauga a 'Terrible Battle.'" *Civil War Times Illustrated* 3 (May 1964): 34–37.

Carnahan, James R. "Personal Recollections of Chickamauga." *Sketches of War History, 1861–1865: Papers Read Before the Ohio Commandery of the Military Order of the Loyal Legion of the United States, 1883–1886.* Vol. 1. Cincinnati, 1888.

Carter, Robert Goldthwaite. *Four Brothers in Blue: Or, Sunshine and Shadows of the War of the Rebellion.* Austin, 1978.

Casey, James B., ed. "The Ordeal of Adoniram Judson Warner: His Minutes of South Mountain and Antietam." *Civil War History* 28 (September 1982): 212–36.

Castel, Albert. *Decision in the West: The Atlanta Campaign of 1864.* Lawrence, 1992.
_____. "Mars and the Reverend Longstreet: Or, Attacking and Dying in the Civil War." *Civil War History* 33 (June 1987): 103–14.

Castel, Albert, ed. "The War Album of Henry Dwight, Part II." *Civil War Times Illustrated* 19 (April 1980): 20–24.
_____. "The War Album of Henry Dwight, Part III." *Civil War Times Illustrated* 19 (May 1980): 32–36.

Castle, Henry A. "Some Experiences of an Enlisted Man." *Glimpses of the Nation's Struggle: A Series of Papers Read Before the Minnesota Commandery of the Military Order of the Loyal Legion of the United States.* 1st ser. St. Paul, 1887.

Catton, Bruce, ed. "Asa Smith Leaves the War." *American Heritage* 22 (February 1971): 54–59, 103–5.

Chamberlain, Joshua Lawrence. *The Passing of the Armies.* New York, 1915.

Churchill, James O. "Wounded at Fort Donelson." *War Papers and Personal Rem-*

iniscences, 1861–1865, Read Before the Commandery of the State of Missouri, Military Order of the Loyal Legion of the United States. Vol. 1. St. Louis, 1892.

Clark, James Samuel. *Life in the Middle West.* Chicago, 1916.

Coates, Earl J., and Dean S. Thomas. *An Introduction to Civil War Small Arms.* Gettysburg, 1990.

Coe, David, ed. *Mine Eyes Have Seen the Glory: Combat Diaries of Union Sergeant Hamlin Alexander Coe.* Rutherford, 1975.

Cooke, Chauncey H. "A Badger Boy in Blue: The Letters of Chauncey H. Cooke." *Wisconsin Magazine of History* 5 (September 1921): 63–98.

Cowell, Charles. "An Infantryman at Corinth: The Diary of Charles Cowell." *Civil War Times Illustrated* 13 (November 1974): 10–14.

Cox, Jacob Dolson. *Military Reminiscences of the Civil War.* Vol. 1. New York, 1900.

Cozzens, Peter. *The Shipwreck of Their Hopes: The Battles for Chattanooga.* Urbana, 1994.

Crosley, George W. "Some Reminiscences of an Iowa Soldier." *Annals of Iowa* 10 (July 1911): 119–36.

Croushore, James H., ed. *A Volunteer's Adventures: A Union Captain's Record of the Civil War.* New Haven, 1946.

Davidson, Cathy N. *The Experimental Fictions of Ambrose Bierce: Structuring the Ineffable.* Lincoln, 1984.

Davis, Charles E., Jr. *Three Years in the Army: The Story of the Thirteenth Massachusetts Volunteers.* Boston, 1894.

Davis, William C. *Battle at Bull Run.* Baton Rouge, 1977.

Dawes, Rufus R. "With the Sixth Wisconsin at Gettysburg." *Sketches of War History, 1861–1865: Papers Prepared for the Ohio Commandery of the Military Order of the Loyal Legion of the United States, 1888–1890.* Vol. 3. Cincinnati, 1890.

DeForest, John W. *Miss Ravenel's Conversion from Secession to Loyalty.* Columbus, 1969.

———. "Our Military Past and Present." *Atlantic Monthly* 44 (November 1879): 561–75.

Dodd, Ira Seymour. "The Making of a Regiment." *McClure's Magazine* 9 (1897): 1031–44.

———. "The Song of the Rappahannock." *McClure's Magazine* 8 (1896–1897): 314–20.

———. *The Song of the Rappahannock: Sketches of the Civil War.* New York, 1898.

Dodge, Theodore A. "Left Wounded on the Field." *Putnam's Magazine* 4 (September 1869): 317–26.

Donald, David Herbert, ed. *Gone for a Soldier: The Civil War Memoirs of Private Alfred Bellard.* Boston, 1975.

Dunkelman, Mark H., and Michael J. Winey. *The Hardtack Regiment: An Illustrated History of the 154th Regiment, New York State Infantry Volunteers.* Rutherford, 1981.

Dwight, Henry Otis. "How We Fight at Atlanta." *Harper's New Monthly Magazine* 29 (October 1864): 663–66.

Eby, Cecil D., ed. *A Virginia Yankee in the Civil War: The Diaries of David Hunter Strother.* Chapel Hill, 1961.

Eisenschiml, Otto, ed. *Vermont General: The Unusual War Experiences of Edward Hastings Ripley, 1862–1865.* New York, 1960.

Ellis, Richard N., ed. "The Civil War Letters of an Iowa Family." *Annals of Iowa* 39 (Spring 1969): 561–86.

Elson, Ruth Miller. *Guardians of Tradition: American Schoolbooks of the Nineteenth Century.* Lincoln, 1964.

Evans, Thomas H. "'All Was Complete Chaos.'" *Civil War Times Illustrated* 6 (January 1968): 32–41.

_____. "At Malvern Hill." *Civil War Times Illustrated* 6 (December 1967): 38–43.

_____. "'The Cries of the Wounded Were Piercing and Horrible.'" *Civil War Times Illustrated* 7 (July 1968): 28–38.

_____. "'There Is No Use Trying to Dodge Shot.'" *Civil War Times Illustrated* 6 (August 1967): 40–45.

Farlow, Joyce, and Louise Barry, eds. "Vincent B. Osborne's Civil War Experiences." *Kansas Historical Quarterly* 20 (May 1952): 108–33.

Favill, Josiah Marshall. *The Diary of a Young Officer.* Chicago, 1909.

Fitch, Michael H. *Echoes of the Civil War as I Hear Them.* New York, 1905.

Fitts, James Franklin. "In the Ranks at Cedar Creek." *Galaxy* 1 (1866): 534–43.

Ford, Worthington Chauncey, ed. *A Cycle of Adams Letters, 1861–1865.* Vol. 1. Boston, 1920.

Frank, Joseph Allan, and George A. Reaves. *"Seeing the Elephant": Raw Recruits at the Battle of Shiloh.* Westport, 1989.

Frassanito, William A. *Gettysburg: A Journey in Time.* New York, 1975.

_____. *Grant and Lee: The Virginia Campaigns, 1864–1865.* New York, 1983.

Fredrickson, George M. *The Inner Civil War: Northern Intellectuals and the Crisis of the Union.* New York, 1965.

Furgurson, Ernest B. *Chancellorsville, 1863: The Souls of the Brave.* New York, 1993.

Fussell, Paul. *The Great War and Modern Memory.* New York, 1975.

_____. *Wartime: Understanding and Behavior in the Second World War.* New York, 1989.

Gabriel, Richard A. *No More Heroes: Madness and Psychiatry in War.* New York, 1987.

Galloway, G. Norton. "Hand-to-Hand Fighting at Spotsylvania." *Battles and Leaders of the Civil War.* Vol. 4. New York, 1956.

Gates, Arnold, ed. *The Rough Side of War: The Civil War Journal of Chesley A. Mosman.* Garden City, 1987.

Geary, James W. *We Need Men: The Union Draft in the Civil War.* DeKalb, 1991.

Goss, Warren Lee. *Recollections of a Private.* New York, 1890.

Gray, J. Glenn. *The Warriors: Reflections on Men in Battle.* New York, 1970.

Greene, Albert Robinson. "Campaigning in the Army of the Frontier." *Transactions of the Kansas Historical Society* 14 (1918): 283–310.

Greene, John W. *Camp Ford Prison; and How I Escaped.* Toledo, 1893.

Griffith, Paddy. *Battle Tactics of the Civil War.* New Haven, 1989.

Grigsby, Melvin. *The Smoked Yank.* Sioux Falls, 1888.

Hafendorfer, Kenneth A. *Perryville: Battle for Kentucky.* Louisville, 1991.

Hage, Anne A. "The Battle of Gettysburg as Seen by Minnesota Soldiers." *Minnesota History* 38 (June 1963): 245–57.

Hagerman, Edward. *The American Civil War and the Origins of Modern Warfare.* Bloomington, 1988.

Hallock, Judith Lee. "The Role of the Community in Civil War Desertion." *Civil War History* 29 (June 1983): 123–34.

Hammond, Mary Acton, ed. "'Dear Mollie': Letters of Captain Edward A. Acton to His Wife, 1862." *Pennsylvania Magazine of History and Biography* 89 (January 1965): 3–51.

Hannaford, Ebenezer. "In Hospital After Stone River." *Harper's New Monthly Magazine* 28 (January 1864): 260–65.

_____. "In the Ranks at Stone River." *Harper's New Monthly Magazine* 27 (November 1863): 809–15.

Harris, Emily J. "Sons and Soldiers: Deerfield, Massachusetts and the Civil War." *Civil War History* 30 (June 1984): 157–71.

Harwood, Nathan S. *The Pea Ridge Campaign: A Paper Read Before the Nebraska Commandery of the Military Order of the Loyal Legion of the United States.* Omaha, 1887.

Hattaway, Herman, and Archer Jones. *How the North Won: A Military History of the Civil War.* Urbana, 1983.

Heitman, Francis B. *Historical Register and Dictionary of the United States Army.* Vol. 1. Washington, D.C., 1903.

Hemingway, Ernest. *For Whom the Bell Tolls.* New York, 1987.

Hennessy, John J. *Return to Bull Run: The Campaign and Battle of Second Manassas.* New York, 1993.

Heslin, James J., ed. "The Diary of a Union Soldier in Confederate Prisons." *New-York Historical Society Quarterly* 41 (July 1957): 233–78.

_____. "A Yankee Soldier in a New York Regiment." *New-York Historical Society Quarterly* 50 (April 1966): 109–49.

Hess, Earl J. *Liberty, Virtue, and Progress: Northerners and Their War for the Union.* New York, 1988.

_____. "The 12th Missouri Infantry: A Socio-Military Profile of a Union Regiment." *Missouri Historical Review* 76 (October 1981): 53–77.

Hess, Earl J., ed. *A German in the Yankee Fatherland: The Civil War Letters of Henry A. Kircher.* Kent, 1983.

Hicks, Borden M. "Personal Recollections of the War of the Rebellion." *Glimpses of the Nation's Struggle: Papers Read Before the Minnesota Commandery of the Military Order of the Loyal Legion of the United States, January, 1903–1908.* 6th ser. Minneapolis, 1909.

Higginson, Thomas Wentworth. *Army Life in a Black Regiment.* Boston, 1882.

_____. "Regular and Volunteer Officers." *Atlantic Monthly* 14 (September 1864): 348–57.

Hitchcock, Frederick L. *War from the Inside.* Philadelphia, 1904.

Hofsommer, Robert D. "On the Death of Reynolds." *Civil War Times Illustrated* 21 (June 1982): 16–25.

Hogarty, William P. "A Medal of Honor." *War Talks in Kansas.* Kansas City, 1906.

Holmes, J. T. *52d O.V.I., Then and Now.* Columbus, 1898.

Holsinger, Frank. "How Does One Feel Under Fire?" *War Talks in Kansas.* Kansas City, 1906.

Holt, Daniel. "In Captivity." *Civil War Times Illustrated* 18 (August 1979): 34–39.

Holzhueter, John O., ed. "William Wallace's Civil War Letters: The Virginia Campaign." *Wisconsin Magazine of History* 57 (Autumn 1973): 28–59.

_____. "William Wallace's Civil War Letters: The Atlanta Campaign." *Wisconsin Magazine of History* 57 (Winter 1973–1974): 91–116.

Hopkins, Vivian C., ed. "Soldier of the 92nd Illinois: Letters of William H. Brown and His Fiancee, Emma Jane Frazey." *Bulletin of the New York Public Library* 73 (February 1969): 114–36.

Hosea, Lewis M. "The Second Day at Shiloh." *Sketches of War History, 1861–1865: Papers Prepared for the Commandery of the State of Ohio, Military Order of the Loyal Legion of the United States, 1903–1908.* Vol. 6. Cincinnati, 1908.

Houghton, Charles H. "In the Crater." *Battles and Leaders of the Civil War.* Vol. 4. New York, 1956.

Houghton, Henry. "The Ordeal of Civil War: A Recollection." *Vermont History* 41 (Winter 1973): 31–49.

Howe, Daniel Wait. *Civil War Times, 1861–1865.* Indianapolis, 1902.

Howe, Mark DeWolfe, Jr., ed. *The Occasional Speeches of Justice Oliver Wendell Holmes.* Cambridge, 1962.

_____. *Touched with Fire: Civil War Letters and Diary of Oliver Wendell Holmes, Jr., 1861–1864.* Cambridge, 1946.

Hubbell, John T., ed. "Stand by the Colors: The Civil War Letters of Leander Stem." *Register of the Kentucky Historical Society* 73 (July 1975): 291–313.

Hyde, Thomas W. *Following the Greek Cross or, Memories of the Sixth Army Corps.* Boston, 1894.

Isham, A. B. "The Story of a Gunshot Wound." *Sketches of War History, 1861–1865: Papers Prepared for the Ohio Commandery of the Military Order of the Loyal Legion of the United States, 1890–1896.* Vol. 4. Cincinnati, 1896.

Jackman, Lyman. *History of the Sixth New Hampshire Regiment in the War for the Union.* Concord, 1891.

Jackson, William Henry. *Time Exposure: The Autobiography of William Henry Jackson.* New York, 1940.

James, William H. "Blue and Gray: A Baltimore Volunteer of 1864." *Maryland Historical Magazine* 36 (March 1941): 22–33.

Jennison, S. P. "The Illusions of a Soldier." *Glimpses of the Nation's Struggle: A Series of Papers Read Before the Minnesota Commandery of the Military Order of the Loyal Legion of the United States.* 1st ser. St. Paul, 1887.

Jimerson, Randall C. *The Private Civil War: Popular Thought During the Sectional Conflict.* Baton Rouge, 1988.

Kaiser, Leo M., ed. "Civil War Letters of Charles W. Carr of the 21st Wisconsin Volunteers." *Wisconsin Magazine of History* 43 (Summer 1960): 264–72.

Kaser, David. *Books and Libraries in Camp and Battle: The Civil War Experience.* Westport, 1984.

Keegan, John. *The Face of Battle: A Study of Agincourt, Waterloo, and the Somme.* New York, 1976.

Kerby, J. O. *On the War Path: A Journey over the Historic Grounds of the Late Civil War.* Chicago, 1890.

Kirkland, Joseph. *The Captain of Company K.* Ridgewood, 1968.

Kniffin, Gilbert C. "A Retrospect." *War Papers, Military Order of the Loyal Legion of the United States, Commandery of the District of Columbia.* N.p., n.d.

Kunitz, Stanley J., and Howard Haycraft, eds. *American Authors, 1600–1900.* New York, 1938.

Leed, Eric J. *No Man's Land: Combat and Identity in World War I.* New York, 1979.

Leggett, Mortimer D. "The Military and the Mob." *Sketches of War History, 1861–1865: Papers Read Before the Ohio Commandery of the Military Order of the Loyal Legion of the United States, 1883–1886.* Vol. 1. Cincinnati, 1888.

Leonard, Thomas C. *Above the Battle: War-Making in America from Appomattox to Versailles.* New York, 1978.

Lewis, John W. "Libby." *War Papers, Military Order of the Loyal Legion of the United States, Commandery of the District of Columbia.* N.p., n.d.

Linderman, Gerald F. *Embattled Courage: The Experience of Combat in the American Civil War.* New York, 1987.

Linenthal, Edward Tabor. *Changing Images of the Warrior Hero in America: A History of Popular Symbolism.* New York, 1982.

Litzinger, Boyd, and Edward K. Eckert, eds. "On the Peninsular Campaign: Civil War Letters from William E. Dunn." *Civil War Times Illustrated* 14 (July 1975): 14–19.

Livermore, Thomas L. "The Northern Volunteers." *Journal of the Military Service Institution of the United States* 12 (September 1891): 905–37.

Logan, John A. *The Volunteer Soldier of America.* Chicago, 1887.

Longacre, Edward G., ed. "'Laughing at the Screaming Bullets.'" *Lincoln Herald* 84 (Fall 1982): 173–80.

Lusk, William Thompson. *War Letters of William Thompson Lusk.* New York, 1911.

Lynn, John A. *Bayonets of the Republic: Motivation and Tactics in the Army of Revolutionary France, 1791–94.* Urbana, 1984.

Lyster, Henry F. "Recollections of the Bull Run Campaign After Twenty-seven Years." *A Paper Read Before Michigan Commandery of the Military Order of the Loyal Legion of the United States, February 1, 1887.* Detroit, 1888.

McBride, George W. "Shiloh, After Thirty-two Years." *Blue and Gray* 3 (1894): 303–10.

McBride, R. E. *In the Ranks from the Wilderness to Appomattox Court House.* Cincinnati, 1881.

McClaughry, Robert W. "The Boys of 1861—and Their Boys." *Military Essays and Recollections: Papers Read Before the Commandery of the State of Illinois, Military Order of the Loyal Legion of the United States.* Vol. 3. Chicago, 1899.

McCook, Daniel, "The Second Division at Shiloh." *Harper's New Monthly Magazine* 28 (May 1864): 828–33.

McDaniel, Anthonette L. "'Just Watch Us Make Things Hum': Chattanooga,

Adolph S. Ochs, and the Memorialization of the Civil War." *East Tennessee Historical Society's Publications* 61 (1989): 3–14.

McDonough, James Lee. *Stones River: Bloody Winter in Tennessee.* Knoxville, 1980.

Mackenzie, Charles. "The Great American Civil War." *War Sketches and Incidents: Iowa Commandery, Military Order of the Loyal Legion of the United States.* Vol. 1. Des Moines, 1893.

McLarty, Vivan Kirkpatrick. "The Civil War Letters of Colonel Bazel F. Lazear." *Missouri Historical Review* 45 (October 1950): 47–63.

McPherson, James M. *Battle Cry of Freedom: The Civil War Era.* New York, 1988.

_____. *Ordeal by Fire: The Civil War and Reconstruction.* New York, 1982.

McWhiney, Grady, and Perry D. Jamieson. *Attack and Die: Civil War Military Tactics and the Southern Heritage.* Tuscaloosa, 1982.

Mailer, Norman. *The Naked and the Dead.* New York, 1980.

Marsh, E. L. "Military Discipline." *War Sketches and Incidents: Iowa Commandery, Military Order of the Loyal Legion of the United States.* Vol. 2. Des Moines, 1898.

Marshall, S. L. A. *Men Against Fire: The Problem of Battle Command in Future War.* New York, 1947.

Marszalek, John F. *Sherman: A Soldier's Passion for Order.* New York, 1993.

Maslowski, Pete. "A Study of Morale in Civil War Soldiers." *Military Affairs* 34 (December 1970): 122–26.

Matter, William D. *If It Takes All Summer: The Battle of Spotsylvania.* Chapel Hill, 1988.

Matthews, Richard E. *The 149th Pennsylvania Volunteer Infantry Unit in the Civil War.* Jefferson, 1994.

Meeker, Edward. "The Improving Health of the United States, 1850–1915." *Explorations in Economic History* 9 (Summer 1972): 353–73.

Melcher, Holman S. "'We Were Cut Off.'" *Civil War Times Illustrated* 8 (December 1969): 10–15.

Mellon, Knox, Jr., ed. "Letters of James Greenalch." *Michigan History* 44 (June 1960): 188–240.

Mercer, S. D. "Forty Years in the Field." *Civil War Sketches and Incidents: Papers Read by Companions of the Commandery of the State of Nebraska, Military Order of the Loyal Legion of the United States.* Omaha, 1902.

Michie, Peter. "Reminiscences of Cadet and Army Service." *Personal Recollections of the War of the Rebellion: Addresses Delivered Before the Commandery of the State of New York, Military Order of the Loyal Legion of the United States.* 2d ser. New York, 1897.

Miller, James Cooper. "Serving Under McClellan on the Peninsula in '62." *Civil War Times Illustrated* 8 (June 1969): 24–30.

Mitchell, Reid. *Civil War Soldiers: Their Expectations and Their Experiences.* New York, 1988.

_____. *The Vacant Chair: The Northern Soldier Leaves Home.* New York, 1993.

Mohr, James C., ed. *The Cormany Diaries: A Northern Family in the Civil War.* Pittsburgh, 1982.

Moran, Lord. *The Anatomy of Courage.* Garden City, 1966.

Morton, Charles. "A Boy at Shiloh." *Personal Recollections of the War of the Rebellion: Addresses Delivered Before the Commandery of the State of New York, Military Order of the Loyal Legion of the United States.* 3d ser. New York, 1907.

Nevins, Allan, ed. *A Diary of Battle: The Personal Journals of Colonel Charles S. Wainwright, 1861–1865.* New York, 1962.

Norton, Oliver Willcox. *Army Letters, 1861–1865.* Chicago, 1903.

Nosworthy, Brent. *The Anatomy of Victory: Battle Tactics, 1689–1763.* New York, 1992.

Noyes, George F. "The Battle of Antietam." *Harper's New Monthly Magazine* 27 (September 1863): 537–41.

Olney, Warren. "Shiloh as Seen by a Private Soldier." *A Paper Read Before California Commandery of the Military Order of the Loyal Legion of the United States, May 31, 1889.* N.p., n.d.

On to Richmond! By Post No. 23, G.A.R., Department of New Jersey, and Its Friends, October 16th, 1881. Trenton, 1881.

Padgett, James A., ed. "With Sherman Through Georgia and the Carolinas: Letters of a Federal Soldier." *Georgia Historical Quarterly* 32 (December 1948): 284–322.

Page, Charles D. *History of the Fourteenth Regiment, Connecticut Vol. Infantry.* Meriden, 1906.

Partridge, Charles A., ed. *History of the Ninety-sixth Regiment Illinois Volunteer Infantry.* Chicago, 1887.

Payne, Edwin W. *History of the Thirty-fourth Regiment of Illinois Volunteer Infantry.* Clinton, 1902.

Peterson, John Stahl. "The Issues of the War." *Continental Monthly* 5 (1864): 274–87.

Pierce, Francis E. "'I Have with the Regiment Been Through a Terrible Battle.'" *Civil War Times Illustrated* 1 (December 1962): 7–9, 28–30.

Pierson, Stephen. "From Chattanooga to Atlanta in 1864." *Proceedings of the New Jersey Historical Society* 16 (1931): 324–56.

Plumb, R. G., ed. "Letters of a Fifth Wisconsin Volunteer." *Wisconsin Magazine of History* 3 (September 1919): 52–83.

Porter, Horace. "The Philosophy of Courage." *Century* 36 (June 1888): 246–54.

Powell, William H. "The Battle of the Petersburg Crater." *Battles and Leaders of the Civil War.* Vol. 4. New York, 1956.

Pratt, Harry E., ed. "The Civil War Letters of Brigadier General William Ward Orme, 1862–1866." *Journal of the Illinois State Historical Society* 23 (July 1930): 246–315.

Prentice, Sartell. "The Opening Hours in the Wilderness in 1864." *Military Essays and Recollections: Papers Read Before the Commandery of the State of Illinois, Military Order of the Loyal Legion of the United States.* Vol. 2. Chicago, 1894.

Quimby, Rollin W. "Recurrent Themes and Purposes in the Sermons of the Union Army Chaplain." *Speech Monographs* 31 (November 1964): 425–36.

"A Rash Deed at Dead Angle." *Confederate Veteran* 12 (August 1904): 394.

Ray, Jean P., ed. *The Diary of A Dead Man: Letters and Diary of Private Ira S. Pettit.* Waverly, 1976.

Riddle, Francis A. "The Soldier's Place in Civilization." *Military Essays and Recollections: Papers Read Before the Commandery of the State of Illinois, Military Order of the Loyal Legion of the United States.* Vol. 2. Chicago, 1894.

Robertson, James I., Jr. *Soldiers Blue and Gray.* Columbia, 1988.

Robertson, James I., Jr., ed. *The Civil War Letters of General Robert McAllister.* New Brunswick, 1965.

_____. "A Federal Surgeon at Sharpsburg." *Civil War History* 6 (June 1960): 134–51.

Robinson, Charles. "My Experiences in the Civil War." *Michigan History Magazine* 24 (Winter 1940): 23–50.

Rodman, Barbee-Sue. "War and Aesthetic Sensibility: An Essay in Cultural History." *Soundings* 5 (Fall 1968): 308–26.

Rorabaugh, W. J. "Who Fought for the North in the Civil War? Concord, Massachusetts, Enlistments." *Journal of American History* 73 (December 1986): 695–701.

Rosenblatt, Emil, and Ruth Rosenblatt, eds. *Hard Marching Every Day: The Civil War Letters of Private Wilbur Fisk, 1861–1865.* Lawrence, 1992.

Rothenberg, Gunther E. *The Art of Warfare in the Age of Napoleon.* Bloomington, 1980.

Rotundo, E. Anthony. "Body and Soul: Changing Ideals of American Middle-Class Manhood, 1770–1920." *Journal of Social History* 16 (Summer 1983): 23–38.

Roy, Paul L. *The Last Reunion of the Blue and Gray.* Gettysburg, 1950.

Saum, Lewis O. "Death in the Popular Mind of Pre–Civil War America." *American Quarterly* 26 (December 1974): 477–95.

_____. "Providence in the Popular Mind of Pre–Civil War America." *Indiana Magazine of History* 72 (December 1976): 315–46.

Schell, Frank H. "'A Great Raging Battlefield Is Hell.'" *Civil War Times Illustrated* 8 (June 1969): 14–22.

Schofield, John M. *Forty-six Years in the Army.* New York, 1897.

Scott, Robert Garth. *Into the Wilderness with the Army of the Potomac.* Bloomington, 1992.

Sears, Stephen W. *To the Gates of Richmond: The Peninsula Campaign.* New York, 1992.

Shannon, Fred Albert, ed. *The Civil War Letters of Sergeant Onley Andrus.* Urbana, 1947.

Shea, William L., and Earl J. Hess. *Pea Ridge: Civil War Campaign in the West.* Chapel Hill, 1992.

Sheridan, Philip H. *Personal Memoirs.* Vol. 2. New York, 1888.

Sherman, Caroline D. "A New England Boy in the Civil War." *New England Quarterly* 5 (April 1932): 310–44.

Sherman, William T. *Memoirs.* vol. 2. New York, 1875.

Skinner, George R. "Impressions and Realities of War." *War Sketches and Incidents, Iowa Commandery, Military Order of the Loyal Legion of the United States.* Vol. 1. Des Moines, 1893.

Slotkin, Richard. *Regeneration Through Violence: The Mythology of the American Frontier, 1600–1860.* Middletown, 1973.

Small, Abner R. *The Road to Richmond.* Berkeley, 1939.

Smith, James O. "My First Campaign and Battle: A Jersey Boy at Antietam—Seventeen Days from Home." *Blue and Gray* 1 (1893): 280–90.

Soltow, Lee, and Edward Stevens. *The Rise of Literacy and the Common School in the United States: A Socioeconomic Analysis to 1870.* Chicago, 1981.

Stark, Cruce. "Brothers at/in War: One Phase of Post–Civil War Reconciliation." *Canadian Review of American Studies* 6 (Fall 1975): 174–81.

Stevens, H. S. *Souvenir of Excursion to Battlefields by the Society of the Fourteenth Connecticut Regiment and Reunion at Antietam, September 1891.* Washington, D.C., 1893.

Stewart, Nixon B. *Dan McCook's Regiment, 52nd O.V.I.* Alliance, 1900.

Stillwell, Leander. "In the Ranks at Shiloh." *War Talks in Kansas.* Kansas City, 1906.

_____. *The Story of a Common Soldier of Army Life in the Civil War, 1861–1865.* Kansas City, 1920.

Sutherland, George E. "The Negro in the Late War." *War Papers Read Before the Commandery of the State of Wisconsin, Military Order of the Loyal Legion of the United States.* Vol. 1. Milwaukee, 1891.

Sweney, Joseph H, "Nursed a Wounded Brother." *Annals of Iowa* 31 (January 1952): 177–99.

Sword, Wiley. *The Confederacy's Last Hurrah: Spring Hill, Franklin, and Nashville.* Lawrence, 1992.

Tanner, James. *Experience of a Wounded Soldier at the Second Battle of Bull Run.* N.p., 1927. Reprinted from *Military Surgeon,* February 1927.

Tapert, Annette. *The Brothers' War: Civil War Letters to Their Loved Ones from the Blue & Gray.* New York, 1989.

Thatcher, Marshall P. *A Hundred Battles in the West.* Detroit, 1884.

Thompson, David L. "With Burnside at Antietam." *Battles and Leaders of the Civil War.* Vol. 2. New York, 1956.

Throne, Mildred, ed. "An Iowa Doctor in Blue: The Letters of Seneca B. Thrall, 1862–1864." *Iowa Journal of History* 58 (April 1960): 97–188.

_____. "Reminiscences of Jacob C. Switzer of the 22nd Iowa." *Iowa Journal of History* 56 (January 1958): 37–76.

Tilley, Nannie M., ed. *Federals on the Frontier: The Diary of Benjamin F. McIntyre, 1862–1864.* Austin, 1963.

Tourgee, Albion W. *An Appeal to Caesar.* New York, 1884.

_____. *The Veteran and His Pipe.* Chicago, 1888.

Trowbridge, John Townsend. *The South: A Tour of Its Battle-Fields and Ruined Cities.* Hartford, 1866.

Twitchell, Albert S. *History of the Seventh Maine Light Battery.* Boston, 1892.

Vandiver, Frank E. *Blood Brothers: A Short History of the Civil War.* College Station, 1992.

Wainwright, Nicholas B., ed. *A Philadelphia Perspective: The Diary of Sidney George Fisher Covering the Years 1834–1871.* Philadelphia, 1967.

Walton, Claiborne J. "'One Continued Scene of Carnage.'" *Civil War Times Illustrated* 15 (August 1976): 34–36.

War of the Rebellion: A Compilation of the Official Records of the Union and Confederate Armies. 128 vols. Washington, D.C., 1880–1901.

Wasson, Stanley P., ed. "Civil War Letters of Darwin Cody." *Ohio Historical Quarterly* 68 (October 1959): 371–407.

Weld, Stephen Minot. *War Diary and Letters of Stephen Minot Weld, 1861–1865.* Boston, 1979.

Wheeler, William. *Letters of William Wheeler of the Class of 1855.* Cambridge, 1875.

White, Patrick H. "Civil War Diary of Patrick H. White." *Journal of the Illinois State Historical Society* 15 (October 1922–January 1923): 640–63.

Wiley, Bell Irvin. *The Life of Billy Yank: The Common Soldier of the Union.* Baton Rouge, 1952.

Wilkeson, Frank. *Recollections of a Private Soldier in the Army of the Potomac.* New York, 1887.

Williams, Charles Richard, ed. *Diary & Letters of Rutherford Birchard Hayes.* Vol. 2. Columbus, 1922.

Williams, George F. "Lights and Shadows of Army Life." *Century* 28 (October 1884): 803–19.

Winsor, Frederick. "The Surgeon at the Field Hospital." *Atlantic Monthly* 46 (August 1880): 183–88.

Woodruff, Charles A. "Our Boys in the War of the Rebellion." *A Paper Prepared and Read Before California Commandery of the Military Order of the Loyal Legion of the United States, November 12, 1890.* N.p., n.d.

Woodruff, Frederick M., ed. "The Civil War Notebook of Montgomery Schuyler Woodruff." *Missouri Historical Society Bulletin* 29 (April 1973): 163–88.

Index

239